HANDWRIT[

Nadya O

ILLUSTR

Nadya Olyanova is one of the pioneers in the science of graphology, and it is thanks to her work as a consultant in both the business and the scientific field that graphology is now fully accepted as a vital and significant tool in character and personality analysis.

Graphology is the one direct and immediate way in which one's untapped potentialities and resources, as well as one's weaknesses and blind spots, can be discovered. There are now over 300 business corporations who will not hire a prospective job applicant without first submitting his handwriting to a graphologist for analysis. In hospitals and clinics across the country psychiatrists and psychologists use graphology to discover hints of unconscious resistances in patients, resistances which would take considerably longer to uncover through more traditional analytical methods. In the field of physical medicine, the science has been helpful as a sub-diagnostic tool where heart disease or motor defects are suspected. The benefits of graphology are not limited to scientists and businessmen; parents anxious to develop the creative and intellectual potential of their children use it to discover character indications that can be revealed in a child's handwriting as early as the ninth or tenth year of life. Couples about to be married use graphology to spot potential incompatibilities.

In this classic volume, Nadya Olyanova illustrates the broad range of application the science covers. She discusses the signs of maturity and immaturity in children and adults, the manifestations of extroversion and introversion, the signs of talent, the indications of inferiority complexes and their attendant compensations, handwriting differences between active and passive people, the evidence and degree of intensity of the sexual impulses in men and women, and the signs of maladjustment in handwriting. She devotes a large part of this book to analyses of the handwritings of great men and women and of outstanding personalities on the contemporary scene: in the arts, the sciences, politics and government—an analysis of every major presidential aspirant in 1968 is included in the book—and business and finance. There is a de-

tailed section on how to analyze one's own handwriting, and the volume concludes with a short history of the science and an explanation of the difference between a graphologist and a "handwriting expert." *Handwriting Tells* should prove indispensable to anyone interested in knowing more about the motivating forces within himself and those around him.

ANTONIO BARONE

Nadya Olyanova has been consultant to the psychiatric service of King's County Hospital in New York and the Menninger Clinic in Topeka, Kansas, as well as to numerous private psychiatrists and psychologists. She is presently a consultant to over 200 business corporations and to her own private clientele.

TO

C. D. M.

IN GRATITUDE

Handwriting Tells

Cover model
Blanche Powers — Los Angeles, California

Melvin Powers
WILSHIRE BOOK COMPANY
12015 Sherman Road
No. Hollywood, California 91605

The Bobbs-Merrill Company, Inc.
A Subsidiary of Howard W. Sams & Co., Inc., Publishers
Indianapolis · Kansas City · New York

ISBN 0-87980-046-1

CONTENTS

PART TWO: HOW TO ANALYZE
         YOUR OWN HANDWRITING

INTRODUCTION

IN ORDER for a skill or art to qualify as a science it must fulfill three criteria: It must acquire a body of systematic observations; it must derive principles based on these observations and tailored to the unique qualities of the skill in question; and it must have a high average in making accurate deductions. All the above criteria find admirable fulfillment in the science of graphology. And no one has labored more diligently for this fulfillment over the years than has Nadya Olyanova.

The scientific study of personality, whether by handwriting or by any other method, is most difficult. In clinical psychology there is a statement about personality called "the projective hypothesis" which holds that personality is an organized whole and consistent, and that all human behavior is a reflection of personality. This is a useful concept that has validity, whether we think of personality as a group of various traits, as a collection of physical attributes, or as a way of relating to people. It does not mean that we reveal all of ourselves all of the time, or that we do not vary our attributes and actions. It does mean that every gesture, every word, and every action of ours is in some manner related to that basic life-style we call our personality.

Binswanger reminds us that the best data gatherer and all-round computer in existence is the human mind—that "subconscious psychologist" that exists in all of us, and that has evolved from generations of experience in interpersonal evaluation.

In obtaining knowledge about others we are helped by the fact that they want us to know about them. Freud asserts that it is impossible for anyone to keep a secret. Deep down, and in a very real way, we do not want to keep our secrets. We want the world to know exactly who and what we are. Paradoxical though it seems, we still give a great deal away even when we are being most taciturn, for taciturnity itself reveals something about the individual. In any event, the secrets most worth discovering are those that concern ourselves—who we are, what we are, and why we do the things we do.

Human beings have managed to accumulate considerable intrinsic knowledge about themselves. But the majority of us are usually not aware of how much we know. Hence the study of graphology (as well as other techniques of personality assessment) often turns out to be a matter of simply discovering the sources in ourselves that have always been there—unknown and untapped.

To the rich data of human history, Nadya Olyanova adds a lifetime of varied experience in professional data gathering and expert analysis, which together constitute a veritable goldmine of graphological knowledge. So concise and vivid is her grasp of graphological dynamics that one need only mention the name of a former client and the essence of his or her personality constellation is instantly recalled by her. More impressive is the way in which the mere mention of, say, salesman or actor or bank president summons to her agile mind a wealth of composite knowledge based on literally hundreds of handwritings produced by individuals who belong to those categories.

In the study of personality and its myriad manifestations, handwriting offers an overabundance of riches. The problem then becomes how to select from such a mass of data the precise information that properly describes a particular individual. Nadya Olyanova has a highly developed ability to sift the wealth of data, and to coordinate and summarize it. In finding common denominators and arranging them by order of importance, she demonstrates the remarkable capacity of the human mind at the height of alertness.

In this book Nadya Olyanova shares with us her special intuitive gifts and her wealth of experience in the field. She now makes available to students of graphology the composite evaluation of literally thousands of handwriting specimens.

It is a privilege to be allowed to call public attention to the art, skill, and experience of one who has given so much to graphology during her lifetime, and who has earned for herself and for her profession the respect of the scientific world.

GEORGE EDINGTON, M.A.
BRADFORD J. WILSON, M.A.

I

Children and Adults—
Maturity and Immaturity

The childhood shows the man
As morning shows the day
—JOHN MILTON

Emotional Immaturity of Children

IF WE ARE TO OBSERVE THE HANDWRITING OF HUMAN-beings with a view to analyzing character, disposition, and talents, we must start with the writing of children, in whom the roots of character have their inception. Psychologists and psychiatrists have concluded that character starts to develop in infancy and that the behavior pattern (or, as Dr. Alfred Adler called it, "the style of life") is already crystallized by the age of five. But since few children learn to write before the age of schooling, we must start from that point.

At the age of six when the average child enters first grade and becomes acquainted with the alphabet and the mechanics of writing, he focuses his attention on the formation of letters and words. Not until writing becomes an unconscious habit, like walking, with more concentration given to the thought being expressed than to the physical act of writing, does the character of the child begin to reveal itself.

The more a child has been taught to act on his own volition and to accept responsibility, the more independent he becomes in his thinking and actions, forming habits that begin to show themselves in individual characteristics in his handwriting. Childish handwriting, whether executed by child or adult, is characterized by roundness of structure. Just as wax before it is molded into a particular form is shapeless and smooth, so it is with undeveloped character as re-

3

vealed in handwriting. And just as wax may be of coarse or delicate texture, inherent traits may be coarse or sensitive, easy or difficult to manipulate. If the pen pressure or the writing is heavy, firm, and even, we are dealing with robust material. If the pen pressure is light or delicate, the material is more pliable; that is, the child is more impressionable, more receptive to constructive or destructive environmental influences.

Where a child (or an adult) belongs in the family constellation should be taken into consideration when analyzing his handwriting; it is important in the development of outstanding traits. The pampering a first born receives usually structures his behavior pattern for the rest of his life. The second child is often in competition with the first and may develop aggressiveness in a desire to outdistance the older one. (This is a trait often found in the handwriting of salesmen, a large number of whom were second children.)

The third child, and so on down the line, will have a mixture of traits ranging from possible feelings of envy or rejection or deprivation to a need to prove himself, because there is bound to be sibling rivalry where there are a number of children. And an only child will often have traits similar to the first born, with graphological signs of self-indulgence. Thus, the position a child occupies in the family constellation can determine vast differences in each child.

Discipline plays a large part in forming a child's attitudes. It is revealed in handwriting by a variety of signs, including the way in which the writing is spaced and how the *t*'s are crossed. Messy-looking papers often reveal a lack of cooperation and may point to some disturbance in the child. It might be the result of a physical defect; if so, it should be taken into account. A child who makes the effort to write neatly will often be neat and orderly in other habits and be courteous and thoughtful of others. His neat writing then reveals his desire to cooperate with others and indicates he has the ability to make social adjustments.

The Intelligent Curious Girl (Age 13)

Despite the childish roundness so obvious in this handwriting, there are signs of good judgment in the single downstroke of the *y*, and the careful spacing between words. Already she shows an interest in the welfare of other people by the return stroke on the *y* in the word "York" (done two or more times the meaning is corroborated; even if it appears once the instinct is there, though it may not yet have become a habit). It reveals a giving instinct, a desire to be useful to others, to make some contribution, and is a sign of cooperation in this kind of outgoing hand. Her expressed love of travel comes from her curiosity to see, to observe, and this shows in the broad *r*

Then I wonder whethe want to go to New Yor instead because I like like New York City where is always going on.

SPECIMEN 1

that appears all through the writing. Taking the over-all picture, we are confronted with an intelligent, visual, optimistic (rising lines), and flexible individual, one who is receptive and suggestible and responsive to constructive influences in the environment.

Environmental Influences in Handwriting

As the child develops intellectual independence and a capacity to accept responsibility the handwriting becomes more angular and individual. We are, most of us, taught the same method of writing in school, yet were we to examine the handwriting of a group of children some five years after they have left elementary school, we would see marked differences in many of them. Even those handwritings that look similar would show some slight difference, readily discernible to the practiced eye of the graphologist.

Development may occur before the child finishes elementary school. In such an instance we may assume that environmental influences have played an important part in developing his psyche and character. His parents might be culturally above average, and the child is thus conditioned to learning and encouraged in his efforts.

In the case of an only child, parental and other environmental influences have a greater effect upon his character development than his schooling has. Parents of only children sometimes send them to private schools where they might receive specialized instruction. This often helps to set the original pattern of the pampered child, resulting in aloofness, selectiveness, and perhaps some snobbishness. The handwriting developed in such a school is recognized by its vertical angle and artistically styled formations (see Specimen 40), and sometimes it employs a style of printing called manuscript writing. In those children who desire to rise above an environment that is distasteful to them, we may see the same kind of handwriting though the child may have gone to public school. Even in private schools there are a number who write a free-flowing, rightward-leaning hand, but these may be children who have brothers and sisters, and the social instincts are therefore more strongly developed. In contrast to an only child, a child from a large family usually develops more expansiveness and consideration for the rights of others, and may choose a career that brings him into contact with other people. An only child, however, often develops many of the traits of the isolate and may have more difficulty in adjusting to a society that will not pamper him. His companions will usually be people in his own social stratum, or those with prestige and position.

The more talented a child is, the more neurotic he is likely to be. In childhood, this will show in an inability to adjust readily to everyday routine, whether at home or in school. He may be a poor student despite a high IQ, and his behavior may cause his parents some anxiety. Often a child will reveal creativity in drawing, painting, or writing at an early age. The arts are replete with people who may have been problems as children, but who have found a solution through creative expression. Through expressing himself creatively a child develops a measure of discipline. And when such discipline is acquired during the formative years, it gives the child a strength he might not otherwise have. Where the child develops a definite purpose early in life, as long as it is a socially acceptable one, the chances for his happiness and fulfillment are greater than if he is permitted to drift without acquiring some form of discipline.

The Intelligent, Emotionally Immature Student

SPECIMEN 2

Something of the child still remains in this older girl, evident by the roundness here; but there is some angularity too, and this tells us she is in the process of development. We see signs of intelligence in the single stroke of the letter *h* in the word "have," which we call a "mental formation." The loop is eliminated, which shows independence of thought. There is, however, a sign of indecisiveness in the *t* bar that does not go through the stem of the letter, and we realize there are still areas of emotional dependency. (This is often seen in the handwriting of the first born, where too much was done for the child, even to making his decisions for him.) As she is on the threshold of choosing a career—she is thinking of becoming an airline hostess—we assume that her choice caters to the restlessness revealed in the indecisive *t* bar. She may change her mind later on, but the adventure connected with her present choice appeals to her during this stage of her development. We may also assume that her handwriting will show more angularity as she gains experience on her own. And as she is forced to make decisions and act on her own volition, her self-confidence will strengthen and so will her *t* bars. She can be persistent, as shown in the looped *t* bar in the word "to."

This means she has the capacity to counterbalance the indecision and dependency, tapping inner resources and ultimately strengthening her weaker traits.

The Healthy Talented Boy (Age 11)

You may wonder why I print lil I just got into the swing of it. In case y handwriting, I will write one small sentenc. eleven years old. I am a lefthanded writer.

SPECIMEN 3

Although manuscript writing (printing) is taught in many schools today, especially in private ones, this boy says he "got into the swing of printing" without being taught it. The reasons are obvious: He is essentially constructive, and so constructs his letter forms. He has an older brother and sister, and although it is a cooperative, well-adjusted family, a normal sibling rivalry still exists, if unconsciously. He has ambitions in a number of directions: he loves sports, enjoys studying French, science, and English, is fascinated by acting and singing, and has taken parts in plays. Roundness can be discerned all through the writing, especially in the *m*'s and *n*'s. The capital *I*, a single stroke, tells us he can get down to essentials without wasting time on inconsequential detail. He is already learning to think and plan independently; he possesses a measure of self-discipline, as shown in the firm *t* bars, some of them bowed; and his excellent memory is revealed in careful *i* dots. He is a left-handed writer who is skillfully learning to adapt himself to a right-handed world.

The Athletic Boy (Age 13)

This boy is beginning to develop emotionally and to mature. This shows in the letters that a few years ago were completely rounded

SPECIMEN 4

but that now lean toward angularity. Here also is a tendency to eliminate initial strokes, as in the words "older," "am," and "as." (When
strokes we are taught to make are eliminated, it reveals a trend toward
individual thinking.) The pen pressure is uniformly heavy; the flow
is to the right and spontaneous; the interests lean more toward physical activity than study, and the writing is larger than in Specimen 1.
The rising lines show animation and energy, further indicated by the
speed with which the specimen was written. The thought expressed
here is spontaneous (not dictated), and except for a desire to give a
good impression by its neatness, no conscious thought was given to
the word and letter forms. As more attention is given to physical
activity than by the previous boy, the spacing between words is not
so wide as in the preceding specimen. It is not unlikely that if this
boy does not realize the high goal he has set for himself, he may effect a compromise and become a physical culture instructor. For
this he would be eminently suited.

The Independent Judicious Boy (Age 14)

In Specimen 5, more angularity is apparent in the letter formations
than in the previous two, though the child is only fourteen. Concentration (small writing) and reliable judgment—indicated in the formation of *y* where the return stroke of the lower loop is eliminated,

SPECIMEN 5

as in the words "boy" and "study"—tells us that the child is unusually well developed for his age, capable of logical, consecutive thought (shown in the connecting of the first two words "I am"). The *t* bar above the stem of the letter (not taught him in school) points to a vivid imagination, a striving for the "higher place," with some of the elements of the perfectionist. Whenever the *t* bar appears above the stem of the letter, no matter in what handwriting, we may be sure the imagination of the writer is above average. In the instance of this boy, in whom apparent good judgment, concentration, and the capacity for independent thought combine with imagination, we may be safe in assuming that his background offers intellectual stimulation, training in cooperation, social feeling, and encouragement. His letter reads: "I am a boy of 14 years of age and am entering high school. My Grandfather and father were prominent lawyers but I have a great desire to study medicine." (For medicine, it is important that a child show all the signs of being a natural-born student. Thus, this boy's goal is well-chosen.)

Although his capitalizing of the word "Grandfather" shows an innate respect for the gentleman, his desire to be superior to his environment is indicated not only in his expression of independence, but also in his unusual handwriting. The *t* bar above the stem of the letter further indicates a spirit of adventure and in this instance a desire to explore a field different from his father's and grandfather's.

Careful punctuation gives evidence of a retentive memory, as well as a desire to be thorough. The emotions, on the threshold of awakening, make him restless, and for this reason the base lines in the specimen show a tendency to waver. However, adolescence presents no problems that he cannot solve.

The Problem Child (Age 9)

SPECIMEN 6

With proper encouragement and patience exerted in the interest of this boy of nine, he could develop into a useful member of society, since he has the energy, intelligence, and ambition to be "somebody." His high upper loops (which normally show idealism) are exaggerated in this case and reveal a fantasy world to which he retreats when he feels that the world of reality does not accept his aggressive maneuvers. The text of the specimen was dictated to him by a parent who wields a domineering hand, disciplining the boy to the point where he rebels. Already we see signs of rebelliousness in many downstrokes of the *t* bar, especially in the word "diligently." Other strong and firm *t* bars tell us he is a willful, demanding child, and the large writing (indicative of extroversion) shows his constant bid for attention. This is understandable when we know he is the second child competing with an older brother whom he is desperately trying to outdistance. While roundness exists here, revealing the child, there is also angularity that tells us he can be demanding, exacting, uncompromising, and uncooperative. The broad r's reveal a strong visual sense, and the wide spacing between letters—noticeable especially in the first and second lines—gives us already a hint of paranoid trends. Given direction by someone in authority whom he likes and respects, this boy could some day apply those traits that now appear as faults to constructive goals. Though somewhat cramped, because of the ruled lines on which he was asked to write, the words are clear and the letter forms more or less uniform; the meticulous dotting of i's shows his excellent memory. The elimination of an initial stroke on the letters d and o indicates intelligence in this kind of writing. The child means business and will get what he wants out of life, even if he has to ride roughshod over others. However, if he can learn to cooperate with others and develop social feelings, he can turn out to be a leader of sorts, even if an officer in the army. He resents having discipline imposed on him, but he himself has all the makings of a relentless disciplinarian.

School Influences

If teachers could understand what causes a child to write poorly, they could be an important influence in helping to correct some of the mistakes made in the home environment. (We are not talking here of children reared in institutions, or the victims of broken homes.) A child whose handwriting is poor or illegible is definitely disturbed in some way. If an older child continues to misspell or to leave out letters in words it may be a serious symptom of brain damage and may become more evident in a child's inability to learn quickly or to concentrate. This is extreme, of course, as with a retarded child, but it is worth considering.

It is a good idea to keep a watchful eye, with patience and understanding, on the recalcitrant child, to confer with parents about his behavior, to ask for an encephalograph to be taken, or even to seek corroboration from a graphologist who has worked specifically on children's handwriting. A rebellious child just might be a mentally sick one, although this does not always follow. Withdrawn children who are unable to cooperate with others, who show no interest in play, and to whom writing is a major effort need special attention.

There is, of course, the healthy intelligent child who dislikes routine yet learns quickly from being exposed to knowledge. His writing may be illegible and unsightly, but it will reveal signs of unusual intelligence and ability and is readily recognized by the graphologist as different from that of the disturbed child. It may even be a healthy type of discontent, as in the instance of the athletic boy whose overprotective mother won't allow him to be physically active for fear he might hurt himself.

Dedicated teachers will soon recognize what motivates the child. They spot the one who prefers to take the lead, the follower, the lazy child—who is often the pampered one. And they have no difficulty in spotting the troublemaker. In examining the handwriting of this last, we often find that he has a vivid imagination, coupled with a creative urge that is not finding expression for lack of understanding and encouragement. His handwriting will show his lack of discipline. In many instances where the handwriting of parents was examined (as was done in a clinic for disturbed children), we discovered why the child was in open rebellion. Any kind of troublemaking was found to be an attention-getting device and turned out to be an indictment against too much domination and not enough love. Parents might be encouraged to cooperate with teachers and together bring out whatever constructive elements the handwriting reveals and take steps to redirect destructive behavior into useful channels.

The line between childhood mistakes and adult failure is a direct one, and unless such mistakes are corrected early the problem child may turn out to be a problem adult. Even severe damage done in childhood, unless it be serious brain damage, can often be corrected as long as the child is made to feel he is wanted and loved and that he belongs.

The child who gets good marks in school will not necessarily become an outstanding adult. He may never be an innovator or iconoclast, whereas the one who is a little devil might. He might be the one who thinks too independently to follow the textbooks, and later become what is often referred to as "a self-made man."

But there is also the rebel without a cause who may end up behind prison bars because of antisocial traits he revealed as a child. His parents will have no idea what led him into crime, nor will they realize that it isn't what happened during his childhood that counted so much as the meaning he gave to it.

Sophistication in Children

Dear Madame

I wish you would tell me along with my character analsys why I am not more popular with boys. I am fourteen. years old.

SPECIMEN 7

The unusually observant growing child, mentally beyond his years, is one who is often reared among grownups instead of with children his own age and who develops a sophistication beyond his years. He is the product of our modern times, very often a child of modern parents who permit the youngsters to sit in at their cocktail parties. The modern mother, interested in her own independent self-expression, whose interests are outside the home rather than in it, does not always take the time or have the patience to play down to the children—if she spends much time at all with them. She encourages them instead to enter into her games, to listen to the kind of music she enjoys, even to reading books of her choice. This results in a kind of sophisticated development of the child, bringing us face to face with many of our present-day problems. We may find such a girl (fifteen or younger) telling her mother where to get off at the same time that she emulates her mother's style of dress and her self-centered habits. The old myth of "children should be seen and not heard" has long ago gone by the boards in our present family gatherings, and in many instances the unchildlike child takes over the conversation and holds forth.

Specimen 7 is an example of what I might describe as a sophisticated girl of 14. One glance at the writing shows its unusual formations; its compactness expresses a mind possessing original ideas, with powers of concentration. The vertical angle, coupled with mental formations (explained in a later chapter), is indicative of a cool, analytical intellect in control of the emotions. Her mental age might well be twice her years. The emotions, not yet fully developed, are repressed and generated into intellectualizing. She is extremely individualistic, unusually critical and observant, and possesses marked talent. She could be a writer, a painter, a musician—anything along creative lines she chooses to follow.

She writes none of the formations taught her in school. Small letters reconstructed from ordinary copybook forms (*s* and *b*) reveal a mind that can formulate ideas independently, and she can make decisions in the same way. Capital letters are also printed, and the severe capital *I* is conclusive proof of clarity of thought and a somewhat detached, sophisticated approach to life. Environmental influences, coupled with an inherently alert mental mechanism, have resulted in this writing. What knowledge she has not acquired through actual experience she has gained through observation in her extensive traveling and avid reading. In this handwriting there slumbers the root of genius. Whether it will blossom to maturity depends largely upon how she develops emotionally in the next few years. (Read her letter: "along with my character analysis . . . why I am not more popular with boys. I am fourteen years old.") She would not attract boys, certainly not in her own age group, because she is so much more mature than they are, and it would be hard to find a meeting of minds with any except a much older man.

Immature Adult

Although this was written by a woman in her early 30's, the mother of three (the oldest 6), her rounded handwriting might readily belong in the category of Specimen 1. We might say that emotionally she is somewhere around 13. She is fairly well organized, however, which shows in the carefulness with which she organizes her writing, the clear spacing between lines and words, a good margin

to take to you when he goes to
country on Thursday. Thank-
again for allowing me the p
of reading "Your Siamese Cat,"
the use of the carrier.

SPECIMEN 8

on the left, careful dotting of *i*'s and crossing of *t*'s. Her home re-
flects her desire for orderliness and cleanliness; her children are
well attended to. She is submissive to the wishes of her husband and
in every respect essentially feminine. There are signs of constructiveness in the printing of some capital letters (the *S* and *T*), telling us
of a desire to improve and do what is right. Her rising lines reveal
optimism. Living a sheltered life as she does, it is doubtful that her
handwriting will develop sharp edges, for even if left to her own
resources she would seek and eventually find someone to take care
of her.

Adolescent Boy (Age 15)

Adolescence is the period when most boys make an attempt to
assert their independence, especially where they have been given
some leeway to make their own decisions, and we have here a good
example of such a boy. There is a strong mixture of angularity and
roundness. His intelligence is above average; his small writing shows
ability to concentrate in studies; the excellent spacing between words
and lines reveals a capacity to organize his effort and time. The un-
embellished capital *T* followed by a mental formation of the small
h, careful *i* dots, and the sign of good judgment in his lower loops,
tell us he has a measure of common sense. That some of the *t* bars
do not go through the stem of the letter, showing some indecisive-

This summer I am going to be a Counselor in Training at a work camp in Connecticut. I shall be taught how to work with kids from 12 up, and will, in addition, have a good time myself.

SPECIMEN 9

ness and dependence, merely tells us he is on the threshold of making his own decisions and he tends to waver. As yet he is still somewhat self-conscious. But in the *gestalt* (the entire handwriting) there is good evidence that he can conquer his dependency in time and become a constructively functioning adult. The short, blunt endings on words are indicative of a reserve that prevents him from expressing himself spontaneously. But working as a counselor in a summer camp will help make him more outgoing and cooperative, and this will set the tone for a useful future in which he will have overcome the weaker traits. (Indecision is not necessarily a trait of a child or adolescent; many adults are indecisive. In an adolescent it is natural; in an adult we must look for other signs of neurosis in the handwriting.)

Adolescent Girl (Age 14)

This specimen might well be that of a mature adult for all the angularity, powers of concentration, good judgment, and independent thinking it shows. And although there are signs of indecision, as expected of an adolescent, there is also a sign that indicates self-assuredness and self-discipline. She is a natural student; her mind is keen, incisive, capable of clear logical reasoning, with occasional

Feb 18, 1964

Dear Miss Olyanova

   I have heard that you are quite good at analyzing handwriting. I would like you to analyze mine and the enclosed letter from Mr. A. W. Lawrence. He is a professor of archeology at Cambridge University, and the brother of Lawrence of Arabia. I would also like the enclosed page from a book analyzed, the writing is that of T. E. Lawrence, Lawrence of Arabia.

   The loose-leaf paper which is also enclosed is a better specimen of my own writing, and would you please consider that rather than this? I am doing a special study on T. E. Lawrence, and feel that the only sure way to get to his personality is through a complete analysis of his handwriting. I'm a 14 year old girl.

SPECIMEN 10

flashes of intuition (shown in the breaks in words). Problems are bound to arise where the intellect has advanced so far ahead of the emotions, but in her curious and searching way, she may find solutions to her emotional problems. Most of her energy is generated into thinking, but the heavy pressure tells us she is also capable of physical activity and strong feelings, and this combination can be unbeatable. There is a chance that the handwriting may become larger and more expansive as she encounters emotional experiences, but the instinct of the introvert, the hermit, will probably always remain a part of her, and it is not likely that she will ever abandon her intellectual pursuits for any length of time. The lines have a tendency to slant downward, disclosing a leaning toward skepticism. The mind doubts until it can find answers. There is so little of the child here that we wonder how she gets on with other children her age, and whether she does not often feel her isolation. Her potentialities for becoming a writer, a researcher, or a scientist are apparent. She also has an interest in music, and could probably learn to play some instrument extremely well.

Where rounded handwriting may in time, and with individual development, become angular, the opposite is true of angular writing. Once it reaches a definitely angular form, it will not become rounded again, unless there is a complete regression to childhood, as happens occasionally in cases of senility. This is a logical conclusion, for in angular writing the experiences have already worn their groove in the inner consciousness. We may encounter instances of people who appear hard or cynical yet underneath they are quite gullible. They are usually the ones who start out in life with unreceptive mentalities (commonly referred to as bull-headedness), but they have thin hides, and through their hypersensitivity they become hardened in self-defense.

II

Extroverts and Introverts

*Some for the Glories of This World; and some
Sigh for the Prophet's Paradise to come;
Ah, take the Cash, and let the Credit go,
Nor heed the rumble of a distant Drum!*
—OMAR KHAYYÁM

EXTROVERTS AND INTROVERTS

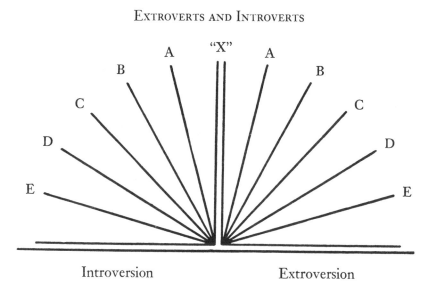

Introversion   Extroversion

THE DIRECTION IN WHICH YOUR HANDWRITING slants points the way "from you to me." In your environmental history and in the experiences that have affected your development during the formative years and influenced your approach to life can be discovered why your handwriting leans to the right or left, or is vertical. If you have been yanked in several directions by conflicting forces in your early life, this will have affected your handwriting, and it may still reveal an inner conflict that has not yet been resolved.

The degree of emotional intensity you are capable of reveals itself in the pen pressure. But how much of this you express is determined in the slant; we will call it the angle of inclination.

If you are a social, gregarious, impulsive, and demonstrative person, with a liking for people—or an absolute need of them—if your energies flow outward, you belong somewhere on the right side of this diagram among the extroverts. Your handwriting will have a rhythmic, spontaneous, rightward flow. The more slant your writing has, the more apt you are to show your feelings.

Introvert tendencies begin to manifest themselves as the slant of the writing becomes less pronounced—swinging first to the vertical angle—then backward—and the degree of the left slant helps to determine the extent to which the person pulls away from other people. Emotions are less in evidence and reason becomes prevalent.

The vertical writer usually has his emotions under control; his mind sits in judgment and checks the impulses, and the person is not as a rule spontaneous in expressing his feelings.

Backhand writers, those who belong on the extreme left side of the diagram, are those in whom introvert tendencies have become habits. They are the ones whose social environment during the formative years developed in them a measure of isolation, inhibition, repression, and selectiveness. They are often undemonstrative, reticent, and withdrawn, though there are exceptions who are not so reticent and who, in fact, can be quite talkative. They do, however, usually reflect before taking action; many of them take rather than give, but there are exceptions who may give lavishly, often to a cause or to what they consider a worthwhile philanthropy.

The interest is more apt to be in things rather than in people, toward whom they often have a detached attitude, and the interest is greater in self than in sharing a social life with others. The need for human companionship is less pronounced than is that of the rightward slanters, and the desire is often to be alone, with emphasis on privacy.

The emotional intensity of D and E on the left side of the diagram is equal in degree to D and E on the right side, but where there is an ease of expression on the right side, on the left the energies flow inward, augmenting the intensity and affecting the attitudes and approach to life of the backhand writer.

Environmental Influences That Develop the Extrovert

Not without reason does the psychiatrist question the patient regarding his early memories and background when making a diagnosis. It is in childhood (as we have said) that the behavior pattern of a human being's adult life begins to form.

In a family where there is more than one child, the social instinct becomes more strongly developed among the members. A bond of affection is often created among the children, as well as a spirit of give and take. The intelligent mother will show no partiality, giving all the children equal attention and privileges, and they grow up normally extroverted, with consideration for one another's rights and desires. However, few mothers show such impartiality, and should there be a particularly delicate or sick child in the family, that one is apt to receive the most attention. This may develop a selfishness in the sick child at the same time that it arouses negative feelings in other members of the family.

One child may become rebellious because "dear little Arthur" gets everything he wants. This arouses in the child feelings of deprivation and a desire to compete for Mother's attention, and this spirit of rebellion and competition may cause in him a desire to show that he is worthy of more than he is receiving. Already we see here the beginning of an extrovert pattern.

Another child, perhaps more sensitive and feeling neglected, may become resentful, and instead of acting in a way to attract the attention of the mother, may withdraw into himself and find relief in fantasies, developing an outer mien of aloofness or superiority. He may feel, and tell himself, he is better than "little Arthur" and doesn't have to be pampered. Or he may decide to show that he is independent of his family and seek approbation from people outside of the home, perhaps his teacher or a neighbor. Thus the extrovert pattern is formed, and the child carries it with him into a world in which he works toward becoming a superior human being.

The only child, often writing a vertical hand, exercises his will over his parents, knowing they will give him what he wants because of attentions they shower on him. After he has left his childhood kingdom, where he may have reigned tyrannically, he often has difficulty in adjusting himself to a world that does not cater to his every wish. He therefore builds up a compensatory self-importance in his own segregated world and develops introverted qualities. He feels that no one understands him, and in consequence does not always make the effort to make himself understood or to cooperate. (Specimen 7 is an example of such a child, except that she has an overcompensation: her mentality is keenly developed, placing her above average intellectually but presenting difficulties in her attempts at emotional adjustment.)

The sickly child in a family group might as well be the only child because of the attention he receives. He is usually pampered and spoiled. His illness becomes an integral part of his behavior pattern and he uses it to command those around him. Here the roots of selfishness and introversion are nurtured, and he grows up with a feeling of exclusiveness that he carries with him all his life. Such childen belong on the introversion side of the diagram in the leftward slant of their handwriting.

Although normally the upright, vertical hand shows reserve and introverted tendencies, a definite exception is made where the writing is very large. Any very large writing shows exhibitionism, no matter what the angle. We encounter it in some models or show people, in individuals in whom narcissism is an outstanding trait. The angle of inclination is, therefore, of secondary importance when drawing graphological conclusions.

The Extrovert

An extrovert is one whose motivating desires and goals bring him into contact with the outside world. He is often gregarious, impulsive, and usually demonstrative. He needs human companionship and has an interest in external objects. His energies flow outward, and there is a greater desire for activity than there is for contemplation. He can usually mix with other people and usually seeks their approval, and his activities are planned to bring him into contact with the outside world. He is able to form human attachments, is usually sentimental, and is frequently guided more by emotion than by reason in forming decisions.

The extrovert acts in accordance with the dictates of his emotions, preferring to share his feelings, whether of joy or sorrow, with others. He is often impelled to give confidences, and he derives a certain pleasure from giving in the material sense also. Friendship is important to the extrovert, in many cases meaning more to him than material possessions. (There are exceptions, of course, but these are determined by other factors besides slant.)

The handwriting of the extrovert leans to the right and will usually be large or medium large. It will have a smooth rhythmic flow, may or may not have flourishes, and may have as many rounded forms as angular ones. Pen pressure may be heavy or medium heavy, in some instances even light, depending on the physical make-up of the writer and his sensory apparatus.

Because of the social nature of the extrovert—the desire to be among people, to feel he belongs, to share—sex impulses will usually be stronger than in the introvert. Pleasures and sensations are more fully enjoyed if shared with someone else. And although he prefers being active to being pinned down to routine or confined to a desk, he may also have periods of reflection when he wants solitude. Such isolated moods are often the forerunners of planned action. He rarely delves into himself to get closer to his unconscious motivations, unless forced by circumstances to be alone a great deal.

There are extroverts who, by virtue of their superior intellects, enjoy acquiring knowledge for its own sake. But such a person will be less of a mixer than other outgoing people, even though his interest in others is not lessened. He may express his interest through the medium of art, music, or literature, and his subject will usually be people. To mingle with them may serve as a means of studying and observing them. In this type of extrovert there is usually an admixture of the introvert, just as in many introverts we discover extrovert qualities. To be a complete introvert would mean living the life of a hermit, and the extreme extrovert could be quite wearing if one had to live with him. The handwriting of the intellectual extrovert is concentrated and may be either small or medium large.

The angle is usually vertical (Specimen 157). Because of this mixture it is often difficult to determine which predominates, extroversion or introversion.

There are extroverts who, having suffered an emotional shock, may renounce the world and withdraw into a secluded life. A disappointment in love or the loss of a loved one may drive a man to a monastery, a woman to a convent. If they have a vocation to the religious life, it is safe to assume there was probably some introversion in the nature to begin with. Those who leave the monastic life do so because the outside world appeals to their extroverted qualities.

The handwriting of such people may lean to the right, but it is in the letter formations and light pen pressure that we see the desire for a life of spirituality and isolation. The spiritual tendencies could have been recognized before the unhappy event that drove them to a life of seclusion.

Not all rightward-leaning writers are purely extroverted, although most extroverts write with a rightward slant. Much depends on the experiences that impelled them to, or prevented them from, seeking outward expression.

Goals of Extroverts

From the time little Ruthie begins to recite in class, or Johnny struts his stuff whenever company arrives (with Mother's approval and encouragement), extrovert qualities begin to show. Ruthie may aspire to be an actress when she grows up, and Johnny a policeman or soldier—in fact any choice in which he might bedeck himself in uniform. Encouraged by parents to mingle with people, and prodded by the environment to seek a position of importance and superiority, the extroverted child finds many paths beckoning him as he seeks extrovert goals.

The ladder of extroverts is a long one and almost as broad as it is long (unlike the narrow, often isolated ladder of the introverts). On the top rung we are confronted with the statesman—an articulate FDR, for instance—and somewhere along the line we find the Billy Grahams and the Senator Dirksens with their qualities of showmanship. At the very bottom of the ladder are a large number of the common variety of show-offs or exhibitionists. The intellectual development determines the particular rung on which the individual belongs. The soapbox orator belongs in this group, too, as do many clergymen, salesmen, movie stars, and limelighted personalities.

One kind of extrovert personality is invariably recognized graphologically by his underscored signature. The personality may be at variance with the character itself, which may have introverted elements, as in the case of George Bernard Shaw (Specimen 91). But the underscore is a confession of the person's desire to enter into the world's game and to be recognized as outstanding in it. To underscore your signature is a way of saying: "I am important. Applaud me." (There is a deep psychological, as well as graphological, significance to the underscore, which is discussed later.) It is an expression of a positive personality and indicates that the goal this person has chosen was designed to bring him the approval of the outside world. It is a gesture of emphasis.

Not all extroverts underscore their signatures, of course. The insurance salesman, the clerk, and the stevedore may have a strong desire for world approval, expressing it when with their families and friends or their superiors. The handwriting of these people may not show anything particularly individualistic, but in the slant we see them as belonging on the extroverted side.

Most extroverts select goals that bring them into contact with people—where they might perform a service, or use physical energy, or have opportunities for conversation—and usually do their work in a spirit of cooperation. The force that flows outwardly must have a definite objective in view or the person is not happy. The more extroverted the person, and the more spontaneous, demonstrative, expansive, and talkative he is, the larger will be his handwriting in its rightward slant.

Handwritings of Extroverts

This man is intense, ardent; possesses strong sex impulses, shown in long lower loops. The nature is impulsive and supersensitive. He has a definite need for people, and he seeks their approval. Decisions are predicated much more on feeling than on reasoning, but there are

SPECIMEN 11

signs of self-control as well as aggressiveness. Although there is some confusion in the letters of the upper line running into the line below, this man manages to fill a useful niche in an extroverted role of working with other people.

SPECIMEN 12

Here is an indication of the mild extrovert in whom there is a mixture of sentimentality and reason. Her need for affection and human companionship is greater than for material possessions, but she is sufficiently materialistic to enjoy the creature comforts of life, especially if she can share them.

This is a combination of extroverted emotions and introverted

I wish to thank you very much
for your kind information regarding
Sylvus book and shall buy a copy

SPECIMEN 13

mentality. The interest is in intellectual achievement, in research that involves a knowledge of human behavior. The angular structure tells us the person has a keen intelligence and is mature.

I don't know if you are at
the same address, but I do hope
that you are still helping people
to know & understand their friends,
enemies and relations —

SPECIMEN 14

This handwriting shows social extrovert tendencies, but there is a selectivity, an aloofness, here, and the person does not mix intimately with other people unless she considers them on her social level. She is friendly but discriminating. She keeps a distance between herself and those outside her social stratum. She has been conditioned to a life of material wealth and prestige, and respects it in others. Tendencies of both extrovert and introvert are seen here. Now, although she shows an interest in other people, most of it is detached, even impersonal. There will always be a barrier between her and other people, despite her capacity for making friends. She might be described as a quasi introvert.

Traits of Introverts

The traits of the introvert become more pronounced in vertical and backhand writing. Impulses are consciously held in check by the mind, which has formed the habit of sitting in judgment. Among backhand writers are found a variety of inhibited, repressed, undemonstrative people, most of them lacking in spontaneity. They are usually reticent in a group of people, but they may talk obsessively on some particular subject when someone draws them out. They do not give confidences readily or invite them. They may be outwardly formal, seldom go out of their way to cultivate new friends, and in many instances are more concerned with possessions than with people.

The energies of the introvert flow inward. Should the person be emotionally ardent (shown by heavy pen pressure), the result is often introspection, intense suffering, unless the emotions are sublimated in some art form of expression. In the introvert, work can absorb the emotional energies and will often come ahead of human considerations.

The left-slant writer does not particularly desire or need the contact of other people, yet once he does form an alliance or relationship, it has deep roots and can last forever. To the extrovert, he appears aloof, independent, self-sufficient, even snobbish, for he does not invite closeness or intimacy. He is usually more self-centered than the extrovert, often preferring to be left alone; if forced by circumstances to mix with others, he can maintain a formality that prevents intrusion into his inner self. He is slow to let go of resentments and is less likely to be as forgiving as the extrovert, who in his great need for people may overlook hurts done to him.

Because the introvert is by his very nature brought into close contact with his subconscious self, he is often more sensitive, more reflective, and more introspective than the extrovert. Often he is more interested in the development of his ego than in being one of a group, and if he has a keen intellectual endowment, he may possess a richer inner life than outer one.

Environmental Influences of Introverts

Much of the introversion of backhand writers is the result, in most cases, of an incident of repression in childhood. As explained earlier, the only child and the sickly child come under this category. The sensitive, impressionable child, victimized by too much parental domination and discipline, may seek refuge within himself in an attempt to escape from his parents' harshness. He finds fantasies much more rewarding than reality, and in his introverted pattern builds a world no one can enter. He may prefer to play alone, to wander off into the woods by himself, to commune with nature. Or books might be his cherished companions. If mechanical-minded, he may show an interest in mechanical toys, perhaps invent some. Often he does not know how to play with other children and they leave him alone. He may become a loner in later life, at which time other people sense this and leave him to himself. This happens if he has been encouraged in childhood to remain by himself much of the time. He may be a studious child, interested in the esoteric; he may turn out to be a physicist or a writer. The possibilities for such a person are legion, but in any work he chooses, he will continue to be an isolate and, as such, different in many respects from the general run of human beings.

In Specimen 7, which we have referred to previously, there is a need for human companionship, which the writer's intellectual superiority prevents her from having with children her own age. Childish games would appear foolish to her, and so she finds refuge in books and in painting.

Where there are other children in the family the introvert may start by being the problem child. Quiet and undemonstrative, or nervous and finicky, he might, under the guidance of a neurotic mother, reflect her distorted view of life, and this will appear in his handwriting at a very early age.

Backhand Writers

In women who write backhanded, the tendency to vivify inanimate objects is often present. In an extreme case known to me, a maternal instinct became so twisted that a pet animal was clothed in human dress and treated as a member of the family. (For the most part, the backhand writers I have known have not devoted themselves to pets.) Others I have known have married men much older than themselves in their search for a father-figure, someone to cater to an indulgent life that began in childhood. Lacking the romantic sentiment of the spontaneous rightward-writing extrovert, the backhanded introvert's choice of a mate is often deliberate and devoid of sentiment. The marriage may be entered into for reasons of physical comfort, if not for prestige or position. They give very little of themselves and, in their choice of older men, aim to receive attention rather than to give it. Although there is a quality of romanticism, it is more the adventurous kind wherein they might indulge in a love of luxury, ease, and traveling. Frequently they are style-conscious and pay a great deal of attention to clothes. Many of them feel they are in a class by themselves—and some of them definitely are.

Among male backhand writers there is often found a detached form of sensuality. They approach sex simply as another appetite to be satisfied, and this same deliberateness is prevalent in their approach to other issues. The desire for power, prestige, individual gratification, is stronger than that of companionship. Should the backhanded writer be a creative artist (as is often true), he finds emotional gratification in his art. He will prefer to work independently of others (most artists do), will not seek the approbation of the outside world (feeling that he is not appreciated or understood), and will tend to evaluate his work by the money it earns rather than by its intrinsic value as a work of art.

Because the introvert prefers his own society to that of other people, because his desire for ego-gratification is stronger than his desire for others' approval, his energies are projected upon himself, and his sex impulses are not apt to be so strong as those of the extrovert. When they are strong, they are still likely to be secondary in importance to ego-gratification, and can therefore be rather disappointing to a sex partner who enjoys spontaneous lovemaking. His approach to sexual matters might readily be a detached, impersonal one; he might even use sex as a means to an end—an ambition or a goal. His preoccupation with self precludes the giving of self, so important in sexual matters. He might rather give of his worldly goods than of himself and will do so generously. This not giving of self is derived from fear generated during his formative years, and it has inhibited him to such an extent that he finds it almost impossible to give of himself without feeling he is losing something.

The introverted members of society, whose exclusive upbringing has made them feel they are special and has developed in them a selectivity, whether of possessions, companions, or estates, are more the result of conditioning influences than of a desire to get closer to their inner selves. They are more likely to inhabit the exclusive beaches, attend social functions, and have their names in the society columns than is the introvert who becomes so because of unusual sensitivity and keen mental fiber. The latter type of introvert (often found at the top of the ladder) may become immortal through creative or scientific or philosophic contributions to mankind. Such men and women are in a class by themselves, and their handwriting does not lean backward. They are not lacking in either sentiment or empathy, but are often timid and supersensitive; not consciously aloof from people, they are necessarily so in order to have time for reflection and for their work. They have gained recognition, without seeking it, because of their genius. (Further on in Specimen 100, the writer Jakob Wassermann is a good example of the introvert described above.)

Because of the need for self-expression rather than for worldly activity or achievement, the person of strong introvert traits is often found in creative fields. Although the theater primarily attracts the extrovert, there are some exceptions. Eleonora Duse was one of these, and so is Katharine Cornell. Miss Cornell's vertical writing reveals many of the elements of the introvert. She has some shyness with regard to publicity, but I have nevertheless been fortunate enough to get a sample of her handwriting (see Specimen 111).

Introversion and Genius

The isolated ladder of genius, on whose few rungs we find greatness and introversion combined, has given us Beethoven, Schopenhauer, Nietzsche, Cézanne, Kant, Newton, Kierkegaard, Lamb, and Ibsen among others. Frustration, due to some physical defect in many of these men, had the effect of forcing them to develop rich inner lives. Their biographies disclose the nature of their defects. Their contributions were their release from overwhelming suffering; through their very torture the world has been enriched.

Seemingly unfriendly, they were often misunderstood, and their closeness to their unconscious in their need for ego-gratification prevented an easy outer communication with other people. They communicated through their contributions. Beethoven, in his deafness, developed an inner ear that helped give birth to symphonies that stir us, often without our knowing why. Were it not for his seclusiveness and introversion, which began in childhood and crystallized later through his deafness, he might not have had this tremendous musical power. (See Specimen 86.)

Handwriting of Introverts

SPECIMEN 15

Here we have the introvert who is trying his vocation in a monastery. The left slant with fairly light pen pressure indicates his

withdrawal from social life; *t* bars are almost consistently bowed
and tell us of a development of habitual self-discipline. Despite evidence of roundedness on the upper part of letter forms, there is an
over-all rigidity pointing to scrupulosity that results in an uncompromising attitude sometimes carried to extremes. He keeps his distance from other human beings, who (he feels) are sinful and con-
taminated by worldliness. There are signs of talent in his printed
letters, coupled with intuition in the breaks in words, much of which
he sublimates in worship or in art designed "for the glory of God."
Yet when faced with practical issues he can use good judgment,
keeps on an even keel within the framework of his circumscribed
environment, and is well suited to his vocation—into which he was
led by desires that go back to his childhood. He would have difficulty
adjusting to the outside world, but he functions quite well within
the confines of a monastery.

SPECIMEN 16

This is the backhand of an intensely emotional individual who is
self-centered and exacting (shown in the angular formations), yet
there are signs of roundness, too, telling us she sometimes is childish in
her demands and can be unreasonable. Not an extreme introvert,
despite the far-left slant due to large writing, she nevertheless keeps
a distance between herself and other people—except for her family,

whom she considers an extension of herself. The hook on the end of the word "though" is a sign of tenacity, and although she is not in perfect health, she hangs on to life, having a strong instinct for survival.

SPECIMEN 17

Introversion here is predominant—shown in the small writing, the upright angle, the light pen pressure. There are signs of culture in the Greek *d* and in the *g* made like a figure 8, and a vivid imagination and a spirit of adventure in the *t* bar, which appears above the stem of the letter. She enjoys adventures of the mind, is scholarly, and can express herself with facility in writing. She can be friendly, as shown in the flexible roundness; she has a desire to cooperate, mostly with people with whom she has communication in areas that interest her. For the most part, she prefers to be alone as long as she is concentrating on intellectual pursuits, but she can be a good listener when in the company of others. Passivity is evident, for most of her energy goes into thinking, but she will share her thoughts with those with whom she has common interests. Essentially a gentle person, extremely sensitive and impressionable, she avoids noise, dissension, and excitement, finding this last in her intellectual pursuits.

This writing (18) leans in several directions, telling us that this is a man of moods, of sudden changes in feeling. When he is not on the defensive, as seen in the down-slanting *t* bar in the word "last," he can be generous and giving (formation of the *y* in "days"). He is impatient, as shown in the quick, erratic rhythm of the writing;

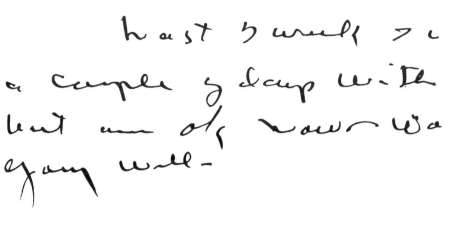

SPECIMEN 18

at times he appears aloof and resorts to pontification, and at other times he withdraws and feels sorry for himself. In the over-all picture we see a person with a number of problems, some of them predicated on paranoid trends, corroborated by the wide spacing between words. For the most part he feels misunderstood, yet he seldom puts forth the effort to make himself understood. When life becomes too much of a burden he is apt to blame others, alternating between masochism and sadism and suffering tremendous guilt feelings. He is unpredictable, and an intimate association with him could be devastating to the other person. Yet the specimen is placed with some order on the page, and the lines between sentences are clear. This tells us that there is some organization even in his disorder. He is a man of good intelligence, but his emotions keep him in a stew and color his judgment. He might be described as an ambivert, but essentially he belongs in the category of the neurotic.

Left-Handed Writers

It does not usually follow that the writing of the person who uses his left hand must veer to the left. There is no reason to believe that because you write with your left hand you are introverted, asocial, or an isolate. If the left-handed person's writing leans to the left, it is because he belongs on the left side of the diagram, and he would be there no matter which hand he used. However, if of his own volition he changes over to writing with his right hand, it gives him an added advantage. For the determination that impelled him to do this will show strength of resolve and affect other areas of his life, besides making him ambidextrous. It is a big mistake, however, for any adult to force a child to use his right hand if he is naturally left-handed. We often find among stutterers people who had been forced as children to change to the right hand, but today this is not likely to happen.

In my experience, I have discovered that most left-handed writers possess some unusual ability in one area or another. If they happen to have difficult problems for which they need therapeutic help, it is for other reasons and not because of their left-handedness. In any event, it takes strength of purpose for a left-handed writer to adjust himself to a right-handed world, and he therefore has the potentiality for making himself outstanding in the work he chooses, provided he is suited to it to start with.

Circumstances arise at times that force right-handed people to learn the use of the left hand. A notable example is Horatio Nelson, who lost his right hand in battle. It took patience and self-discipline, the sign of which is shown almost consistently, in the following two specimens, in the significantly bowed *t* bar.

In the right-slanted one, we see an ardent, outgoing, impulsive person, strongly sexed but controlled. His involved capital *H* shows a tendency to get into tight situations, from which, by logic and strategy, he could emerge. The embellished ending on the signature is larger than the rest of the writing, gives us his sense of the dramatic, and shows a dominant personality.

In the sample written with his left hand, ten years after he lost his right one, the angle is notably changed and vertical, showing a prevalence of reason over emotion. Intuition has developed in these intervening years, as shown in breaks in words, which did not appear as often in the earlier sample. His capital *N* now takes on an old-fashioned form, revealing a paternalism which became more distinct after his adventurous life. Both specimens show some similarities, as in the capital *B*. He had become more realistic and less romantic in his approach to life; his emotions were tempered by reason, and he derived pleasure from reading and reflecting, where formerly he was a man of action.

Horatio Nelson

WRITTEN WITH THE RIGHT HAND

SPECIMEN 19

WRITTEN WITH THE LEFT HAND

SPECIMEN 19A

The following two specimens (20 and 20A) were written by natural left-handed writers. The first one discloses several angles—vertical, right, and far right—telling us that the writer is volatile, changeable, subject to changing moods. But he can exercise self-control where necessary (as shown in his bowed *t* bars), and *t* bars that appear above the stem reveal his spirit of adventure and vivid imagination. There are signs of talent and versatility, and the unique

way he forms his capital *N* shows individuality. Essentially the
angle is rightward and shows his leaning toward people and his need
for human companionship.

SPECIMEN 20

SPECIMEN 20A

Another left-handed writer, this one writes in a fairly consistent
vertical angle. It is a kind of reserve that is mitigated by the essential
roundness of the writing, which tells us that the person is pliable,
flexible, and yielding, although her conditioning influences—she
was the first born—caused a sense of isolation. But the writing is
medium large, showing more extroversion than is usually shown in
vertical writers. She has talent for the stage and for literary achieve-

ment (see the *g* made like an 8), and she possesses intuition. There is a hint of the rightward turn on the downstroke of the *y*, so altruistic tendencies are here, along with a desire to make a worthwhile contribution to the outside world.

(See Specimen 112 for an example of a woman painter who is a left-handed writer.)

III

Talent and the Choice of Vocation

*Talent is developed in retirement: character is
formed in the rush of the world.*
—GOETHE

Hobbies and Interests of Children

PARENTS WHO REALLY CARE ABOUT THE OVER-ALL
development of their children will note their children's interests and
encourage them in achieving their goals. Unfortunately, parents may
also insist on certain goals that are not suited to the child's native
talents, and it is then that discontent follows. A parent whose own
ambition has been frustrated may try to realize it through his child.
A father may choose a career for his son without considering the
son's aptitudes or desires. He may want his son ultimately to carry on
the family business, not realizing that the boy may be better equipped
for an artistic or professional career. This is perhaps the main reason
why there are so many square pegs in round holes, why men who are
eminently suited for a career in law or medicine are laboring unhap-
pily in the rank and file of business offices.

The hobbies of children offer clues to their interests and capabilities. A child can often do best what he has a natural liking for. The
boy who derives a keen pleasure from his collection of tools may develop into a craftsman or inventor. A child may express a desire to be
a teacher or a lawyer or a surgeon because of someone he admires.
Boys who look up to their fathers as heroes may express a desire to
follow in the same work.

Children who enjoy manual work, where they have a chance to use
their hands, and who are adept in the use of tools may later develop
into furniture designers, or if the aesthetic quality in the child is stim-

ulated, into architects. In handwriting, this will become evident very early, in the constructing of severe capital letters or the printing of small letters, apart from the copybook formations the child is taught to make in school.

Many children express a desire to become pilots because they have a strong spirit of adventure. If the writing reveals mechanical tendencies which the child also manifests in his hobbies, and if he has a natural bent for mathematics, the parents should encourage him. This same bent may lead to a career in engineering or banking or accounting. So much depends on the ultimate wishes of the child and the encouragement he receives at home.

Too often, however, parents turn a deaf ear to the expressed desires of children, or belittle their ambitions. This can create in the child feelings of inferiority, so that he keeps his cherished ambitions to himself. He may develop a disrespectful attitude toward the parent who belittles him, for children are more sensitive to criticism than parents realize. Waving aside the ambition a child has may cause deep-seated resentment and rebelliousness, although it can also strengthen his determination.

Children whose writing is upright (vertical) tend to enjoy activities they do not have to share with other children. This may be true of either the quiet, undemonstrative child, sensitive and studious, who reads a great deal, or the one who busies himself with tools, building airplanes, boats, or furniture.

Social Children Choose Extrovert Goals

Children who enjoy activities with other youngsters have handwriting that is larger, sprawling, and leans more to the right than that of the loners. It is more difficult for them to decide their goals, for the range of social goals is so wide. The little girl playing with dolls may talk of wanting to be a nurse, yet be physically unsuited to it. Here, also, it is wise to watch the hobbies of growing children. The physical type of child, interested primarily in athletics, may be a poor student, yet excel in the one thing that holds his interest. He may, with proper education and encouragement, become an athletic instructor or a professional athlete—as in the case of Specimen 4, who became a baseball pitcher. The alert, studious child who is forever asking questions should be encouraged to go to college.

The school subjects in which the child does well may also be a determining factor. The child who gets good marks in composition may later follow a literary career, and the one who excels in arithmetic may turn out to be an engineer or an accountant. Such children start early to eliminate extra return strokes on lower loops of *y* and *g*, making the letters resemble the numerals 7 and 9. (See Specimen 5. The boy's ability to figure things out with mathematical accuracy points also to scientific leanings, augmenting his chances for studying medicine. He tends to be more interested in the scientific aspects of medicine than in treating patients.)

The little girl who delights in sewing dresses for her dolls may be more absorbed in the act of sewing than in the care of the doll. Here is the beginning of a constructive faculty finding a practical means of outlet. She may become a seamstress or a dress designer, depending on her imagination and her feeling for line, fabric, and color.

Desires of children to be on the stage should not be discouraged. Even if it does not develop into an active theatrical career, the training helps the children to develop self-confidence and poise. The handwriting of stage-struck children will often reveal underscored signatures, for here the personality is already beginning to assert itself, and such children will perform at the least provocation, to win applause.

Creative Ability in Children

Nervous, sensitive children, unable to follow classroom routine, who may be good in drawing, quick to learn to play the piano, and finicky about sounds, colors, and odors, should be given special attention. If the child is nurtured with care, not overindulged, and guided by an observant mother, creative urges may assert themselves even before he approaches adolescence. If misunderstood, overdisciplined, and scolded because he is "different from other children," he may develop into a neurotic, become seclusive, and never get enough experience with social activities to be able to deal with them except through escape.

The handwriting of such children may reveal anything from keen mental development (as in Specimen 7) to sluggish, messy, illegible strokes. Nervous children (in whom the neurotic pattern has its beginning), who are more sensitive than average children, possess roots that may yield unusual accomplishments, but if they are conquered by destructive elements in the environment, such children may turn into misfits and maladjusted adults. It is therefore important for parents to understand the reasons for such symptoms in children as poor appetite, temper tantrums, or extreme shyness, and encourage them to become interested in something constructive for which they have a natural bent. When I encounter the handwriting of such a child, I do not pass judgment until I have studied the writing of the parents; in a majority of cases I find a neurotic mother who is unsuited to guide the child's activities. The apple doesn't fall far from the tree, and in the handwriting of problem children, I invariably find signs of trouble that can be linked with neurotic symptoms in the parents' handwriting.

The death of a parent or some other shocking experience in childhood may have the power to redirect the originally expressed goal of the child and be in keeping with the child's later development. We have the case of a boy wanting to be an engineer who finds himself the head of the family on his father's death and is confronted with having to get any kind of job to help support the household. The feeling of responsibility that prompts such redirection of a definite goal may give him the desire to succeed in the work he now does. Yet it is only natural he would not be wholehearted in such work if it is not the engineering he set his heart on, and his handwriting will reveal this halfheartedness in some way, either in *t* crossings that are strong, coupled with drooping lines (disappointment), or in the development of executive ability as the head of the family with added responsibilities.

Backward children are the problem of the psychiatrist and often the result of ill health on the part of one or both of the parents. Or they may be the products of a union of people of advanced age. The writing of such children is easily recognized (if they write at all), for the formations are without uniformity, extremely large, and the entire specimen looks like diffused scribbling.

Choice of Vocation

Social Vocations: Marriage, Teaching, Nursing, Medicine, Politics, Law, Statesmanship, Welfare Work, the Priesthood and Ministry, Social Secretarial Work, Clerical Work, and the like.

Constructive Practical Goals: Invention, Mechanics, Engineering, Skilled Work, Craftsmanship.

Creative Art: Painting, Sculpture, Surgery, Literature, Music Composition, Architecture.

Interpretative Art: Dancing, Singing, Dramatics—all Performing Arts.

Adaptive Art: Interior Decoration, Designing (Craftsmanship), Advertising.

Business: Executive Work, Finance, Salesmanship, Agriculture, Farming.

Science: Bacteriology, Archeology, Physics, Medicine, etc.

Vocational Aptitudes in Adults

When determining through handwriting what vocation the adult is suited for, it is first necessary to find out what his goal is, or has been at one time. Knowledge of the early history, along with specimens of handwriting over a period of years, reveals the person's development, making vocational deduction easier for the graphologist.

Many people seeking vocational guidance write me: "I don't know what to choose as a career." My question is usually, "What have you always wanted most to do?" People who seemingly have no definite goal in mind are usually those who have lost it either through lack of encouragement, or through economic stress that forced them into a field that would produce a livelihood.

After I find out what the person desires most to do, it will become evident in many cases that the handwriting shows some aptitude for such work. There are exceptions, where people lack the necessary ability to follow the desired course. This may be due to faulty encouragement by overzealous parents, which gives the individual a false sense of his own value.

The energetic person with a smattering of talent may achieve a greater success through hard work and continuous striving than the naturally gifted but ambitionless person. The striver may even gain public approval or recognition. Such approval is no indication of talent, but may be the result of a driving ambition that brooks no interference in the pursuit of the desired goal, and such striving for recognition and superiority will be disclosed in the handwriting.

It may be that the vocational preference has its origin in a spirit of adventure more than in actual talent. During adolescence, such is often the case. The 15-year-old girl who had visited the circus and expressed a desire to be an animal trainer is a case in point. Her writing showed a maternal instinct and a spirit of adventure, resulting in her choice. This she later modified by opening a dog kennel, with the expressed ambition to own, in time, a silver-fox farm.

The physical demands made upon us by our natures play an important part in the selection of a goal in life. The field of sports or other work that requires physical activity will be chosen by the more robust members of society, while the mental, spiritual, and many artistic goals are selected by the less physical—with many exceptions, of course.

Sublimation or Redirection of Maternal Instinct

Many women find a sublimation for a frustrated maternal instinct in their chosen vocations. The teacher, nurse, social worker, physician, and even the artist are in this group. Many interior decorators, in whom the interest in homemaking finds expression artistically, are in this group, except that here the materialistic leanings are stronger than the social. Interior decorators frequently write vertical hands, as in Specimen 39.

In men, goals and vocations tend to be decided by education and environment rather than by instinctive preference. The ability to participate in work that has no relation to an instinctive paternal need, as with women, gives a man greater scope for dealing with abstractions. The power to create outside of himself is stronger in men than in women and helps to determine their vocations.

Once the person's choice of vocation is known, the handwriting will indicate whether he is more extrovert than introvert, and to what type of humanity he belongs. The type of humanity is determined by his interest: social, material, constructive, or spiritual. Where the social (extrovert) person's goal will usually include human contact, the material goals (although they embrace first the interest in concrete objects) may also incidentally include the need to associate with people. Among the material goals (contrary to belief) are many of the artistic and constructive choices, which require adeptness in the use of the hands.

The spiritual goals or vocations, indicated by a preference for the pulpit or missionary work, have their origin in lesser physical demands made upon the person by his elemental nature. People choosing such vocations are often lacking in physical robustness, or are denied emotional expression through some physical debility. Spiritual vocations are usually definitely selected by the person, often long in advance of maturity, though I have had cases where such persons have asked whether their handwriting showed such aptitudes.

Social Vocations

Marriage: As a vocation, marriage may be made an art, a business, or a mess. If the handwritings of two people entering such an alliance show tolerance and a broad sense of humor, success is in most cases assured. (See Chapter V, "Choosing Your Mate.")

Teaching: The first requisite of a person seeking success in this goal is a love of teaching. This is indicated in handwriting by uniformity of letter formations; slow execution, revealing patience; leaning to the right, expressing extroverted tendencies. Another requisite is a retentive memory, shown in careful punctuation and good spacing between lines and words. The teacher specializing in one subject will show the above-mentioned manifestations, except that the entire writing will be smaller and concentrated. The more educated the teacher is, the smaller will become his writing, and there will be more evidence of mental formations.

Nursing: The first essential of a nurse is a good physical constitution. (See Part Two, section on pen pressure.) Angle may be either vertical or rightward, but sympathy must be expressed in the writing by rounded formations or signs of altruism. Nurses often show in handwriting similar traits to teachers. Practicality, another essential trait, may be seen in signs of good judgment and caution manifested by many closed small letters. The requirement is, from the very outset, education to gain entrance to this field. The progressive nurse continues to study and creates for herself greater opportunities for advancement and specialization. Capital letters and good spacing will indicate whether the nurse has executive capacities, and such is usually the case where there is a preponderance of practicality over sympathy—in handwriting, angularity over roundness.

Medicine: It will be found that the person choosing medicine as a profession is usually a born student. The handwriting will show signs of drive and perseverance. In that of the research worker or specialist, it may be small and concentrated. The pen pressure will be either heavy, medium, or moderately light, but usually uniform. A retentive memory is an important requisite, as are common sense and a spirit of cooperation.

Physician

SPECIMEN 21

Written with a rhythmic drive that reveals energy and the ability for concerted action, we have the physician dedicated to his profession. The writing is medium small, mildly rightward-leaning, veering in an upward direction (showing optimism). Angularity discloses keen perception, a number of high *i* dots show imagination. The capital *I*'s and the capital *M* in the word "my" are modest in size and tell us he is more interested in his work than in himself. This physician is a student of graphology and gets a sampling of his patients' handwriting to help him corroborate his diagnostic findings. His capacity for self-discipline is indicated in the bowed *t*-bar formation in the word "practice," and his early history discloses his having overcome many obstacles in his youth, thus giving him a built-in strength to accomplish his goals.

Politics, Law, Statesmanship: One common sign in the handwriting of people dealing with the law, especially where diplomacy is revealed (often described as shrewdness), is in the tapering of letters at the end of words. Many times letters will be mere slurs. Often the angle will lean to the right. In observing the handwriting of President Lyndon Johnson, we see an exception in the vertical (upright) angle. (This will be analyzed later on.) The more brilliance the person possesses, the more evidence will there be in mental formations; the writing is apt to be small and angular. In politicians, signs of aggressiveness are often in sharper focus (in *t* bars and ending strokes). In the handwriting of lawyers, we see this in the downstroke of the *t* bar, which tells us they are argumentative. Signs of logical thinking are shown in connected letters, sometimes connected words. In statesmen, the signature is often underscored, and formations will resemble those of the lawyer. (We shall deal more with the underscore later on.) Lawyers who write vertically are more apt to choose the fields of research, probate, or patent law, whereas the more extroverted one with a flair for dramatics has a greater chance for success in trial (or criminal) law and is likely to choose it. The dramatic instinct is invariably shown in the underscored signature, corroborated by other signs in the writing. Politicians, like lawyers and statesmen, must be shrewd and capable of compromise, yet too often we find them governed largely by personal attitudes and prejudices instead of the hoped-for detachment.

Specimen 22 was written by a man in the diplomatic service. He has a keen, critical, incisive mind, coupled with an aloofness (vertical angle) that tells us his reason prevails over emotion. He is self-con-

Diplomat

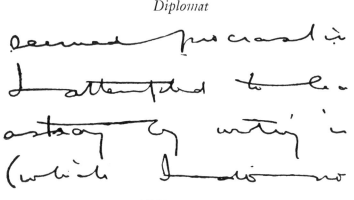

SPECIMEN 22

tained, poised, dignified. Connecting words indicate not only a capacity for logical reasoning but also an ability to connect ideas. As seen in the slurs, it is not easy for others to know what he is thinking, for he tells them only what he thinks they should know. Although time is taken out for reflection, the long *t* crosses tell us he is a man of determination and will power, with a capacity for hard work. Some breaks in words give us a clue to an intuitive faculty that gives him insights into more than might be happening externally. He goes beneath the surface, and his consistently sound judgment adjusts his antennae so that he can sense whether he is on safe or dangerous ground. This man is not easy to rattle, and in his smooth and clever way he can point up the weaknesses in people or situations with cool objectivity.

Welfare Work: This field, as well as that of teaching, is usually chosen by those who have a strong social consciousness and desire to improve the lives of others. Education is an important requisite. Organizational ability, important as an adjunct in helping welfare (or social) workers achieve greater success, is revealed in the careful spacing of margins and lines, with some signs of independence in high but simple capital letters. *T* bars should be fairly strong, though not so strong as to appear aggressive or dominating. The person must be cooperative and show elements of tolerance and open-mindedness; but mainly the interest must be in people.

Teacher

We've had a rough couple of
months - mom had been ailing
but she's better now and ter
ribly eager also for your

SPECIMEN 23

In this handwriting, characterized by roundness, with angular tops in the letters *m* and *n*, we find the gentle, outgoing, patient individual, suited for teaching. Lines are well spaced, as are the words; signs of good judgment and refinement of tastes are seen in the Greek formation of the small *e*; fairly high upper loops show idealism, and the entire specimen discloses a cooperative, intelligent, disciplined person who can win the confidence of her pupils because of interest in their progress. Just as the handwriting looks pleasant and harmonious, so is the writer. She has a major in music, which is shown in the rhythmic flow; the angular lower loop in the word "for" tells us she is not readily sidetracked from her purpose by obstacles. (Many nurses, welfare workers, and homemakers show similar traits in their handwriting.)

Specimen 24 is a good example of a social worker. Extroversion is shown in the rightward angle, not too pronounced; pen pressure is medium light, and there is a combination of angularity and roundness. The *t* bar above the letter, as in the word "together," tells us the

Social Worker

SPECIMEN 24

writer has a vivid imagination, which, along with signs of intuition, gives him the ability to understand other people and to imagine himself in the other fellow's place. There is an easy flow in this writing that reveals his easygoing, pleasant nature, and his expansiveness is evident in the spreading out of many words. The literary g made like an 8 indicates not only that he is adaptable and flexible, but also that he should be able to express himself in writing.

Priests and Ministers: The predominant characteristic a man of the cloth should possess is selflessness. This is, unfortunately, not always present, but when it is, we also find in the handwriting a light pen pressure, signs of altruism in the right turn of the downward stroke of the *y*, and a leaning toward people seen in the rightward angle. There should be signs of generosity, tolerance, and adaptability, as well as a respect for conventions.

Jesuit Priest

SPECIMEN 25

This is a good example of a man who is suited to his calling. He is a Jesuit priest. The sign of altruism appears consistently in his handwriting. The pen pressure is light, so that the entire writing looks fine with a hairline sensitivity. Keenness of mind is shown in the angularity; an ability for leadership and logic can be seen in the connection of the words "is published" and "I am." Excellent spacing between words and lines indicates a capacity for reflection and meditation. (Not all Jesuits write in this way; some have even shown heavy pressure, indicating sensuousness and materialism, but usually the mind has been keen and capable of what has come to be known as "Jesuitical" reasoning.)

Secretarial Work: This vocation is usually chosen by persons who enjoy accepting another's responsibilities at the very outset. The first requisite is education, whether formal schooling or self-acquired. There must be signs of tactfulness (explained fully in section on uniformity), a well-ordered mind (shown in good spacing where the letters of the words in the line above do not run into the line below), and enough extrovert qualities to indicate the person can mingle with others. Aptness for detail, efficiency, and a retentive memory should all be present in the handwriting. There should be signs of angularity (keenness of perception) and a time sense. (See Specimen 47, Administrative Secretary.)

Beauticians: For the most part, beauticians are extroverted, for they choose work that brings them into contact with other people. The writing will show signs that may also appear in the handwriting of nurses, competent housewives, or any capable, versatile individual. The hair stylist will usually write artistic formations and may be somewhat introverted, though this does not always follow. If you see a circle dot over the *i* in such writing, you know the writer is manually adept, has a feeling for design, and enjoys using her hands. (See another explanation for circle *i* dots in Part Two.)

Veterinarians: The writing should show signs of kindness (roundness), also practicality and physical endurance. Usually veterinarians lack aggressiveness and are peace-loving, but we sometimes come across a veterinarian who is rough or aggressive, and he is apt to be more concerned with the business end of his calling than with the animals themselves. The veterinary surgeon will have as much skill as a medical surgeon, but there will usually be another sign, found in a lover of animals or children (the helpless ones), and that is the protective *A*, *M*, and *N*—an old-fashioned formation. (Farmers have it too.)

Right in the salutation of this specimen is a modern version of what we described as a protective formation of the capital *N*. Paternalistic, this man is equally concerned with his family. The open capital *D* indicates his openheartedness as well as his frankness. The rightward angle shows his leaning toward people and his ability to deal with them in taking care of their pets. His is a keen, quick, logical mind with intuition. The even spacing between words and letters is a sign of a well-organized individual. He is constructive (the capital *S* in the word "speaking"), adaptable, and efficient—as the angularity shows. Sensitive, impressionable, he is also mildly compulsive (we often find compulsiveness in a talented person, a sign of dedication). This veterinarian is dedicated to his work, is an excellent surgeon, and a thinking, responsible human being. A rare combination. Although not a robust man, he has good recoverability and a capacity for self-discipline. (I would utterly trust him with my pets.)

Veterinarian

Dear Nadya,

Thanks so much for your good wishes. Why we become veter is a complex question. Speaking of myself, I would say it was a boy wish to own a dog that probably le me to veterinary medicine. As a very

SPECIMEN 26

Constructive-Practical Goals

Invention, Mechanics, Engineering: These vocations are usually chosen by people who have a natural bent for mathematics. Many are technical or mechanical-minded. The writing is more often than not heavy in pen pressure; capitals are invariably printed; frequently the entire specimen is printed. The writing is often vertical, although it can be rightward-flowing at a moderate angle. These people are seldom good mixers; their interest in things—structures such as bridges, as well as abstractions—is greater than in people. An ability to deal with detail will be revealed; and usually there are powers of concentration, another important quality, seen in small letter forms, or if medium large, in strong *t* bars (expressing also self-discipline). The writing of inventors often shows original capitals; mechanical leanings have long lower loops, not always as rhythmic as in the handwriting of a musician, but then many musicians need (and have) mechanical deftness in handling their instruments. Engineers, when not printing, write legible hands, with letters of words usually connected.

Following are two specimens written by the same man (who has engineering training)—one printed, the other written. Notice the good spacing between words and sentences in both specimens. Pen pressure is on the light side, telling us of a sensitive, gentle person, and these traits are corroborated in the rounded formations of 27A. An element of self-consciousness appears in the short *t* bar, but this man has poise and reserve. His interest in people extends primarily to his family.

5. ALTHOUGH I CAN RECALL CONDITIONS WHIC
AT ABOUT 3 TO 4 YEARS OF AGE, THERE SEEMS
THESE MEMORIES ARE CONSISTENTLY PLEASANT I
THINGS AS MY FATHER COMING HOME ON HIS BICYC
AND FORTH TO MY GRANDPARENTS AND OTHER TH
TO TAKE PLACE BEFORE THE AGE OF FIVE. I
EMERGENCIES INVOLVING PERSONAL INJURY AND SUC
BE TRANSFERS FROM LATER FAMILY RECALL.

SPECIMEN 27

Cabinetmakers, Skilled Workers: Such people will have in common heavy pen pressure, constructed or printed capitals; the angle may vary depending upon the temperament. The more skillful the individual, the more originality will be revealed in letter forms. Where meticulousness characterizes his work, angularity is very evident.

Since I normally print, there is some
whither or not I remember how this writer
will account for the change to printing but
at this time I am actively considerin

SPECIMEN 27A

Creative Art

Painting and Sculpture: The handwriting of artists shows a definite departure from copybook forms. It may look as if it were done with a brush (many artists use a brush in writing letters), or with a hand accustomed to wielding a brush. Rhythm, love of line, form, color, and structure are usually indicated in the harmonious shading of pen pressure. This is not always so, but where it appears the writing may even resemble a design or painting. Often there are signs of sensuousness and usually of imagination. The emotions tend to predominate. Manual dexterity will show in firmness and heaviness, with signs of self-assurance, although there may be evidence of changing moods. The angle may be in any direction, depending on the artist's subject matter, whether people, landscapes, or abstractions. The versatile artist can create all of them. Any handwriting with good margins, constructed capitals, uniform spacing—all of which indicate aesthetic appreciation—gives us a clue to artistic leanings, and if we delve deeply enough we may discover undeveloped talent. Very often we see signs of weakness in weak or varying *t* bars, but this is characteristic of many artists who, dealing with a world of fantasy, do not always finish paintings. It is often the perfectionist in him that makes an artist feel keenly the discrepancies between his mental picture and his ability to put it on canvas.

A well-known painter ventured the opinion that no painting is ever really finished; the artist merely stops working on it, and he must use judgment in knowing when to stop. While signs of self-discipline, so essential to the artist, should show in the writing, there are not many who possess this valuable trait. Where will power is strongly in evidence, we have the hard worker, sometimes with a minimum of talent. In some of the most talented artists, the handwriting will show signs of procrastination; the more creative the artist, the more signs of procrastination are likely to appear. Compulsiveness is a common trait of the instinctive artist, whether he be painter, writer, or musician. It is a strong drive with neurotic overtones and has in it elements of dedication; it was characteristic of Van Gogh, and it is easily recognized in handwriting.

Painter, Illustrator

SPECIMEN 28

This is an excellent example of the creative artist. Notice the swing and rhythm of the writing, the original formations; yet here also are *t* bars that start thick and end in a spearpoint. The interest often lessens after the inspirational inception; then comes the matter of self-discipline, which shows in the formation of the *t* bar in the word "night."

Sculptors often write an almost identical hand, although there might be some slight differences in pen pressure or angle. With sculptors the pressure may be heavier, due to the habit of working with tough materials rather than with paints and brushes. There are a number of painters who turn to sculpture, and many of them are instinctively musical. The instinctive artist is not usually a specialist.

He makes an art of everything he does; he reacts more sensitively to life itself, embodying in his creations his subjective reactions to life.

Sculptor

SPECIMEN 29

In Specimen 29 we have a sculptor's handwriting. Notice the difference in rhythm between it and that of the painter. Strokes are firm, many small letters are printed; and though it has form, structure and rhythm, it is not so spontaneously written as the painter's is. (This sculptor also paints, but his paintings have clean structural lines that appear chiseled.)

Architecture: The architect has many traits in common with the painter and the musician, but his writing may show signs of more practicality. The aesthetic quality is equally evident; so are signs of originality in letter forms, depending on the extent of the talent. The engineer with artistic talent is often led into the field of architecture, and there is something of the engineer in every architect.

Specimens 30 and 30A were written by a young architect. The unusual formation of many of the *t*'s in the cursive writing signals a neurotic disturbance in the man, but it does not interfere with his work. In work he finds compensation for a neurosis that seems to stalk him; his unswerving meticulousness is part of the neurotic structure. Though it sometimes amounts to an obsession, this meticulous-

Architect

While I enjoyed my stay in
was also able to get away and
the Netherland's beautiful and
esque countryside, dotted with
and protected from the sea by

SPECIMEN 30

WHILE I ENJOYED MY STAY IN AMSTE

ALSO ABLE TO GET AWAY AND SEE S

NETHERLAND'S BEAUTIFUL AND VERY

COUNTRYSIDE, DOTTED WITH WINDMILL

TECTED FROM THE SEA BY DIKES.

SPECIMEN 30A

ness is very useful in his work. The almost machinelike printing corroborates his striving for perfection and shows him to be a good
draftsman. There is, however, much roundness in the writing itself,
and this tells us there is still much of the child in this man and that he
is emotionally immature. But his talent is indisputable, and he may
go far in the field of architecture as his social qualities are developed.

Surgery: This may be considered a fine art, certainly the finest
of crafts, or a combination of art and science, depending on the intellect of the surgeon. The handwriting of surgeons shows traits in
common with creative artists. One marked difference is in the *t* bar,
which goes firmly through the stem of the letter and is bowed. This
often appears in combination with heavy pressure, but the pressure

may also be medium heavy and, in some instances, light. Angularity will usually be present to reveal exactness and a high efficiency. There are always signs of good muscular coordination and a sure hand in firmness of letter forms. An occasional surgeon may regard the body he's operating on as a sculptor might regard his marble, or the painter his canvas. Others will have an awareness of the human entity they are operating on. All are interested in making their contribution through constructive endeavor.

Surgeon

Professor R. Nissen

dankt für die guten Wünsche und erwidert

sie aufs herzlichste.

With kindest regards

Truly yours

Prof. Nissen

SPECIMEN 31

This specimen is the handwriting of an outstanding surgeon who operated on Fritz Kreisler, Albert Einstein, and other people of note. The angularity is severe, and we see signs of culture, intuition, and altruism. Dr. Nissen gave up practicing surgery some time ago to teach at the University of Basel in Switzerland. He may be a hard taskmaster with his pupils, but they are taught the rigid disciplines of which he is capable. He is a man who does not permit his sympathies to sway him. His first interest was his patients, and he worked on them with a sure and unswerving hand, just as he now instructs his pupils to do.

Writer

have always gone in for the "I
hen" straightforward interview approa
and are normously suspicious of an
systematic methods of character analy
The Germans and the French are mor
open-minded, I'm told. I'd be

SPECIMEN 32

A combination of mental formations accompanying signs of culture in the small *h*, and the capital *I* made in a single stroke, along with the Greek *d* and the literary *g*, reveal literary ability in this handwriting. Talent shows in the small printed *s*'s, and the entire tempo of the writing is quick, as is the mind. Intuition (in breaks between letters) indicates the writer has insight into more than appears on the surface; he can often see through a situation and is able to take a short cut to a conclusion. Other capitals are also simply constructed and indicate an ability to get down to essentials without wasting time on unnecessary detail. The writing may be difficult to read: This kind of illegibility is a sign of so rapid a mind that the hand finds it difficult to keep up with the thinking. The good spacing and margins are signs of an organized thinker, and the vertical angle shows the prevalence of reason over emotion; the signs of good judgment reveal a common-sense approach to many things.

In Specimen 33 we have a combination engineer, industrial designer, painter, musician, and craftsman. It is a rounded rhythmic writing, and although the angle is vertical, showing a measure of reserve, this person is flexible and responsive and has curiosity. There

Industrial Designer, Craftsman, Musician

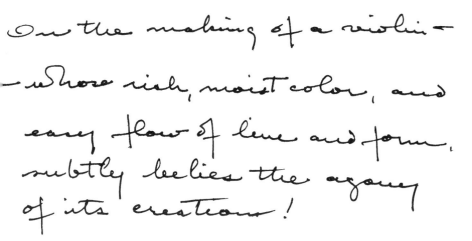

On the making of a violin —
—whose rich, moist color, and
easy flow of line and form,
subtly belies the agony
of its creation!

SPECIMEN 33

are signs of culture and of literary taste, and the writer has the self-discipline so essential to his achievements. He is not a robust individual, but he has, nevertheless, managed to fill his working life with much variety, from ceramics, leather work, and ship design to his latest task—making a violin. Work is done meticulously, and with more ease and patience than is present in many an artist. And though there is imagination as well as aspiration, there is an absence of the compulsiveness which so often characterizes the creative individual. Instead, there are signs of sound practical judgment and an ability to plan, to look ahead, and to provide the practical needs for the future. The entire writing is characterized by a lack of pretentiousness or "artiness" as seen in the simple, recognizable formations. Though he can be frank and outspoken (the open formation of the simple capital O), he can also listen, another art at which he is adept. And the vertical angle, besides showing his mild aloofness and detachment, also tells us he can face reality and deal with it in practical terms. There is no sign of sentimentality here, despite underlying sentiments, and his sense of humor allows him to see the humor in pathos, shown in the combination of a wavy *t* bar (in the word "moist") and the altruistic formation of the *y* in "easy"—which also is the sign of giving, coupled with a desire to make his contribution to the world.

Poet

SPECIMEN 34

In Specimen 34 we see the signs of the poet and part of a poem she wrote. The handwriting of the poet is often printed; the spaces between letters indicate intuition, and letter forms may be varied— some are original, others are conventional. In this writing there are the printed capitals and small letters; the vertical angle indicates the observer whose mind is in control of her emotions; the small writing shows concentration. Roundness tells us she is still somewhat immature and flexible emotionally; *t* bars vary and give us a clue to neurotic overtones. She is talented and has good potentialities, but is still in the process of growth, and like the young girl in Specimen 7, she has a pseudo-sophistication that is in keeping with the world in which she moves. She is in her twenties. Although the good spacing and margins reveal a desire for some organization in her life, there is a tendency to take the line of least resistance, seen in the type of *t* bars in the word "streets" (repeated elsewhere); she is "feeling" her way toward goals that often recede because they are not fostered in determination and will power.

Versatile Artist

Dear Nadya.   Saturday

I just wanted to wish
you "happy holidays" and
thank you for the nice card
you sent us.

Hope everything is fine
with you - and I hope to
see you soon.

Dear
Nadya

Thankyou
for remembering
me on my birthday—
Hope
you are
enjoying your stay up there
I'll definitely see you
when you get back to the
hot, wicked city. Keep well.
Love, Bonnie

love,
B.

SPECIMEN 35

Another girl in her early twenties, Specimen 35 reveals versatility of talent, signs of culture, and an unusual capacity for achievement in unusual letter formations. This is borne out in her printing, but the handwriting itself shows a shading that indicates a feeling for color, rhythm, structure, and line. The old-fashioned formation of the capital letter *N* in this type of mental hand tells us of her interest in the classics, evidenced in the type of music she plays on her flute. (She has received scholarships for painting and music.) The severe capital *I* is an indication of a mind that can get to essentials, cutting through unimportant detail; the rightward turn of the lower stroke on *y*'s show masochistic trends, a factor in her neurotic structure. But there is a capacity for concentration, meticulous workmanship, and discipline, where the interest is focused and lends some excitement to her vivid imagination. (This is a middle child, sandwiched in between two brothers, and her position in the family has had a great effect in determining not only her goals but also her attitude toward members of the opposite sex.) She is much too old for her tender years, and this has created a number of problems, although they seem not to militate against her productiveness when what she is doing gives her an opportunity to be creative and original.

Ballet Dancer (Child Student)

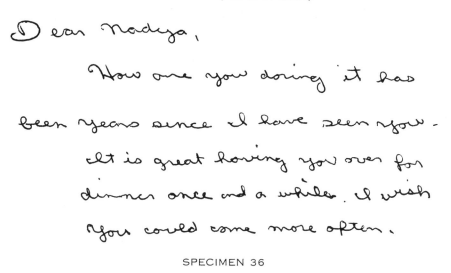

SPECIMEN 36

Here we have the handwriting of a young girl studying ballet. The vertical angle shows a detached aloofness, although roundness indicates emotional pliability and flexibility. (She is only 13.) The light pen pressure is expressive of a spiritual quality, and in watching her dance we might be seeing a spirit raising herself gracefully into the air. She is intelligent and already is developing a critical faculty, but this is because she can also be practical in coping with everyday reality. The small writing shows powers of concentration coupled with some introversion. Lines and words well spaced tell us she seeks some order in her life and habits, and the lack of length and swing in the lower loops shows a lack of interest in material things. She lives very much in a fantasy world, as many ballet dancers do, but whatever touch she has with reality is factual. The acute hairline sensitivity in the tenuous way her pen touches the paper is a sign of delicacy, and she is greatly conditioned by an aesthetic sense that determines most of her choices. This is seen in the spacing, but the *gestalt* picture is that of a somewhat timorous child who feels happiest when dancing.

Actress

SPECIMEN 37

Written by a dramatic actress, this handwriting shows emotional intensity in the combination of heavy pen pressure and the rightward-leaning angle. There are signs of culture as well as of enthusiasm; the angularity shows a desire to perfect herself in any role she undertakes. The altruistic formation of the *y* tells us she takes seriously the reactions of her audience, whose interest she has at heart. This is one type of dramatic actress, possibly one of the old school; in the handwriting of Kim Stanley, however (see Specimen 107), we have an altogether different type. But the handwriting of Bette Davis (Specimen 106) falls more into this category, with similar fervor and a desire to give of herself to the utmost.

Adaptive Art

Interior Decorating, Designing, Craftsmanship: Such vocations have this in common: Whatever the person creates can be put to practical use. Therefore, the handwriting will show signs of artistic talent plus practicality. Often the writing will look like a design. More often than not, it is vertical. Many times the circle *i* dot appears and reveals manual dexterity. (This kind of dot has another significance, explained later.)

Fabric Designer

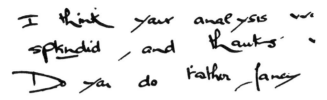

SPECIMEN 38

Written by a designer, this specimen hardly needs explanation. Here are the printed formations, the rhythm, and the signs of sensuousness to forms, color, structure, line; the original capitals. This woman designs fabrics, but she can also paint, do ceramics, and create an unusual background in her home.

Interior Decorator

This is a sample of a
56 years old. He is retired + di
He is a cousin + also my best
Please do an analisis for me.
thanks.

SPECIMEN 39

Although this person is the product of a private school and has many of the elements (selectiveness, mild snobbishness, self-centeredness) often found in such writers, her practicality was able to handle the circumstance that led her into the business world. Here she applies a native talent for artistic arrangement, a feeling for line and structure, although the roundness tells us she is still something of a child in some respects and can decorate children's rooms. In a sense, she is self-indulgent and somewhat dependent emotionally, but as she was an only child, this is to be expected. Pliable and suggestible, she is much more influenced by people in positions of prestige than by those she considers "ordinary." And the largeness of her writing is a clue to her desire to do things that show. In short: she is not apt to hide her light under a bushel.

Psychotherapist

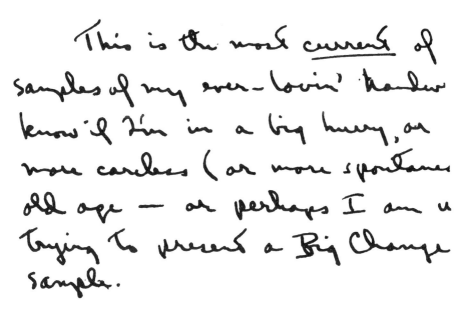

SPECIMEN 40

An unusual combination of formations here tells of the versatility of Specimen 40. Besides being a therapist who is dedicated to helping emotionally disturbed people, he is also a musician, a writer, an original thinker. The intellect is keen, as shown in angular formations; the nature, although reserved, has a combination of flexibility and friendliness, with a kind of impersonal detachment. The upward trend of the *t* bars shows aspiration as well as imagination. Yet the angle also reveals he can be realistic, and the careful *i* dots show an excellent memory. He is also a good mimic, can be entertaining when not being formal and reserved. The heavy pen pressure in such a hand tells us of a sensuousness to forms, colors, art, and music, and the good spacing reveals his desire to be organized and, incidentally, to help others organize their lives, too. He is essentially logical, as his connected letters in words show, but he has flashes of intuition that usually turn out to be certainties because of his perceptiveness and good judgment.

Business Executive

Dear Miss Olganova:

Your questions of May

are interesting to me.

Coats asks all those up

to father's work of his

SPECIMEN 41

A good example of an executive with more than average mental acuity—possessing constructive ability (in printed capitals), angularity of letter forms, and large writing—is indicated here. He has a strong will, a sense of direction, and a capacity for organized, judicious planning. His heavy, even pen pressure indicates healthy physical appetites, as well as a sensuousness for forms, colors, music. He is versatile and has a taste for literature (the *g* made like an 8); he can express himself with facility in writing. Although outgoing and extroverted, he has an element of reserve, shown in the closed capital *O*. His intuitive breaks tell us he thinks quickly and sometimes jumps to conclusions, but his first impressions are usually correct because of signs of good judgment in the single downstroke of the *y* in the word "May" and in the elimination of the upper stroke in the loop on the word "father's." He could succeed as a publisher if he made this his goal, but whatever the direction his energies take, his apparent purposiveness and his ability to cooperate should bring positive results. He has salesmanship, but more than that, he could direct and make plans for other salesmen.

Advertising Man

SPECIMEN 42

This is an advertising man (Specimen 42). The writing is large and shows a desire to do things on a grand scale; small letters are not always uniform and tell us that he finds difficulty in concentrating because many ideas come to him, often at the same time. He has drive and salesmanship, besides the ability to formulate ideas, which he dramatizes. He is robust and has humor; is restless unless engaged in something exciting and stimulating; he paints and has exhibitions, catering to an exhibitionistic trend and a capability for showmanship. Somewhat self-centered, he still needs companionship, but he tries to avoid whatever threatens to be boring or dull. He has drive and persistence and can be tireless when engaged in a project that interests him and touches off his compulsiveness.

Salesman

SPECIMEN 43

Here we have, in Specimen 43, the sign of the salesman in the downstroke of the *t* bars in the word "that," indicating aggressiveness (this is also the sign of the rebel); a keen mind in the angularity; good judgment in the single downstroke on the *g* in the word "writing"; and self-control and determination in other firm *t* bars. The writing flows to the right, and in combination with other formations mentioned it tells us he has an interest in being of service to other people, despite his trying to impose his will upon them. But he can do it tactfully, as shown in the tapering of the word "writing." The lines are well spaced and show a talent for organization; this man has the potentiality for being an organizer of other salesmen, of winning their confidence, and of being cooperative in his dealings with salesmen and customers alike.

The creative salesman who has intuition that can be called inspirational, as shown in so many breaks in words, is illustrated in

Creative Salesman

SPECIMEN 44

Specimen 44. He has a definite interest in the needs and desires of other people; can see through situations and if necessary take short cuts to a conclusion or destination. He is a man of culture and mental keenness, of self-discipline and constructive ability. His mental formations place him above the average, no matter what work category he falls into, and his outgoing nature, tempered by reserve, tells us that he can mix with all kinds of people yet never lose his dignity, showing an empathy for those who have problems.

Banker

SPECIMEN 45

There is hardly such a thing as a typical banker. Some, as this one, show signs of culture; one president of a bank paints and writes in his spare time. Here are signs of a keen mind accelerated by intuition, and a consistent drive, shown in *t* bars that have a hook on the end (tenacity); the second one in the word "interesting," above the stem of the letter, tells us of a spirit of adventure derived from a vivid imagination. His history reveals some outstanding innovations in the banking field, but he would be capable of such in any field to which he bent his effort. Notice how his *g*'s resemble the figure 9, which tells us he has a talent for figures. He has an excellent memory, seen in the careful dotting of the *i*'s. That the specimen is meticulously written and pleasing to the eye gives us a clue to regular habits from which he does not readily depart, and a sense of responsibility that is ingrained in him. He has powers of concentration, enjoys mental gymnastics, and has excellent physical resistance, as seen in the even medium heavy pen pressure.

Scientist

SPECIMEN 46

This specimen was written by a noted bacteriologist. It reveals his keen mentality and capacity for logical deduction, but occasional flashes of intuition enliven his mind and give him insights into more than may be obvious on the surface. From these he is inspired to make discoveries. (He maintains that, at one time, he discovered the origin of life and had his findings in a test tube, but his lack of initiative—shown in the type of *t* which has nothing but a hook on the end—prevented him from setting forth his findings for the world to know.) The sign of altruism is also present. (We always find this sign in the handwriting of individuals who feel they must, in one way or another, make some contribution.) This man felt impelled to enrich the world through his scientific researches. An occasional long lower loop indicates good physical resistance with healthy appetites that are conditioned by a strong aesthetic sense. There is also a tendency toward asceticism indicated here that ties in with his idealism. This man has sacrificed much in the interest of science, and has written many theses that remain in our scientific archives.

Science

Bacteriology, Archeology, Physics: These mental types are recognized by small, angular writing. Angle of inclination varies according to the individual temperament of the person, yet in all the introvert is fairly strong. These people, usually interested in the abstract or esoteric, in formulas and mathematical equations, usually have the capacity for unlimited concentration. The archeologist is, perhaps, more on the materialistic side, and his handwriting will therefore be heavier in pen pressure, with other corroborative signs.

To illustrate traits and attributes essential to the secretary, we have in Specimen 47 an example of what might be termed an administrative secretary. In other words, she is more than just a shorthand taker. She is outgoing and optimistic, has drive and determination (shown in the many long *t* bars), is compulsive to the point of dedication to a project to which she lends her enthusiasm (shown in the *t* bar that flies away from the stem), and has the altruistic sign in the word "days," which tells us she cares what happens to other people, especially those she considers deserving. The high upper loops point to a consistent idealism and desire for perfection, and she applies this kind of perfectionism to work to which she commits herself, as well as to causes in which she wholeheartedly believes. She goes about her work without having to be told what to do; can take over responsibilities of executives less knowledgeable than she is, and be-

Administrative Secretary

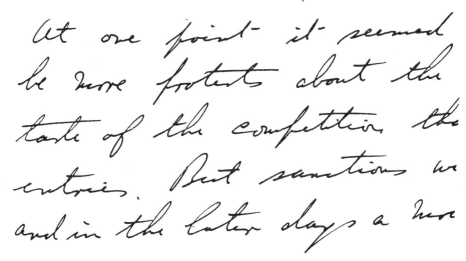

SPECIMEN 47

lieves that any worthwhile job is worth doing efficiently. The angularity reveals her exactness, and the occasional roundness tells us of some pliability in her nature, which she keeps guarded because she understands her own vulnerability.

Specimen 48 was written by a nun. It reveals an almost childlike pliability in its roundness, spirituality in the light pen pressure, simplicity in taste and desires in the simple letter forms and capitals, and the sign of self-discipline in the bowed *t* bar in the word "to" (third line). The simplicity and legibility of the entire specimen tell us that she lives a life of simple faith about which she does not intellectualize. She can be practical despite her dedication, and goes about her work helping others without questioning that this is part of the work to which she has dedicated her life. She is cooperative, gentle, responsive, easy to talk to, and capable of listening. Her memory is retentive, and although she is for the most part serious, she does not lack a sense of humor. Her life is uncomplicated because she has found herself in the innate belief that she is performing a service from which many human beings benefit.

Nun

Elizabeth spent a few days
at St Elizabeth House this past
summer on her way to visit
the Poor Clares in England at
the advice of her Confessors. They
suggested to her that it would
be better if she tried her vocation

SPECIMEN 48

Clerical Worker

been doing clerical work
establishments in New York
father and mother are stil
I am of Spanish descent.

SPECIMEN 49

In 49, the handwriting of a clerical worker, many signs appear
that are seen in the nun's handwriting: Both individuals can do work
that requires attention to routine and detail. Thus, the nun, if forced
into the outside world, could find a niche in an office, though it is
unlikely that the writer of 49 could live in a convent.

IV

The Inferiority Complex and Compensations

The feeling of inferiority rules the mental life and can be clearly recognized in the sense of incompleteness and unfulfillment, and in the uninterrupted struggle both of individuals and of humanity.
—ALFRED ADLER

Inferiority and the Need for Compensation

CHILDREN WHO ARE MADE TO FEEL INFERIOR IN their environment seek, often unconsciously, to compensate for such feelings. It may be expressed in their behavior, or in their striving for unusual achievements, artistically or intellectually. The child who feels deprived of affection at home may seek it from playmates, teachers, or even strangers.

The child who feels inferior because of constant chastisement and punishment may resort to lying or to stealing from his parents in order to buy from others the love he wants. Lying often results from fear of punishment, but it can also derive from a vivid imagination in which the child makes himself important in his fantasies.

Inferiority and Rebelliousness

Whenever dominance of an older person, whether a parent or the oldest member of the family, forces the child to subordinate his will to that person and stifles individual self-expression, rebelliousness is bound to be the result. The rebellious child, feeling inferior in school and unwilling to accept what he considers dull routine, plays truant, or, seeking the adventure he craves, runs away to look for it. The child who is subjected to physical cruelty by a bad-tempered parent

78

may compensate by getting into fights with schoolmates and even becoming a bully.

Rebelliousness usually rears its head in childhood in resentment over too much parent domination, and the pattern persists with the adult who continues to rebel at superiors. He wants to be the one in authority, and by driving toward a goal that will give it to him, he develops an overcompensatory aggressiveness. Such people carry a chip on their shoulders, and this is revealed in handwriting in the more obvious down-slant form of the *t* bar.

Parent Domination and Inferiority

Where respect is demanded rather than earned, by a domineering father whose iron will inculcates fear in the child, the result is that complexes relating to it dominate the haunted victim later in life. The intimidated child, not permitted to act spontaneously and independently, may hesitate to take the initiative, even when the impulse is beneficial to others, for fear of being punished. He already has the beginnings of a masochistic trend, for having been led to believe that he deserves punishment, he finds reasons to impose it upon himself, or he may unconsciously gravitate to those who are sadistic.

Where the child is overly sensitive and seemingly lacking in spirit, he becomes submissive and is unable to make decisions for himself, knowing from experience that whatever he decides will meet with disapproval. He is a pawn in the hands of a martinet and may go through life weak, indecisive, and dependent upon others. The handwriting will usually show this weakness in ineffectual *t* bars that do not go through the stem of the letter; if there is a preponderance of these in the adult's writing, it is a sign of a neurotic person who is indecisive, self-conscious, emotionally dependent, and lacking in self-reliance.

Many children find it easier to obey than to defy the one who makes the rules. It gives them a feeling of security. Others obey because they fear punishment. Thus the habit of obedience is formed very early in life and becomes an integral part of the character.

The domination of parents is a confession that they lack confidence in the child, and thus the child grows up lacking self-confidence. When parent domination results in rebelliousness, however, this pattern is carried into maturity. Take the time-worn example of the minister's renegade son: forced to swallow religion in toto without being given a chance to digest it, he shows his rebelliousness by extreme defiance, and when he leaves home he often kicks over the traces, denies parental beliefs and may even become an atheist.

Whenever an individual's handwriting shows an inability to assume responsibilities, I feel that he was not given sufficient responsibility in childhood, or else that he was given more than he could cope with, which caused him to rebel. Where force, rather than love and understanding, is used, the will of the child is weakened or broken, but if he rebels sufficiently and aims at a constructive goal, he can get out from under and assert his own will.

I cannot stress enough the necessity for parents to teach children self-reliance, cooperation, a sense of responsibility; for mothers to sever the umbilical cord before it becomes a noose. Let the child feel his parents believe in him, trust him to do the right thing, and he is exalted. He will then make every effort to be responsible and trustworthy and will develop into a strong, purposeful and secure adult.

Unfortunately, parents are too often victimized by their own inferiorities and seek to compensate for them by imposing their will on their children. They feel that by ruling autocratically they become important, whereas if they ruled by love they would become infinitely more important to the children, who thrive on love and encouragement. The handwriting of parents may reveal the reasons for questionable behavior of the children.

Physical Handicaps and Compensations in Children

Children can be very cruel to the little boy who limps and plays games awkwardly. It is no wonder that the crippled or disabled child develops a deep-seated sense of inferiority in childhood and a supersensitivity that remains an integral part of his later behavior pattern. The feeling of inferiority resulting from such handicaps produces a strong desire for compensation. The child who is encouraged to have confidence in himself may develop a compensatory pattern in a creative endeavor. The pampered, indulged child—given special attention because of his handicap—may either remain a misfit, or overcompensate.

We have but to remember the character Philip in Somerset Maugham's *Of Human Bondage* to imagine the extent of a crippled child's suffering. The handwriting of physically disabled children is not apt to show the physical robustness of a healthy child's scribblings. The "jerkiness," usually a lack of muscular coordination, coupled with extremely light pen pressure, or pressure of varying shades and intensity, will give the writing a disturbed or "sickly" look.

An excellent example of a child's efforts to compensate for physical handicaps is the case of Danny, an orphan in the kindergarten of a city hospital in Manhattan. Under the guidance of a very capable instructor, Danny, disabled through infantile paralysis and unable to use his hands, learned first to write with his toes and later with his mouth. When the following specimen was written, he had outgrown these primitive methods and used his hand. It was a tiring, painful process, but Danny's efforts were encouraged by his patient instructor. He learned later on to work in clay, to plan and build artistically. Danny was 10 when this was written. The roundness shows his childlike qualities, but the strong *t* crossings show the will to overcome obstacles; although the one in the first "the" is slightly trembly, the one in the second "the" shows excellent self-discipline. The broad *r* in "birds," expressing a visual sense, is corroborated by his expression: "See the lake!" His self-confidence will see him through any other vicissitudes he might have to face later.

See the lake!
Wake up the birds!
This is my school lesson.

SPECIMEN 50

Inferiority and Vanity

We are not always conscious of our inadequacies until we are brought into contact with other people who, by their seeming outward superiority, bring into sharper focus our own feelings of inferiority. There is always someone who knows more than we do, someone who is better looking or physically stronger; and in one area or another, most of us have feelings of envy, indulge in wishful thinking, and seek to feel important. Those who seek compensation by trying to be superior in the outside world, where greater opportunities prevail, are often motivated by ambition. If forced by circumstances to remain in the environment of childhood, we may seek to develop a personality to make us outstanding in that environment. In all of us there is a striving for superiority of some sort. If we excel in one direction, we find ourselves inadequate in others. The more aware a person becomes of his inadequacies, the more apparent does his striving for superiority become.

In handwriting, signs that immediately attract the eye—ornamentation, flourishes, unnecessary underscoring of words—all point to compensating factors. Signs of weakness may not be obvious immediately in the handwriting (just as our inferiorities are not readily discovered by other people), but when ferreted out they will point to weaknesses or inferiority in the character for which the positive signs are compensations. Even the minus, or weak, signs in handwriting may be found to have within themselves some compensating graphological signs of strength. And this strength may be in the character itself, in some talent, in the personality, or perhaps in a compensating physical attribute.

We all have seen the person in a group who insists on taking the center of the stage. He appears superior to his environment by commanding the attention of everybody in the room. He may speak most convincingly, relate experiences, expound political theories. He may speak quite loudly and gesticulate. Perhaps, psychologically, his loud speaking and calling attention to himself may be his compensation in shutting out the inner voices of unfulfillment, which might disturb his sense of self-importance and force him to recognize his basic feelings of inferiority.

Specimen 51 is an example of such a person. The ready rightward flow in such extremely large writing, coupled with evident speed in execution of the specimen, indicates an ease of expression. The person does everything on a lavish, extravagant scale—even his writing. To him the gesture of an act is often more important than the act itself. His positive personality, which commands the attention of those with whom he comes in contact, shows in his forceful, downward-slanting *t* bars. (The signature, not shown in this specimen, was underscored.) He will argue at the drop of a hat and with heated persistence. He does not concentrate on the cause of things, as does the microscopic writer, but creates the entire picture of an issue in his mind first—and it is colored by his extravagant emotionalism. To concentrate would mean to reflect, and in the process of reflecting, he would be brought into closer proximity with his inner self, which he does not want; for it would make him aware of his inferiority. In his desire to do everything on a grand scale, he finds a measure of compensation for a lack of something definite within himself. There is also a compensation of caution for his generosity, shown in the capital *D*, which is closed with a loop. This may seem out of keeping with such unrestrained writing, but it mirrors the seat of his inferiority complex. His large capitals express his personal vanity and have a direct relation to his desire to make an imposing appearance. The loop above the capital *D* points to some element of flirtatiousness, a typical exhibitionist, a bluffer. But he can usually back up bluffs because he has a strong will. Besides, his vanity would not permit him to bluff unless he could "show color."

Where the inferiority complex has its origin cannot always be decided as obviously as in this specimen. The best way to find out where the roots of the inferiority lie is to know something of the early history of the individual. The handwriting will show that some sense of inferiority exists and will give a clue to the form the compensation takes. This is particularly true when the writing discloses some unusual ability.

Certainly this unusually large writing is startling to the eye and reveals showmanship. His gestures are recognizable and unique and not easily forgotten. He has found overcompensation for an earlier inferiority complex; some would say he has a superiority complex.

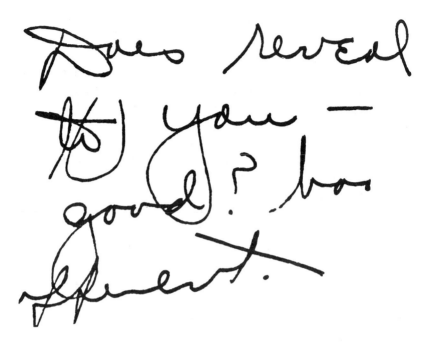

SPECIMEN 51

Nothing timid or inferior would be revealed in his actions, for he could be domineering and controlling yet be considered a good guy (the rhythmic roundness).

Inferiority and Intellectual Compensation

Here is a case of a brilliant young man married to a flashy, flirtatious woman. He seeks in her what he lacks, to complement—and compensate for—his negative personality. She injects color into his life. To her, he is a stick-in-the-mud because he is reflective and studious. She is intelligent enough to feel her need of what he possesses—which she lacks—intellectual fiber. This is one of the reasons for his attraction for her.

Because of the difference in their intellectual approach to life, there is a conflict between them, and both have feelings of inferiority on different scores. She feels inadequate when she cannot follow his line of reasoning, or when she is among his intellectual companions. To compensate for this, she seeks to enhance her beauty so she will be attractive to other men. In her husband's presence, she will flirt with men more obviously attractive than he is to make him feel inferior, in retaliation for the inferiority he causes her to feel.

For her lack of intellect, she has a compensating physical beauty, and she uses it consciously. For his lack of physical attractiveness, he imposes his conscious knowledge of his superior mentality on her, finding in this his compensation. Thus the very factors that attracted these two people to each other are the causes for their feelings of inferiority while in each other's company.

Specimens 52 and 53 were written by this couple. Hers manifests a superficial, pleasure-loving, coquettish nature. Her vanity is expressed in her capitals, especially in the *M*, where the last upper stroke is higher than the others. The long lower loops running into the line below indicate her liking for anything novel or unusual, and in such glamorous attractions she finds an escape from the reality of her conscious inadequacies. Such formations, without clarity between lines, never appear in the handwriting of clear-thinking persons, for they indicate a slight confusion, where fact and fancy run into each other and become tangled.

In her, the desire for activity is greater than for contemplation. Concentration is difficult (large writing), and she acts first and thinks later. *T* bars are weak; when coupled with such confused formations as loops running into the line below, they indicate material self-indulgence. In this and in the vain capitals is seen her compensation for the inferiority shown in the weak *t* crossings.

His writing, small and concentrated, expresses a studious, conservative person, critical and analytical. The weak and downward-slanting *t* bar, not going through the stem, points to an arrogant weakness, a lack of self-confidence, yet also an inner rebelliousness of spirit. The personality is negative (seen in the signature, similar to the rest of the specimen), yet the lower loops—long, exaggerated in comparison with the rest of his letter forms—show his flair for the exotic and unusual (his beautiful but vain wife). His severe capitals indicate egotism, though there is no overestimation of his abilities.

SPECIMEN 52

Both handwritings have in common some lower loops and weakness of will. As often happens, the weakness was the factor of their mutual attraction. In minus signs, they reveal their inferiorities; in the compensatory plus signs, they go off in different directions. His is mental, hers physical. Each has diversified interests. His is in intellectual pursuit, in abstractions; hers is in physical activity, dancing, personal contacts, and those things she can use to further enhance her appearance and personality.

SPECIMEN 53

Where he is interested in the causes of things, getting down to fundamentals (small writing), her mind skims the surface and deals with externals and generalities (large, unrestrained writing). The extrovert is strong in her, mild in him, for he leans toward introversion in the vertical angle in the specimen.

In inflated capital letters, there is always a sign of vanity with regard to appearances, more so when there is an initial stroke before the capital letter. Long lower loops, rhythmically executed, show animal spirits in any writing, indicating strong sex impulses. As their handwriting has this in common, this is undoubtedly their strongest bond—sex.

Inferiority and Creative Compensation

To find evidence of inferiority in handwriting, we look for signs of obvious expressions of superiority. Where there is an abundance of flourishes and fancy formations, we know they are the ruffles that hide the inadequacies or deficiencies.

Accepting the fact that in all of us some feeling of inferiority exists on some point, how then are we to distinguish the inferiority complex that makes an individual want to accomplish something worthwhile in order to overcome the deficiency?

The most definite clue is in the underscored signature. Great men have become so because of their desire to compensate for some inferiority through superior achievement. Many of the recognized personalities underscore their signatures from habit, even after they have achieved a measure of recognition. People in the public eye—musicians, actors, writers, statesmen, and all those desiring the approval of the world through accomplishment—underscore their signatures. The more a person feels his inferiority, the greater must be his achievement to compensate for it.

He will encounter obstacles along the way, and the more determined he is to resist obstacles, to forego momentary temptations that might sway him from his course, the greater will be his need for a firm and unrelenting will.

Thus, in the handwriting of a man finding compensation for his inferiority complex there will be signs of this strong will, together with foresight—the combination of imagination and practical judgment. His conflicts may be evident in some of his actions and will show up in his handwriting.

When the writing shows weakness of will and indecisiveness, as well as exaggerated capital letters (or other exaggerated signs such as long lower loops), a definite, active inferiority complex exists in the character. Long lower loops in handwriting with weak *t* bars show that the writer seeks an escape from responsibility through indulging his physical appetites.

Physical Inferiority and Compensation

Physical handicaps in a world where physical perfection is admired and envied must necessarily create in the physically disabled person feelings of inferiority. One day I received a letter whose writing, slightly disturbed in rhythm, revealed some physical disturbance. The capital letters had flourishes, showing a compensating vanity. I realized this was a man with an obvious inferiority complex.

The history of the man disclosed that he had lost both his arms in an accident during childhood; the specimen he sent me had been executed with his toes. This achievement, which he regarded as superior, gave him feelings of superiority, expressed in the fancy capitals. (See Specimen 118.) Nature's law of compensation tends to strengthen one part of the body to compensate for the loss of another part.

V

Choosing Your Mate

*Ah! a man's love is strong
When fain he comes a-mating.
But a woman's love's is long
And grows when it is waiting.*
—LAURENCE HOUSMAN

IF YOU WERE GOING TO INVEST MONEY IN A BUSINESS partnership with another person, it is highly unlikely you would accept that person on faith without making some investigation regarding his abilities and integrity. Why then enter a marriage partnership blindly, without first understanding the needs and demands —physical, mental, and emotional—of the individual with whom you have decided to share your life?

In any human relationship a certain degree of faith is essential. But to be aware of another's weakness beforehand, and to understand it, can create a strong mutual attachment. Human weaknesses, when approached with tolerance and a sense of humor, have a way of binding people together. To have an intelligent appreciation of your prospective spouse is to be aware of the causes of weakness and strength, the motives that lie hidden in the inner self.

Many mistakes and much unhappiness could be avoided if every couple contemplating marriage were to submit their handwriting to an expert for analysis. The impersonal diagnosis, uncolored by emotional involvement, might disclose some shocking truths. But it is better to know the worst before marriage than afterward. Besides, it offers an opportunity to help each other conquer weaknesses, and might help to avoid future unhappiness and misunderstanding.

During the period of courtship, when the element of pursuit inspires the man to appear at his best so that he may win the lady of his choice, when she also is on her guard and best behavior so as not to divert him from his course of pursuit, weaknesses are hidden under the guise of pleasantries and considerations. But after marriage, when the keen edge of desire has dulled through fulfillment and a need to face practical problems, Prince Charming becomes human, the veil of romantic coloration is torn aside, and both are often revealed in their true aspects. One can still be romantic and aware of the partner's weaknesses. To be honest with each other is the first essential of marriage, for through this is mutual confidence created. To be "touchy" and supersensitive means to invite hurts which can often be avoided when the motive is understood. To possess a broad sense of humor is to alleviate much unnecessary pain on the part of both, especially when two people of some differences must live in close proximity. This is often developed with maturity of vision, and the most successful marriages are often those entered into by two people who are mature in their outlook on life, and willing to "give and take."

Physical Compatibility

The first thing I look for when the handwriting of prospective marriage partners is submitted to me for analysis is physical compatibility. If one person's writing shows strong sex impulses and the other's does not—unless there are compensating factors in the latter's writing, I sound a note of warning. Though sex attraction is not the only consideration, it is, after all, the magnetic force that attracts two people to each other, and a foundation on which a lasting structure can be built. Though not always obvious, perhaps even hidden under the guise of platonic friendship, unconscious in either or both persons, it is true that the first attraction between two healthy persons of opposite sex is almost always based on sexual desire.

There are, of course, exceptions to the rule of physical compatibility being the first consideration. With older people the desire may be for companionship, or for economic security. There are instances of women and men being attracted to each other for the material advantages offered by a mutual relationship. But we are concerned, essentially, with the normal healthy approach to marriage, based on the need of men and women for each other.

Animated, easy-flowing writing, usually leaning to the right, with rhythmic long lower loops, reveals obviously strong sex impulses. When these appear in a vertical hand, the sexual drive is strong but held in check by the mind, and can therefore be diluted in its intensity by reason. Present in both handwritings, with accompanying harmonious traits, such formations assure mutual sexual attraction and show good potential for achieving sexual harmony. But other factors must also be present in both handwritings on which to build mutual understanding; the more interests two people have in common, the more chances there are of creating a permanent bond of understanding.

Our ideals and tastes change as we develop and mature. Our physical appetites may become tempered with our aesthetic development. Even our ideals, realized to some degree, may be replaced by others. Should two people, marrying before either is matured, develop together, there is a chance for continued mutual happiness. But two handwritings that show compatibility before marriage may, five years after marriage, show decided differences, indicating real causes for disharmony.

Marriage may foster in women certain instincts, dormant before the event, yet act as a damper to some men. Marriage might be stabilizing to a restless, nervous woman, but unnerving to a man who was easygoing and irresponsible before marriage. The responsibilities incumbent upon marriage, both emotional and economic, exact a toll, especially since we are all instinctively polygamous; therefore, marriage requires that adjustments be made continually. It presupposes a need for tolerance, cooperation, self-control, sociability, and sympathy, and the more of these qualities two people have in common, the greater their chances for finding permanent happiness in marriage.

Determine Whether Extrovert or Introvert

To achieve mutual harmony, two people must be able to see and understand each other's viewpoint. This is comparatively easy when both persons write in the same angle. It is obvious that two people whose energies flow outward (the right side of the diagram in Chapter II) will have more in common in their approach to life than if one wrote a backhand and the other a rightward-leaning script.

There can be compatibility between any two people attracted to each other if the corresponding angles of their handwriting are D with E, C with D, B with C, or even "X" with A. Such angles harmonize on either the left or the right side of the diagram. But there can seldom be compatibility when one person writes leftward and the other rightward. In such instances, their approach to life, their perspective, is in direct opposition, and they would have too little in common emotionally, temperamentally, and in interests to ensure a lasting relationship in marriage.

Too often are such direct opposites attracted to each other. Extroverts, sensing some mystery in the aloof, reserved introvert, become attracted to him in the hope of bringing him out of himself. But they usually find that the twig has been bent for too long, and they give up in despair, and find someone else more in harmony with their extroverted natures.

Attractions between extroverts and introverts rarely jell. When they do, it is because both have admixtures of extrovert and introvert qualities, creating a common bond between them. It might be said that the extreme extrovert is East, the introvert West, and "ne'er the twain shall meet" in complete harmony.

To stay on the safe side, where marriage has the possibility of permanence and happiness, means to stay on your side of the diagram.

Determine Tolerance and Harmonious Traits

Because human beings are so variable and changeable, so often affected by experiences of intimacy with each other, an essential element in any marriage is tolerance—a toleration of each other's weaknesses. (Acceptance of them is even more desirable.) It is easy to be tolerant when both have the same approach to life, seeing it through the same or related lenses, so to speak, and when there exists between them a physical compatibility. Yet our conditioning in early life often creates prejudices in us with a resulting intolerance later on. This must be tempered or abandoned if we are to get along with people different from ourselves.

It is difficult to tolerate attitudes and beliefs contrary to our own, but with reasoning, education and sympathy, we may learn to see the other man's point of view. It is usually when the senses of an aesthetically receptive person are offended that tolerance is difficult to attain, for, as Emerson wisely put it: "At short distances the senses are despotic."

To overcome this takes a generosity of spirit, a philosophical attitude. In handwritings where both show signs of altruism and adaptability (the *g* made like an 8, the stem of the *y* made with a return stroke instead of a loop), accompanied by social qualities, we find broad tolerance. And such signs indicate a maturity of vision. Generosity of nature, essential to the development of tolerance, will show in broad spacing between letters in words and between words themselves, in wide margins, and in open formations of the small *a* and *o*. These may be accompanied by the open formation of capital *D*, which shows an openheartedness.

These formations are rarely present in an extremely angular script, the very angularity showing a measure of exactness and intolerance. Thus, the more rounded the writing, the more evidence there is of generosity, pliable emotions, expansiveness, and an instinctive sympathy that gives rise to tolerance.

Women, remembering that many men are still children to a marked degree, would do well to develop the art of flattery, if only to minimize the man's weaknesses to himself. He will be loath to leave an environment—or relationship—in which he is considered a superior being. This is important in the development of tolerance toward each other, and may be applied with equally good results by men to women. In such an intimate relationship as marriage, judicious and sincere flattery can act as a soothing salve to alleviate painful hurts or disapproval. The amount of flattery or encouragement offered will vary according to the individual's need to bolster his self-confidence and self-esteem.

Harsh criticism can be very corrosive, developing a rift between two people who may be deeply in love with each other. Care should be taken when criticizing your partner, and if it must be done, then temper it with consideration and love. Using sharp criticism can be tantamount to using a knife, and not many people have the kind of hide that can take it.

Ideals and interests should be taken into account. If the man enjoys solitude, it would be wise for the woman to find outside interests to absorb her during such periods. The woman's writing should show evidence of self-sufficiency, though she may be yielding and emotionally submissive at such times as her husband manifests a responsiveness. If the man is pleasure-loving, responsive to stimulation, the woman's writing should show some adaptability, or the capacity to be stimulating. If she is aware that she has no such resources, then she should show tolerance for the side of his nature she cannot satisfy. This is provided, of course, that his nature does not lead him into irresponsible channels which force her to make continual adjustments. At best, however, women are called upon to make the greater number of adjustments in marriage. And this will be understood and accepted if they realize that marriage is, primarily, their forte and protection.

Tolerance implies an ability to see the humorous side of any trying situation. It necessitates a conscious attempt to refute in oneself any desire for competition with one's partner; to be agreeable, unpossessive, and respectful of the other person's rights.

In the more enlightened person—where emotions are subjected to the light of reasoning, where broadmindedness replaces prejudices —tolerance and humor are more apt to exist. For, "Life is a comedy for those who *think*; a tragedy to those who *feel*." Handwriting will reflect such philosophic approach and generosity of vision. And it must be remembered that people who give (extroverts) are apt to be more tolerant than those who take (introverts).

The true introvert should not—and rarely does—marry. When introverts are married to each other there is seldom a fusing of emotional feeling to bind them closely, but they may not feel the need for it. Shared interests, whether artistic or intellectual, have the power to bind such people together. Such a union has the possibility of permanence, for there is little danger of too much familiarity— which in many instances breeds disrespect and contempt for discovered weaknesses.

But an introvert married to an extrovert invites disharmony from the very outset. It will be a give-and-take alliance—except that the extrovert will do the giving and the introvert the taking, causing resentment in the one for a lack of response in the other.

The campus is huge and there are thousands of students so it is completely different than the college I'm used to. Here you are just a number to most of the faculty and administration and unless you

SPECIMEN 54

Modern Handwriting is the refined manifestation of these symbological beginnings and retains much of the significant characteristics in the individual subconscious mind.

SPECIMEN 55

Specimens 54 and 55 were written by a man and woman of above-average intelligence, and their marriage can be called a success. Despite a disparity in age (she's in her forties, he's in his sixties), there is a meeting of minds; both are interested in intellectual pursuits, but both handwritings lean in a rightward direction and reveal the need for human companionship, which they find in each other.

... most of time.
Calling the stay way
last thing to do, for I
don't anything ... and
it's such a lousy hotel ..
don't seem to know wh
are -

SPECIMEN 56

Her handwriting—small and rounded with signs of intuition and talent, coupled with good spacing of lines and words—tells us she is a woman with a variety of interests. Essentially a student (she went back to college after her children were grown), she enjoys mental stimulation, which he, from what is indicated in his handwriting, can give her. They are both optimistic, as shown in the rising lines, more evident in his than in hers. She has good control and discipline, as seen in strong *t* bars, several of them bowed. She does things quickly and without apparent effort, whereas he has a slower pace, and the angularity in his writing shows his desire to be accurate and efficient. Mental formations are evident in both handwritings, as is the rightward turn of the downstroke on the *g* and *y*, and the success of their relationship can be said to rest on their mutual give-and-take. Both show a sense of humor, and she seems more flexible than he does. There are compensations on every level for what may be lacking to fulfill the desires of each, and the fact that they can talk things out together, with no fear of censure or undue criticism, tells us that they have gone past the tolerant stage and truly accept each other.

writing of Katuva, but I may be
Please let me know the cost
long forgotten - am going to Sth
for 3 weeks then come back +
join an airline in N.Y on Oct
I'll get to see you I hope - un
warmest regards - still an ache -
but it's over + done with - take

SPECIMEN 57

Both have the capacity for making adjustments, through judgment and common sense on her part, and responsiveness on his. They are both cooperative and aware human beings.

Conversely, the next two specimens belong to individuals who were unable to make a go of it. A glance at the vast differences in their handwriting gives the major clue, which even a rank amateur graphologist could discern. She (56) is a neurotic woman whose manner sometimes suggests a better-than-thou attitude, with evident narcissism and a desire for self-indulgence; he (57) is a mixed-up, very sensitive man, nervous and compulsive, with a neurosis developed in a childhood fraught with unhappiness. Whereas she is sadistic—shown in the heavy pressure, coupled with the vertical angle, and the blunt downstrokes (in the d in "and" and the l in "hotel")—he is masochistic and defensive. His neurosis compounds hers, and since at the very outset the attraction was based on a neurotic premise, it could not possibly endure. They might be described as antipodes, and after the physical attraction waned, there was little on which to base a mutual understanding. They spoke different languages, not only literally—he is American and she is Scandinavian—but also in the different set of meanings each had as to what life meant and demanded of them: he had an unconscious desire to be punished (as a child he was often punished and got to feeling he deserved it); she had a desire to mete out punishment, through which she asserted her superiority. And whereas sex to him was flavored with romanticism, to her it was just an appetite to be satisfied, as shown in the sensuality of her pen pressure. His light pen pressure reveals his supersensitivity, and his long *t* bars show nervous energy and drive. He is a compulsive talker, and one can visualize her looking at him haughtily and saying "Nonsense!" This does not make for a harmonious relationship. There is extreme disunity expressed here in the differences in their pen pressure, angle, letter forms, and structure; even their neuroses did not mesh.

Humor—Indispensable in Marriage

A well-known Viennese psychiatrist referred to humor as the "weapon of superiority." When there is obvious conflict such a weapon can break the tension, but it must be used with skill and adroitness. It is a rare quality, but it can be developed. Humor, judiciously applied, can become the saving grace of a relationship where other common factors are lacking. To a happy marriage it is indispensable.

The ability to share laughter, in its various shades and expressions, shows up in handwriting in a number of ways. Humor ranges from broad comedy to subtle, critical wit.

When there is ego conflict between two people, the weapon of humor may be sharpened by cleverness, sarcasm, acuteness of wit. Where there is such competition between two individuals, each will try to outshine the other in wittiness, and the atmosphere sometimes becomes charged with tension.

In handwriting, sarcasm is revealed in lancelike formations, both in *t* bars and in single downstrokes of the *y* and *g*. When sarcasm is tempered by an element of sympathy, the result may be remarks that are witty but not cutting. The desire to soften the sharp edges will often show in roundness or signs of altruism (the rightward turn of the downstroke on the *y*). A relationship may be destroyed by the unskilled use of humor. (Where there is intuition a person may sense when he has gone too far.) Continually resorted to, sarcasm— usually part of a keen critical faculty—can in time destroy mutual confidence. It must have the compensating factors of kindness and judgment, otherwise it can really become destructive.

SPECIMEN 58

In Specimen 58 we have an example of critical, sharp, clever humor. The *t* bars are consistently lancelike, starting heavy and ending in a sharp point. Some of them tend to slant downward, augmenting the thrust through argumentativeness. Some *i* dots are tent-shaped, as usually happens in combination with angularity. Here the steel is tempered by the sign of altruism evident in the word "plays." There are also signs of good judgment, and sensitivity is shown in the medium-light pen pressure. This, combined with signs of intuition, tells us the writer can sense when he has made his point, goes just so far and then stops. (Incidentally, the writer is an avowed homosexual with the kind of wit many of them possess. Other common denominators found in handwritings of homosexuals are present here: masochism, narcissism, a defensive attitude.)

The critical person of keen mentality and pliable emotions can evoke humor from pathos. Chaplin is the master of such humor, and this is bound to be evident in his handwriting. Comedy and tragedy are opposite sides of the same coin. However, when people laugh at funerals, as sometimes happens, it is because of hysteria and not because there is anything humorous in the situation.

Jolly Good Humor

The jolly, good-natured person whose laughter is often infectious and whose spirits spread sunshine in a gloomy house is the one to whom most people are drawn. It is joy that draws us to another person, whereas gloom is apt to live and die alone. It follows that a cheerful, optimistic person has many friends. And in the following specimen (59) we may be certain that the writer is pleasant, good-natured, and full of a love of life. It is easy to see it in her large, flowing, rightward-leaning writing—with consistently rising finals, *t* bars that are curved, *i* dots that are parts of circles, and a buoyant, optimistic rhythm.

Such a person is made-to-order for marriage. She approaches the relationship with expansiveness, which goes hand-in-hand with tolerance. Her attitude is: "Nothing is so bad that it couldn't be worse," and even unfortunate experiences make her feel they are good for something. She has tact because of her natural consideration for others, though instinctively she is impetuous. Some words taper, others grow larger. She is essentially a social being, aware of the needs of other people and always ready to lend a helping hand. It requires no effort on her part to cheer up another person, and she frequently does so by her very presence.

A woman with such a disposition blossoms in marriage, often infecting a less genial partner with her good humor. She is charitable and tends to bring out this trait in others. She is not competitive and practices what she believes, which is to live and let live. Her writing is more rounded than angular, though she may readily be attracted to someone writing in the latter manner. She is a leavening influence.

The type of humor described above is the exception to the rule that most forms of humor have in them an element of cruelty. The person who can laugh at himself has the power to disarm another person's cruelty. The weapon may be disguised in the form of a joke, but if he can make others laugh, he is performing a service.

SPECIMEN 59

Notice how often groups—a TV audience, for instance—will laugh at almost anything that is said by a so-called comedian. It shows our great need to be amused, to be diverted from our troubles—and the world's. The raconteur, the retailer of jokes, always finds an audience, though many of these jokesters often live lives of turmoil or desperation, which they mask with outward raillery.

Uncharitable, Exacting, Narrow-Minded, Humorless People

Exacting, efficient persons who write a tight, angular hand and in whom a sense of justice exists are often lacking in humor. They are forever concerned with receiving their full share in all their dealings with others. To them the Mosaic Law ("an Eye for an Eye") is a predominant ritual. They are impelled to pay back in kind; they take themselves seriously, are often self-righteous and sometimes pontifical or pompous. They are the supersensitive ones who often see hurts where none are intended. It is difficult for them to project their imagination into the feelings and needs of others, often because they live in a narrow, caulked-in world of their own. Often they live according to rule, measuring those who cross their paths with the same yardstick; they are inflexible in their attitudes, uncharitable toward those who may be guilty of even a minor infraction. It is difficult for them to see a joke, because they feel it may be on them. They are intolerant of people who see the humor in life. What is there to laugh at? they wonder.

Such lack of humor goes with intolerance and is usually found in extremely selfish people. They will not even share humor, for it is difficult for them to share anything. The handwriting of such people is usually angular and cramped, often tightly closed, with the words closely spaced together, and there may be an absence of margins on both the left and right sides. These are repressed, inhibited people, single-tracked in their thinking, intolerant of anyone who disagrees with them. Often they are as tight with money as they are with their emotions.

SPECIMEN 60

Specimen 60 is an example of a narrow-minded person without much humor, although there is a sign, in one slightly curved *i* dot, that he might laugh if sufficiently provoked. He is cautious, reflective, despite the rightward angle: caution shows in the closed *a*'s and *o*'s; reflection, in the spacing between words, which is inconsistent with this kind of hand. In the rightward flow of the writing such spacing augments the caution, indicating paranoid trends. He hesitates before spending money or energy. There is no easy rhythmic swing to the writing, no expansiveness or looseness. He is practical and can exercise good judgment when his emotions are not involved. He is serious, ambitious, but unable to see the humor in a situation in which he figures. Often *i* dots in angular writing will be tent-shaped and therefore consistent with sharpness. This is not evident here, so he is not consistently a sourpuss. With no roundness in a specimen to temper a critical faculty we assume that humor may take the form of ridicule. This is likely to be the case here. As the angle is to the right, and there is a hint of an impulse to give (usually repressed), he will expect something in return. He is intolerant of humor and good nature in others, is supersensitive, and (in paranoid fashion) may construe others' laughter as being ridicule of him.

The introverted person, somewhat withdrawn and lacking emotional expansiveness, whose writing is vertical and closely written, with angularity predominating over roundness, will also show a lack of humor. He is greatly concerned with himself, his own reactions and musings; his energies flow inward, and the seriousness with which he regards life demands he be taken seriously. People with whom he comes in contact may consider him a queer duck. Occasionally he may show a peculiar type of humor, but it is likely to be colored with bitterness and resentment as a result of feeling misunderstood. Often these people make no effort to be understood, for they live in a world of private meanings.

As announced over radio recently. enclosed

SPECIMEN 61

In Specimen 61 we have the selfish, humorless person, discontented, intolerant, angry. She is obviously repressed (angular, vertical, heavy-pressure writing), and the *t* bar is short and abrupt, indicating a measure of self-control. But the fact that she feels the need to exercise control causes her resentment. To the casual observer she appears aloof, unsocial, seclusive, for she neither gives nor invites confidences, and does not enjoy sharing humor.

The critical, fault-finding person, sensitive about her own feelings yet entirely unmindful of how she may be hurting others, is often one with a deep-seated inferiority complex. She may suffer from guilt feelings which put her on the defensive. She may see the humor in situations that do not point up her own feelings of inadequacy; for example, she might laugh at a person slipping on a banana peel, glad it didn't happen to her. The fault-finding trait is usually revealed in *t* bars that slant downward but do not go through the stem of the letter, as well as in tent-shaped *i* dots with an admixture of angularity.

The more that small, rounded handwriting tends to be vertical, the more subtle the humor is apt to be, usually corroborated by other signs. The less the desire is to share with others—whether themselves, possessions, or humor (as in the extreme backhand writer), the less balanced is the sense of values. For a good sense of humor is a fair indication of a good sense of values.

The Bad-Tempered Person

Temper is negatively directed energy. When someone is denied the natural expression of his emotional drives (whether in childhood or later) and his emotion struggles for expression, the result may be resentment or temper. Adults may have temper tantrums just as they had in childhood, but as adults they are better able to rationalize them. Frustration is often at the root of temper, and in many instances an explosive release may clear the atmosphere. (The person who explodes on rare occasions may otherwise be good-natured.) This ability to blow off steam is one way of getting rid of excess energy—which is not difficult for an extrovert to do. But the introvert, whose energies flow inward, has already formed a pattern of resentment and vindictiveness, and when his control breaks down there is an outburst.

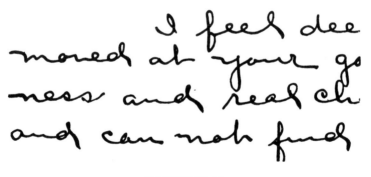

SPECIMEN 62

In Specimen 62 we are confronted with a resentful, vindictive person who may not appear to have these traits. She appears calm on the surface (the vertical writing), but the blunt finals that go downward in heavier pressure than the rest of the specimen tell us something is smoldering in her. And a temper tantrum may erupt without our knowing what set it off. She harbors grudges, is suspicious and possessive. When her energies find no constructive outlet, they find release in a destructive direction. She may be in a white heat, nervous and trembling with rage; she can be deliberately sadistic. She doesn't have the mental equipment to temper her cruelty with judgment, but she may try to come to terms with later guilt feelings by a mildly generous act; this is seen in some open *o*'s and in the extension of the *r* stroke in the word "your." It is further corroborated in the width of her words, which gives us a clue to some expansiveness, but she hesitates to express it for fear someone may take advantage of it.

SPECIMEN 63

In Specimen 63 we see signs of extroversion with a modicum of expansiveness, impulsive ardor, and responsiveness. But here the signs of a bad temper show in the black strokes at the ends of words. The firm *t* bars tell us that, for the most part, the temper is controlled; but the very effort of having to control it creates tension that mounts until it reaches a peak. Then she loses her temper, says things for which she may later be sorry. The fiery quality can take the form of enthusiasm if constructively directed. Although rounded formations show she has an innate sympathy, she is a determined individual, often uncompromising; when she does not get her way she is likely to force it. We see her as a controlling person who can be a hard taskmaster.

SPECIMEN 64

This writing has signs of mental illness. The writer may laugh at something that her distorted mind finds humorous but which she cannot share with others because she lives in a world of private meanings. She has withdrawn into a world of fantasy, but there remains some connection, however tenuous, with the outside world. She is neither good-natured nor cooperative, and is rather difficult to please. Lines that tend to slant downward indicate depression, and the poor rhythm tells us there is no harmonious coordination between her thinking and feeling. She is nervous and tense in her movements. She is an emotional cripple, and it is difficult to tell whether her physical deformity crippled her emotions or vice versa. There is no sign of humor here, nothing to lighten her burden, unless it is some fantasy—which she does not disclose to others—that shows in the high placement of the *i* dots. Omitting letters of words can point to brain damage, as is often the case in a handwriting which definitely reveals disturbance.

Choosing Employees

By reading a book on graphology—this one or one of a dozen others—you will not become an expert in choosing the right man for the right job. But you will get clues you can track down, and you can look for warning signs that will help you avoid hiring a troublemaker, a malcontent, or a mentally or emotionally disturbed person.

Though it is not wise to draw conclusions from a few signs, there are some that have the same meaning no matter in what kind of writing they appear. Where the angles go in different directions, as in Specimen 18, the writer is guided so much by moods as to act the prima donna. And where you see a number of *t* bars that do not go through the stem of the letter, with some of them slanting downward, you can be sure the writer is indecisive, restless, and lacks stick-to-itiveness. He will be difficult to pin down because he doesn't know what he really wants. It is a sign of instability, and the writer is not reliable for the long pull. He has probably had many jobs, none of which he stuck with, even though he may have gotten off to a good start. It is therefore safe to assume that a neurosis absorbs his energy at some point. And he may become a problem.

If you are choosing a salesman, look for the sign of the salesman —the aggressive *t* bar that slants downward and goes through the stem of the letter—especially if you are looking for a go-getter. If it's a sales manager you want, be sure his handwriting reveals an interest in people, in his salesmen, whose confidence he must win. He can't perform very well if he lacks confidence in himself, which shows up in weak *t* bars, corroborated by other signs of weakness.

All through this chapter there are examples of individuals in different kinds of work. Be guided by these to some extent; but in making a final decision, it would be wise to have applicants tested —either by psychological or aptitude tests, or by submitting their handwriting to an expert who is experienced in selecting personnel. Remember: Strong, long *t* bars show determination and a capacity for hard work, and when there is a hook on endings of *t* bars and other strokes, you have a tenacious person who doesn't give up easily.

For cooperation—an important element for employees who have to work with other people or contact them on the outside—look for the angle showing extroversion, with signs of generosity in the width of the writing. If there are signs of intuition, so much the better, as it means he has insight and can take a short cut to a conclusion or destination—provided there are also signs of good judgment.

The best salesmen are born psychologists, and their handwriting reveals a combination of imagination, intuition, and judgment, with an altruistic bent indicated in the rightward turn of the downstrokes on *y*'s and *g*'s. Again it will depend upon what he is selling, although in the long run he is selling himself. Beware of handwriting that is narrow and cramped (resembling Specimen 60); the writer is narrow-minded, intolerant, humorless, hypersensitive, difficult to please. Try to make sure that your candidate for a selling job is concerned with his customers' needs and not just his own. If you see signs of ill-humor, temper, viciousness, or selfishness, as shown in some specimens in this chapter, you may run into trouble. Reflect deliberately and when in doubt *reject!*

These are hints that may prove useful. There is a fine line between the troublemaker and the troubleshooter. The former's handwriting will show weakness in a lack of self-discipline (again the weak *t* bars). He looks for excitement when he becomes bored with his work and may find it by stirring up trouble. He won't be bored if he likes his job, it absorbs him, and he has a definite goal. The troubleshooter may have traits similar to the troublemaker, but his handwriting will reveal constructive signs that include those of self-discipline and judgment.

It is difficult not to form conclusions from outward appearances, but they can be misleading. A man may talk convincingly, but that may be as far as it goes. He sells himself, his personality, and this may take you in, but his handwriting will show whether his character is strong and in harmony with the personality he presents.

The sourpuss may be a good worker in an office by himself but be uncooperative where people are concerned. In such cases, check to see if he's suffering from some physical ailment; this might be the cause of his sourness.

A good employee, like a good husband or wife, is a cooperative human being. This includes consideration for the rights and feelings of others, a measure of humor, a desire to be useful. Someone who shows cooperation, along with accuracy (seen in angularity), would be a good risk and an asset to most firms. Frequently a beginner will show a willingness to listen and learn and may prove more of an asset than an experienced man who thinks he knows it all and refuses to listen.

The person who talks a great deal, who can't listen without becoming bored or impatient, is often self-centered and may become a nuisance in an office where many people work. The open capital *D* that is in a handwriting that has a preponderance of open formations of *a*'s and *o*'s, though revealing openheartedness, also shows frankness, and in many instances gives the major clue to the person's orality. This is especially true when the rhythm of the writing is swift, whether the angle is vertical or leaning to the right.

The more silent ones are often the vertical writers, whose writing may be small or medium small to medium large, with curtailed endings on words, and whose reserve prevents them from spreading themselves around. Those who do spread themselves around have handwritings that spread and sometimes resemble a scrawl.

If you are looking for complete honesty—and it does exist—be sure the writer does not habitually make dwindling formations. These people often have something to hide; they may be manipulative, and they do not show their hand. The person of integrity, who is above-board, trustworthy, and loyal, has a handwriting whose every letter and word is clearly written. It usually has firm *t* bars (a few may be weak, but that is no detriment, for we must allow for some human weakness), and careful punctuation shows attention to detail.

The totally legible hand may not be that of an intellectual giant, but the employer can be certain of loyalty, obedience to the rules, and an even disposition. Much depends upon the job. If it involves politics, law, or work that demands an element of shrewdness, then the dwindling formations might be an advantage.

If a job seeker refuses to submit his handwriting for analysis, be suspicious. He may not trust others because he has little trust in himself, and he may turn out to be a problem. People who won't cooperate in supplying a sample of handwriting may be uncooperative in other areas too. These are the adults who have not been taught cooperation in childhood, and life often becomes more or less of a burden to them.

So it's cooperation, a sense of humor, a willingness to listen and perhaps do more than is expected, and a positive attitude that make for a good employee. Lucky is the employer who has a number of such individuals in his organization. They are usually the ones who lift the morale of an organization and who can counterbalance any disharmonies.

VI

Active and Passive People

God loves an idle rainbow,
No less than labouring seas.
—RALPH HODGSON

The Optimistic Ambitious Person

THE SPEED WITH WHICH A SPECIMEN OF HANDWRITing is executed determines the amount of energy the person uses in accomplishing his tasks. The person propelled by desire, by an inner enthusiasm, will have more ambition, for his inner resources act as the engines that drive him to greater activity.

Where physical force is needed to achieve an end, the muscles are called into play, and the handwriting will show this in the heavy pen pressure, in the firmness of muscular coordination disclosed in the rhythm and pressure combined. Where nervous energy is applied, the specimen will be lighter in pen pressure, but the enthusiasm will show in tenacity hooks all through the writing. Wherever ambition is the driving force, the lines of the writing tend to rise at the right, showing the rising of the spirits, optimism, and hopefulness that usually accompany striving. Ambition and optimism go hand in hand, for without hopefulness and singleness of purpose, ambition would be wingless and the voltage behind the effort of the individual lessened.

If you are ambitious to attain a world goal, one in which you will stand out because of your accomplishment, or one where you are forced to compete with others to attain a measure of superiority, your extroverted qualities will first be obvious in your rightward-flowing writing. Your will power will have behind it the voltage that gives momentum to your energies, and your *t* crossings will therefore be long, forceful, and obvious.

110

The active, ambitious person is recognized by signs in his handwriting of foresight, self-confidence, and sound judgment—coupled with optimism. Pessimists are rarely ambitious. They do not believe effort worthwhile, for to them it leads to naught. Optimists make continued efforts, even after failure, for they always feel that somewhere ahead lies success. Consequently, only disappointed optimists commit suicide: those who realize the futility of their hopes.

Forceful writing, which almost leaps upward on the paper, will show ambition, especially when it reveals strong, lengthy, determined *t* bars in heavy-pressure writing. In lighter pressure script, signs of tenacity in the hooks on ending strokes, whether finals or *t* bars, also reveal ambition, but the tenacity used takes nervous energy rather than physical strength. (Wherever hooks are encountered, we know the person does not give up readily, for even the pen is loath to leave the paper, as in Specimen 65.)

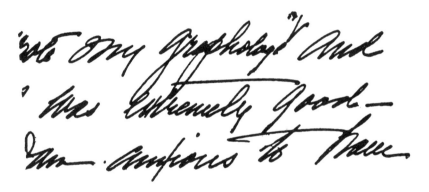

SPECIMEN 65

The Mentally Active Person

Ambitious individuals in whom the mind is a major driving force will usually be recognized by small, well-spaced writing, rising lines, signs of culture in the Greek *d* and *e*, and the letter *g* that looks like the number 8 or part of it. There are frequently signs of self-discipline, especially where the individual is dedicated to his work. He may be a writer, professor, scientist, connected with the field of education. Depending upon his temperament, there will be various signs of strength and weakness, but where he is actively engrossed in his endeavors, signs of strength will predominate.

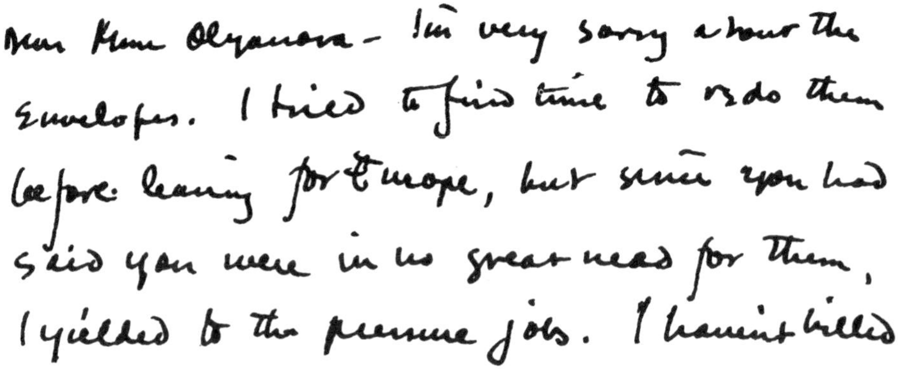
Dear Mme Olyanova - I'm very sorry about the envelopes. I tried to find time to redo them before leaving for Europe, but since you had said you were in no great need for them, I yielded to the pressure jobs. I haven't billed

SPECIMEN 66

Here we have a man of culture, refinement, and innate talent. He is versatile, artistic, extremely sensitive. He is also critical in his observations (as much the observer as the doer, for the writing is vertical), serious about any project he undertakes. Essentially an intellectual, he is also concerned with the plight of underprivileged people and works in their behalf. His goal is to help provide the greatest good to the greatest number, and he can express this in action as well as literary achievement. The simple capital *I* is a major clue to his clarity of thought and is in harmony with the rest of the writing. He is a man of unusual intellectual endowments.

Physical Activity and Muscular Energy

The athletic person, the baseball or football player, the man who takes naturally to skills that require the use of physical energy and a harmonious coordination between mind and body, comes under the heading of the physically active. To excel in athletic goals he must have good muscular coordination, which will be expressed in handwriting in firm, even pen pressure, usually heavy. The more that nerve control is employed, the firmer the strokes will be in the writing—just as the strokes used in golf or swimming. Long, swinging lower loops in heavy-pressure writing invariably point to the writer's desire for physical activity, and this often includes the capacity to enjoy dancing.

The more accomplished people become in physical skills, the more such achievement will reveal itself in the writing. Impatience with details will manifest itself by initial strokes on letters, and the same enthusiasm which is used in pursuing a chosen goal, forming an outlet for the physical energy, can be recognized in the tempo and firm rhythm of the heavy writing. These people dislike doing routine work, are usually fond of travel, possess robust appetites, and prefer to keep on the move. They become restless if confined to a desk.

Nervous Energy

The person with nervous energy who desires physical activity has an inner enthusiasm that has its seat in the imagination. These people, whose own nervous demands force continued activity, may show more resistance in times of illness than their more robust-looking fellows. They are tense, active, enthusiastic, often very talkative; they find relaxation difficult to achieve, for their active imagination drives them to attain an objective, and their nervous ardor colors all their activities.

The writing may look jerky and nervous, but there will be signs of tenacity and often of manual skill disclosed in printed capitals. The small letters may also be printed. Hooks will appear throughout the writing, especially on horizontal strokes (finals and *t* crossings). Specimen 62 is an example of a person who has both physical and nervous energy; the physical robustness shows in the heavy pen pressure, coupled with the quick, firm tempo of the writing; the nervous energy is revealed in the hooks.

Strangely enough, nervous people who seem unable to concentrate for long on one particular thing have been known to do the finest detail work with their hands. Embroidery, needlework, metal work in minute detail—all have been done by highly nervous people.

When the energies are overtaxed—as often happens in those whose enthusiasm carries them beyond their physical capacities—we have resultant nervous ailments, insomnia, poor appetite, hysteria, and attending illnesses. They are not consciously aware, many of them, that they are dissipating their nervous energy until forced to relax by circumstances. In such cases of illness, it is difficult to determine whether the mind influences the body or vice versa. But in nervous diseases the mind does play an important part, and the handwriting will always show a vivid imagination. Permitted to run riot, this same imagination has been responsible for catering to neurotic tendencies in people.

Effects of Geographical Location on Handwriting

It is a known fact that climatic conditions affect the temperament and habits of a nation. We know that in the north, where there is always a battle with the elements, there is more practicality, resourcefulness, and isolation in the character of its people than in the south, where the hot sun is not particularly conducive to hard work. Most of our eminent explorers, men of isolated temperament who have traveled alone, have been Northerners. These were men of practicality and vision, constructive in their pursuits.

The farther north we go, the more isolated the temperament of the individual becomes. This is natural, for the northern places are colder and less inhabited than the south. (For lands south of the equator, the opposite is true, of course.) The farther south we go, the warmer and more expansive the nature of the inhabitants becomes. They are apt to be less practical, less ambitious, yet more romantic and more lethargic than their northern brothers. It is natural, then, that the temperament of people, affected by the north or the south, should be reflected by characteristic signs in handwriting.

In the United States, where the climate of the North is so different from that of the South, we find this difference reflected in the temperament, ambitions, interests, and character of the people. The Northerner, more resourceful in his need to deal with harsher elements, will show this in his conservative, practical handwriting. I speak here more of the New England and North Atlantic states. The Southerner we recognize by his lethargic, easygoing manner, reflected in his musical and lazy drawl. Affecting his mental processes, his temperament, and his approach to life, this lethargic quality is indicated in his handwriting as well. The characteristic Southern handwriting will almost invariably show signs of procrastination and inertia. We know that such mental inertia often gives birth to superstition, religious cults, and beliefs that would not be digested by the more alert thinker.

The sign of procrastination, in which the *t* bar does not go through the stem, is characteristically Southern. Even in the more ambitious Southerners, this sign is present, perhaps to a lesser degree and counterbalanced with positive, or plus, signs. Even the Southerner who comes North to live and work does not easily relinquish his easy-going approach to life, any more than he entirely loses his Southern drawl. Those Southerners with ambition and foresight who want to be progressive do not permit themselves to stagnate in the hot sun. And their handwriting will reveal an attempt to conquer traits of inertia instilled in them by their environment.

SPECIMEN 67

Specimen 67 was penned by a Southerner. The tempo of this writing shows a quality of activity that is diluted (the *t* bars are short and weak and do not go through the stem in many instances). Although seemingly active, this person does not accomplish anything to her own satisfaction. The word "working" is an excellent example of physical inertia in handwriting: A wide, swinging lower loop would reveal consistent physical activity, but her lower loops have no rhythm.

The Diffused Energies of the Scatterbrain

The scatterbrain, whose handwriting, like her brain, is all at loose ends, has no one definite goal toward which to aspire. She starts several things at once in her desire to keep active, yet leaves them unfinished. She is unable to concentrate on one task long enough to complete it, and she is easily distracted.

The writing will be large, often diffused-looking, like an over-enlarged photo in which details are blurred or seem to run into each other. Angles may vary from vertical to rightward, and occasionally there is confusion (letters of the line above running into the line below). *T* bars may be weak or strong or both. She may be quite alert and determined in some respects, yet about most things she'll be vague and in a fog.

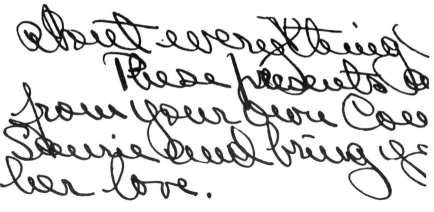

SPECIMEN 68

Specimen 68 is an example of a scatterbrain type. The writing is large, the pen pressure varies. Downstrokes are dark and show obstinacy, and the entire lack of clarity or spacing between words and lines indicates her confusion and self-centeredness. The backward angle here means that she has reacted to her conditioning, in which she was taught to be aloof from those not in her own social stratum. She cannot communicate what is on her mind to others with any semblance of lucidity. Her mind, in short, is slightly out of focus; she "stews in her own juice."

She is attracted to the glamorous or unusual, as a moth is to a flame, but has the fortunate balance of caution. She does things with a lavish gesture, often several at a time, and will be unable to separate one thought from another, constantly harking back to what she has said before.

The scatterbrain is either a victim of faulty home conditioning or of inherited weakness, the offspring of parents whose sexual vitality at conception was at low ebb, or of a traumatic experience in infancy.

Active People on the Minus Side

All of us have met people who, although apparently busy all the time, seem to accomplish nothing definite. They are the ones who lack singleness of purpose, who are quite versatile and capable of doing many things well. But they lack the perseverance to finish what they start. They seem unable to maintain a sustained interest and are often restless and ill-adjusted. There is within them a continual conflict between their emotions and their minds. Possessing no definite goal, they become very enthusiastic over something novel or glamorous or unusual while they are planning its execution. But by the time they are ready to perform their enthusiasm wanes, and they turn to something else.

Their handwriting shows both enthusiasm and inertia. The *t* bars begin with a hook, and either do not go through the letter, or become weaker and hairlike in the finishing stroke.

These are the whimsical, changeable people, often self-indulgent, who live only for the moment. They do not project their vision, for their moods and whims interrupt their thinking. We refer to them as the fickle ones, for they seem forever to be seeking new interests and their lives seem to lack a definite pattern. Often they have a continued desire to escape from the demands made by their inner selves. To concentrate on one thing at a time might bring them into intimate contact with facts about their lives that they do not wish to face. The result is continued activity without reflection. Their actions seem to produce nothing finished or concrete.

Among this group are those who seek compensation for what they lack (a definite goal) in gambling, drinking, useless hobbies.

When inactive they become bored, and their desire to go places and do things usually leads them into groups where much activity takes place in the pursuit of self-indulgent, often hollow pleasures.

In this category are the drifters, the shiftless individuals who switch from one thing to another, who never concentrate long enough on one pursuit to show results, and who are always finding excuses for their shiftlessness. The fault usually lies in the person's early conditioning and influences. It may be because he is a square peg in a round hole.

In analyzing such handwriting, it will be necessary to evaluate the plus and minus traits carefully, for the writing may look strong and show signs of talent, versatility, and obvious force, whereas a thorough examination will reveal a preponderance of weak signs (especially in the *t* bars), which will give the main clue to the weakness that offsets the strength.

lot more healthy then I left it, it is just like taking L.S.D. I am very glad to be back in this less then perfect world. It is true when I'm being taken into La Crepe I look around and feel guilty about

SPECIMEN 69

Here in Specimen 69 we see a woman who is discontented because she has never found the kind of work for which she is best suited and from which she can find a measure of happiness. She is supersensitive, and this robs her of the initiative (shown in a number of *t*'s that end in a hook instead of being crossed) to make the attempt to assert herself. As a result, she got into a rut that had secondary benefits and provided a measure of financial security. But her vivid imagination and spirit of adventure (shown in the *t* bar above the stem in "this" and "then") found no release in her work as a dental assistant, and she chafed against the yoke for many years. There are signs of optimism in the rising lines, of constructive ability in the printed capitals, of the ability to cooperate (roundness, plus graceful endings of words); in work for which she has a natural bent, she could put these to use. Having some elements of the perfectionist (which the high *t* bar also indicates), she may have some difficulty in adjusting to reality. A sign of sound practical judgment appears in the downstroke of the *y* in "guilty," and despite signs of compulsiveness she should be able to make adjustments as long as she is in a niche in which she feels useful and can find expression for her artistic potentialities. Although there seems to be a slight disturbance in the writing (varying angles), this can be a sign of the "divine discontentment" that would impel her to give up a job that offered financial security but did not arouse her interest. She will change (just as her handwriting shows signs of change) when she is expressing herself in a channel that makes more creative demands upon her. She has keen intelligence and insight, as well as a sense of humor, which should help her in making adjustments.

Passive People on the Plus Side

We often wonder at people who seem passive and inactive yet who have obviously accomplished a great deal. These are the people who fit naturally into their chosen goals, and who have no need to strive for achievement. They are apt to be reflective rather than active, but when active they can accomplish a great deal in a short time, because they know just what they want to do and enjoy doing it.

They don't need a driving ambition to spur them into physical or mental activity. Their mental activity may produce abstract theories or discoveries that enrich the world. For example, a man may lie on his back contemplating the stars for many years, and ultimately make a discovery that will revolutionize the world of science. Through his sedentary behavior and his contemplation, he is way ahead of the man who is forever busy yet does nothing to enrich even his own life.

The scientist may have periods of physical activity in which he records his findings, but they are brief compared with the time he has spent contemplating. Such physical passivity is as useful to humanity (often more so) as the visible activity of the consciously ambitious and materially productive person. The handwriting of passive men will show mental formations and concentrated, microscopic formations. Pen pressure will be light or medium heavy, as physical appetites are secondary. *T* bars may be, and often are, weak. But there is no need for a strong will, for the passivity itself takes a plus direction. The trait is essentially that of the introvert, and the writing may even disclose signs of genius in its divergence from the accepted pattern.

SPECIMEN 70

Specimen 70, though not essentially introverted, as seen in the extroverted angle of the writing, shows a lack of conscious effort or drive. *T* bars are altogether uncrossed. The man, a musician of unusual talent, has periods of reflection and contemplation, yet swings to the other extreme in periods of activity to further his interest in music. Inspiration and intuition are seen in the continual breaking up of words. The unusual formations show originality; mental formation of the small *h* indicates he has a keen mental receptivity, and he is equally responsive emotionally. It is during his inactive moments, when he relaxes and lets thoughts come to him—instead of consciously reasoning—that he receives his greatest inspiration.

Lack of Physical Energy and Vitality

Physical weakness or lack of vitality is a good reason for signs of weakness in handwriting. Inactivity may be an advantage to such a person, for every effort consciously made may tend to sap the already depleted vitality. Yet there are many people—driven by enthusiasm rooted in imagination, desirous of accomplishments to justify their very existence—whose enforced inactivity because of ill health creates discontentment. They aggravate their condition by overtaxing what energy they possess and are forced, sooner or later, to go to a hospital or a sanitarium. Such people must be encouraged to rest by creating for them an environment where there is no need for activity.

We find them writing nervous and jerky hands, in which the *T* bars are stronger and blacker than the rest of the writing. Their lack of vitality is disclosed in the shortness of the lower loop that lacks the firmness of muscular coordination. The pen pressure will be extremely light, often unhealthy looking, for even the act of gripping the pen is an effort for a devitalized person.

Such nervous and unfirm writing may show breaks in the letters themselves, and where exertion overtaxes the energy the lines will begin to droop at the right. Though the enthusiasm of such an individual may produce an upward, soaring swing in the line, occasional words will droop, for the very enthusiasm saps the energy. When the writing shows that a person is overtaxing his reserve strength, it is time for the graphologist to sound a note of warning, and caution the writer to take it easy.

A devitalized, inactive person whose writing shows a lack of volition and driving power may preserve her remaining strength by the very inertia expressed in the script. Specimen 71 is done by a woman with little physical vitality whose weakness of will and lack of driving power are to her advantage. The writing is done quickly, and the

SPECIMEN 71

lower loops are long and swinging, which means she has a desire to get things done—with guilt feelings because inactivity makes her feel she is pampering herself.

VII

Sex Impulses

> *Amoebas at the start*
> *Were not complex*
> *They tore themselves apart*
> *And started Sex.*
> —ARTHUR GUITERMAN

Sensuality and Sex

PEN PRESSURE IN HANDWRITING RELATES TO THE senses. The person who is guided by his physical impulses, in whom animal spirits or sensuality are predominant, will write a heavy, rightward-flowing hand, often quite dark in appearance. The intensity with which he wields the pen is transferred to any and all of his pursuits. The pen pressure will often appear somewhat muddy, and the lower loops will be wide and swinging, especially where sensuality is obvious in the person. The heavy pen pressure will be the first noticeable feature in the writing, the formations of which are usually large, and the impressions made will be so heavy they can be seen on the other side of the sheet of paper.

Where the same handwriting shows mental development and signs of self-control in horizontal strokes (*t* bars) as strong as vertical strokes, we have a person whose sensuality is under control. In a highly intellectual person whose pen pressure reveals sensuality, the angle may be vertical, indicating further his ability to check his sensuality, or to divert it into constructive or artistic endeavors. The combination of sensuality and intellectuality in the same handwriting, with an accompanying aesthetic sense, points to unusual subtlety in the character of the writer.

Sensuality, the indulgence of gratifying bodily appetites, is naturally apparent in the writing of a physical type. Here the appetites

123

are all-important; other traits are secondary and are used as a means toward gratification of the physical appetite.

In a handwriting where possessiveness is evident, there will also be signs of sensuality. The person regards the object of his lustful desires as his property, for through this object he can gratify his desires. Sensuality exists in the person whose animal instincts are strong and whose reasoning is used mainly as a means of physical gratification.

Sex to such people is merely another appetite. The enjoyment derived from its gratification is essentially physical, and is of greater importance to the sensual person than the individual who supplies such pleasure. The more endowed the sensual person is with an aesthetic quality (indicated in wide margins and generous spacing between words and lines), the more discriminating he will be in his choice of the person who provides his sensual pleasure.

Sensuality may be present in intellectual individuals, or in ignorant ones. The animal force is the same, but the expression it takes depends largely on the effects civilization has had on each one.

Unrestrained, Undisciplined Sensuality

The sensual person reacts first to everything physically. When imagination is indicated in the writing of the sensual person we refer to it as sensuousness, for here both mind and body react. There are people who are sexually aroused by color, music, odor, movement, or any form of art that excites the senses. The sensually unrestrained and undisciplined person will usually write a "pasty" hand, without the balancing strong t bars or other strong horizontal strokes that are essential in such extremely heavy writing to indicate that the physical desires are held in check. Where they are lacking in an impulsive, rightward-flowing script of extreme pen pressure, we find the writer is guided by his animal impulses. In his pursuit of sensual gratification he often runs the danger of conflicting with the laws of society. The sensually unrestrained person often acts for the moment, without thinking of consequences. His one consuming thought is his desire for the object with which to satisfy his physical craving, whether for food or sex. Caveman fashion, he is likely when starved to take what he wants.

Such a person is usually selfish and inconsiderate of the needs of others, except where others' needs do not conflict with the fulfillment of his own desires. Where consideration enters, we have an accompanying quality of imagination. This is in keeping with the sensuous, rather than the sensual, person's emotional pattern.

Among the handwritings of men guilty of brutal murder, rape, and other less violent crimes I have encountered such evidences of "pasty" pen pressure. The handwriting of a youth who killed his pregnant sweetheart showed signs of such sensuality, along with an extreme rightward angle, indicating his impulsive ardor.

SPECIMEN 72

Specimen 72 reveals sensuality without a strong will to hold it in abeyance. The *t* crossings are weak. But the roundness of the formation lifts it from the brutal class, showing instead a maternal possessiveness. Definite brutality expresses itself graphologically in handwriting that is "pasty" in pen pressure and more angular than rounded, with *t* bars that start thin and end with a clublike thickness. The club-shaped *t* bars show a temper that is slow to grow, but unreliable when it reaches its height.

Sublimated Sensuality

Where a handwriting discloses signs of creative or constructive ability in combination with sensuality (in muddy or pasty pen pressure), it reveals a person who may, with the proper encouragement, be inspired to sublimate his sensual reactions into painting, sculpture, or surgery. There is a straight line running from the murderer to the surgeon, but the latter has fitted his "cruelty" to the needs of society, taking a constructive, rather than destructive, direction, and he stands on a higher rung of the same ladder because of his culture and education.

Many musicians show signs of sensuality in their writing, but this will result in musical expression that stirs the senses of an audience. Where the sensual person's handwriting shows signs of talent combined with self-discipline and control, we are confronted with an unusual creative force that is startling in its intensity and beauty. Here the sensuality, which is a part of the creative temperament, is diverted into sensuousness by the accompanying creative imagination.

Repressed and Controlled Sensuality

The controlled or redirected sensuality appears often in the handwriting of surgeons. The *t* bars here are usually bowed through the center of the stem, indicating a higher type of self-control, which combines mental and muscular elements and is guided by a spirituality in the writer's nature. And there will also be signs of evident culture. The angle may be vertical or even backhand, depending on the individual's approach to his goal. By the backhand or vertical-writing surgeon, people are regarded impersonally, as just so many bodies to be operated upon.

SPECIMEN 73

The sensual backhand belongs, primarily, to the inhibited, repressed person who may derive pleasure from his reactions to inanimate objects instead of human beings. Architects, craftsmen, sculptors may receive as sensual a pleasure from the contour of a building or a piece of sculpture as the rightward-leaning sensual writer would from the contours of a woman's body.

The sensual person in whom exists a spiritual quality, one which gives him a desire to conquer his earthly demands, to rise above them to a higher plane, will show this plainly in the bowed *t* bar above the stem of the letter. In a criminal's writing where this spiritual sign appears, we know that his conscience guides his actions, and that his physical desires are curbed.

Specimen 73 shows repressed sensuality. Here the vertical angle indicates a prevalence of reason over instinct and emotion. The tight upper loops corroborate the repression.

Sensuality and Hypersensitivity

The sensual person, concerned with the gratification of his physical appetites above everything else, will often lack the imagination to understand other people's negative reactions to his approach and tactics. He is often not interested in how his actions affect them. His concern is mainly with himself. He is therefore apt to be hypersensitive—if sensitive at all—for his deep-rooted emotions are not lightened or mellowed by reasoning. His touchiness will appear in his handwriting in letter formations rather than in the pen pressure. The little final hook on a *t* without a bar, usually at the end of a word, when seen two or three times in one specimen, is the indication of such hypersensitivity. Some form of star-shaped *t* will augment the meaning of the foregoing when appearing in the same script, and incurves on the first stroke of capital letters are further evidence of exaggerated sensitivity. It's not that the person is sensitive to the subtleties of emotion, or to another's reactions. He is simply hurt when he thinks that his physical capacities, of which he is proud and aware, have been disparaged in some way, and he will proceed to prove that his physical prowess has been underestimated.

Sensuousness and Sex

Sensuousness is discerned in handwriting in letter formations rather than in pen pressure, though the latter may be heavy. Sensuousness is the combination of sensuality and imagination, coupled with an aesthetic quality that adds discrimination to the writer's tastes. In the same script we will often see signs of intuition.

The sensuous person, when extroverted and sex-conscious, will enjoy the thought of sharing an emotion with another person, and the anticipation of being near someone who satisfies the imagination as well as the senses evokes a reaction from the sensuous person. The touch of a hand, the sound of a voice, the remembrance of an episode wafted into consciousness by a familiar scent, will stir the sensuous person to emotional heights. His desire for sexual fulfillment is often stimulated first through his senses, where the imagination has full play, and sex becomes to him more of an adventure than a mere gratification. Sentiment augments the intensity of desire in the imagination of such individuals, for the memory takes on the fanciful coloration inspired by odors, music, and the like. The literary person may have a sensuous reaction to a particularly well-turned phrase.

Sensuousness and Sensitivity

Where sensuousness is accompanied by signs of intuition and other evidence of extrovert qualities (angle and size), showing that the writer seeks approval of other people and has consideration for their rights and feelings, we know that sensitivity exists. Intuition enables one to sense how another person is reacting, and the considerately sensitive person will often gauge his own actions to harmonize with the demands of others. This type of sensitivity is not evident in handwriting by any one sign, but rather by a combination of signs discerned more readily by the expert than by the layman. It is a quality that comprises consideration and sympathy and will usually be disclosed by signs of altruism in a light-pressure handwriting.

Specimen 74 reveals sensuousness in pen pressure, and the uncrossed *t* bars, those ending in a hook, tell us the writer is hypersensitive, easily upset by tastes in food and by odors that are not to her liking. She can be frank in expressing such dislikes, as shown in the open capital *D*; she is often blunt, seen in blunt endings on words (see "medical"), and is difficult to satisfy. The literary *g* in "go"

Dear friend, Thanks for your kind wishes. — I have not been well at all and had to take a medical rest since April last, and cannot go back to work until July. I'm exhausted

SPECIMEN 74

means she can adapt herself to situations, provided her senses are not offended; she has a preference for strong colors, stirring music, even books that arouse her sexually. She is not a particularly cooperative human being, and this is one reason she has remained unmarried to middle age, but she is competent, efficient, and exacting, as shown by the angularity of the writing and the consistent dotting of her *i*'s. She becomes exhausted by her own intensity, and although she lacks the initiative in many instances to change the order of her life for something more rewarding, she is nevertheless constructive (see capital *T* in "Thanks") and can formulate ideas for practical use.

Lack of Sensuousness and Sensuality

The handwriting that shows a lack of either sensuousness or sensuality belongs primarily to a sensitive person, though it is the type of sensitivity which has to do with mild physical needs, from either a delicate physical structure or a lack of ardor. This kind of writing typifies the instinctive old maid, although not all spinsters write so. The pen pressure will be light, the line almost hairlike. The letter formations will look thin and compressed, and upper loops will be tall and thin, often tightly closed. There may be an absence of lower loops; if they appear, they are short and ineffectual.

These are the people who are interested in fostering the spiritual needs of mankind and who do so without conscious effort. They may choose teaching or missionary work, or they may devote their lives to caring for an invalid relative. They cater, primarily, to those they feel need them most, and we rarely find them in creative fields. An exception to this type is Ralph Waldo Emerson, who expressed his desire to attain a spiritual goal in his writings after he had abandoned the clergy. In the field of creative art, William Blake is an exception to the general rule, and his spirituality is seen in his poems and paintings.

Frustration and Sublimation of Sex in Women

We all have met the old maid whose unfulfilled desires are due to repression. Then there is the woman widowed in her youth who never marries again or permits herself sexual expression. The former may devote her life to teaching children or to welfare work or some related activity. The widow may devote her life to work that brings her into contact with children, or if she has a child of her own, to fulfilling his needs.

The handwriting of the spinster who has not missed a sexual outlet will often show signs of understanding and above-average intelligence; her choice of a single life may be due to unpleasant experiences. There are some women who have been married more than once whose handwriting will reveal finicky old-maidishness, whereas there are spinsters who show liberal, progressive ideas and domestic talents that might well make some man happy. However, the reasons for her choosing a single life may be deep-rooted in childhood influences, some of which have had a prohibiting effect on her wanting to share her life intimately, but she may be capable of cooperation and sharing in other areas.

The sex instinct in women will always find expression in some direction if denied a normal outlet. Maternal women, strongly protective and often equally possessive, write much heavier hands than those who are impelled by duty to fulfill maternal roles.

The maternal heavy-pressure writer will, when sex frustration occurs, find expression in some form of art, and her creations may express her frustration in some manner. Among women painters, sculptors, and photographers we find interpreters of children, kittens, and puppies, and among designers we find creators of children's toys, apparel, and nursery furniture.

They may find a compensation for maternal frustration in individual expression that relates to the home—interior decoration or cooking—or in writing on these subjects. Where this occurs, the handwriting will usually be vertical or backhand and will show signs of independence and self-reliance that compensate for the very frustration that the letter formations in combination with the angle will reveal.

Inhibitions and Puritanism

The phlegmatic or undersexed person may be so because of his physical make-up, or he may become so because of some experience or shock. The light-pressure and vertical or slightly backhand writer belongs in this category. (Light pen pressure among backhands is the exception.) Should such writing be extremely angular, we are confronted with the calculating, cold, unfeeling individual whose inhibitions have created a pattern of don'ts, and who has formed the

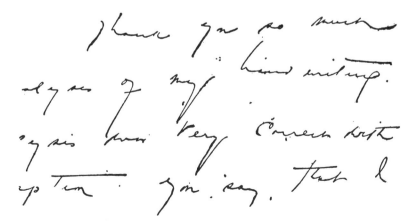

SPECIMEN 75

habit of self-denial. This is somewhat different from the rightward writer who fears what other people will think if she breaks down restrictions and inhibitions learned in childhood.

The puritanical hand will always be light in pen pressure, with the letters closely formed. The heavy-pressure writers whose sex impulses are repressed and inhibited, who find an outlet in superstition, religion, or in such activity that permits them to impose inhibitions on others, come under the self-righteous, blue-law-advocates subdivision. Their handwriting will invariably show a combination of intolerance, narrow-mindedness, and sexual frustration, seen more readily in the constrained letter forms than in the pen pressure.

Specimen 75, with its extremely light pressure, its altruistic formations of *y* in the right turn of the downward return stroke, and the thinness of line, bears the instinct of the puritan. This person is, however, taken out of the narrow-minded, bigoted group by the signs of culture (Greek *d* in "handwriting") and imagination (the high, flying *t* bars). She is capable of self-sacrifice.

Dominant Maternal Instinct

Definite signs in handwriting that point to a predominant and undisputed maternal (or paternal) instinct show in the old-fashioned capital letters *A*, *M* (as those in Specimen 76), and *N*.

SPECIMEN 76

These people are interested in the welfare (mainly physical rather than intellectual) of others. The writing will usually be heavy and rounded. Where the individual is more enlightened or cultured, we usually find signs of altruism and a rightward-slanting angle. This combination may indicate a reformer instinct, for such a writer has an overwhelming desire for betterment. The pen pressure will help to determine whether the improvement desired takes a material or spiritual direction. If the pressure is heavy it is apt to be materialistic; if light, spiritual.

If these traits are constructively directed, and if they are found in an intellectual person's script, they indicate a philanthropist, altruist, humanitarian. If uncontrolled, permitted to dominate the writer, and unchecked by reasoning, we have the person who makes useless sacrifices, who gives indiscriminately, and whose kindness is a fault.

Abraham Lincoln's handwriting revealed such signs in a controlled, constructively altruistic combination of traits (Specimen 77). See the capital *A* in his signature.

SPECIMEN 77

A lengthier specimen would reveal the altruistic *y*, cultured *d*, high imaginative loops, and excellent margins and spacing—indicating combinations of exalted emotion, ideals, and a desire to help the underdog.

This capital *A*, referred to graphologically as the protective *A*, points to the parental instinct. The emotion is directed toward the downtrodden, the ones who need protection, and spurs such persons to energetic activity when decisions involving human welfare fall within their jurisdiction.

SPECIMEN 78

In Poe, this instinct manifested itself in another form. Protective by nature but essentially the poet, Poe gave it expression in poems such as "Annabel Lee," in which he had a vision of his child-wife. (Specimen 78 has the same form of protective *A* in the signature.)

Specimen 76 is an excellent example of the dominating maternal instinct. Note the consistency with which the writer makes the old-fashioned formations of *M* and *A*, and carries it further in the capital *P*. Pen pressure is heavy, indicating physical vitality, and letter formations are rounded, augmenting maternal gentleness. (Graphologically, this type has been referred to as philoprogenitive.)

Women in whom the maternal instinct is strong and overpowering often defeat their own ends by indulging this instinct. They are the overindulgent mothers, those who weaken the will power of their children by making decisions for them. Their sacrifices are often made to retain their children's affection and presence, and when their children marry and dare to live their own lives, such mothers feel their sacrifices were unappreciated and in vain.

Dear Miss Olyanova,

    I have just finished reading your book ' The Psychology of Handwriting ' and found it fascinating and most Enjoyable - I would like to

SPECIMEN 79

In contrast to Specimen 76 with its old-fashioned formations, the modern woman is unhampered by the frills and trappings of her grandmother's day. She has replaced the Victorian styles with more modern ones, the baroque gilt frames with those of simple lines; she has eliminated cluttered mantels, antimacassars and useless trappings. Her capital letters are simple and without flourishes, and sometimes even severe. This severity is reflected in her attitudes, which include a desire for more independence.

In Specimen 79, there is a streamlined version of the old-fashioned capital *M* in "Miss," yet the rest of the writing is simple, with many printed formations, and tells us this woman is talented and has a maternal instinct. However, her short *t* bars reveal that she is somewhat indecisive and that she lives in the past to some extent; there may even be an element of envy for the less complex life of yesteryear. No clutter here. A desire for the simple things in life is revealed in the legible, uncomplicated letter forms in the handwriting of this intelligent, intuitive, sensitive human being. However, as the simple version of the protective capital *M* appears here, and it is likely that the accompanying *A* and *N* would show in a larger specimen, we can reasonably assume that this woman is interested in antiques.

VIII

Why Sex Is Not Indicated in the Writer's Handwriting

*Women are wiser than men because they
know less and understand more.*
—JAMES STEPHENS

Masculine Traits

HANDWRITING DOES NOT DISCLOSE THE SEX OF THE writer because there is a mixture of masculine and feminine in all of us.

So it is always best that the writer's sex be known to the graphologist before an analysis is made. The expert may intuitively form an impression based on his observations of many specimens of handwriting of both sexes, but this is not according to scientific graphological formula and cannot be relied on.

There are characteristically masculine and feminine traits determined by the preponderance of certain signs in the writing, but signs that we characterize as strength in a woman's handwriting might be interpreted as weakness in a man's handwriting.

I have discovered after analyzing many thousands of handwritings that the born executives and planners, the realists, in whose handwriting appears a predominant factualness, are women. Men, observed through the same graphological microscope, are essentially the dreamers, the sentimentalists, the romantics.

No doubt it is a woman's biological mission that makes her so, just as men's causes them to take their emotional functions less seriously. A handwriting may show strong masculine traits and yet be written by a woman. What then shows masculinity in handwriting?

136

The working of a man's mind, dealing primarily with abstractions because his emotions are not directly tied up with his biological mission, is different from a woman's: He thinks with his mind, whereas she "thinks," for the most part, with her heart.

Where women tend to act and are more interested in people (owing to their job of running the family), men are more prone to reflection, and possess a broader horizon of interest that reaches to the world beyond the home. For it is there a man's goal lies, and in that world he may try to become an outstanding figure.

The scene is changing, however, and many women have developed ambitions in fields that were once the exclusive province of men. Even in independent women, there usually is the desire to express feminine interests, and many women who have careers outside the home are married and have children and enjoy all their roles.

The alterocentrism of the typically feminine woman is lacking in most men. So, as a rule, is the versatility so essential to the woman who must deal with a variety of tasks and problems every day.

Where the essentially feminine hand will show spontaneity and the ability to make decisions on the spur of the moment, men are more apt to be analytical, to seek reasons for their decisions, and to be more logical. A sick child may run a temperature while a man is deciding whether he should call the doctor; a woman will call the doctor first and do her thinking later. Where man is actuated by his reason, woman relies more on her emotions to guide her in important issues.

Mental Make-Up

Logical thinking shows in connected writing, often in connected words, indicating a consecutiveness of thoughts and ideas. There are fewer signs of emotional domination in the essentially masculine hand, and when there is creative ability, the signs in the handwriting are also more obvious.

More men than women are really introverted, seen especially when there are signs of mental development, as in small, well-formed writing where the angle tends to be vertical or slightly backhand. This is more comprehensible when we consider that the woman's biological mission forces her into a more social, more extroverted pattern.

Intuition is primarily a feminine trait, arising from woman's original place in the cultural development of civilization: Education was at one time given solely to men, leaving women to learn by instinct. Intuition is often evident in the handwriting of men, and when it occurs it is frequently accompanied by signs of good judgment. Though men do get intuitive hunches, they do not rely upon them as consistently as do women. A man may reason out his hunch, tracing it to its possible source. A woman may say, "I don't trust that person; I don't know why," and her actions will corroborate her instinctive feeling.

Intuition shows in breaks between letters, where the hand lifts unconsciously from the paper, allowing a flash of intuition to enter the consciousness. The good judgment will show in the omission of initial strokes, and where this occurs there is usually corroborating evidence in the omission of return strokes on lower loops, or in upper loops that start with a single stroke. (In such cases y and g will look like figures 7 and 9.)

Because woman, through necessity, has acquired a habit of mind that sees many things at the same time; because she has, in the past, been denied higher education and has been relegated to the limited area of the home—to say nothing of bumbling through life by following her instincts—she has learned to assimilate knowledge readily. This is especially true in her ability to understand human beings. A woman will size up another woman at a glance, sensing the other's reactions. She not only will notice the hat another woman is wearing, but also will determine whether she is sincere or merely putting on an act. She sees through people and is instinctively more critical than men. This is what makes her more gossipy, and when we meet a man who has this trait, we think him an old woman.

Man's mind is constituted to deal with abstractions and is less concerned with emotional experiences and their importance in his scheme of life. A woman may be considered well educated because of what she has learned from her emotional experience, for her natural practicality causes her to apply such knowledge to her everyday life. Women know many things without having to learn them, whereas men, in order to know, must be taught.

A cultured or educated hand can therefore be referred to, graphologically, as a masculine one, even though it has been penned by a woman. Conversely, the emotional, practical hand will show a greater number of feminine traits and is referred to as feminine. There may well be a mixture of masculine and feminine traits in one specimen—thus the need for astute study before attempting a character analysis from handwriting.

Dominant Ambitions

There are few fields of endeavor that women have not invaded, including creative art and science. There are women who have in their make-up enough masculinity to inspire them to express their creative instinct, not just biologically but also artistically.

Because the dominant ambitions of a man bring him into contact with the outer world and its problems, whether through conscious striving or otherwise, he is less concerned with problems in the home. The adventurous spirit of the explorer, the desire to build or conquer empires, is essentially masculine. We hear occasionally of a woman explorer, but she is the exception. Her handwriting, just as the man's, will reveal this spirit of adventure in the flying *t* bar above the stem of the letter.

Amelia Earhart is a good example of such combination of masculine and feminine traits. Her handwriting shows that emotionally she was extremely feminine. (See Specimen 97.)

There are few household tasks women undertake that cannot be mastered by men. The best cooks, for instance, have been men in whose handwriting may be seen some feminine traits. Women will make it their duty to be good cooks; men will approach cooking either as an art or as an experiment.

Living in a patriarchy as we do (although there are signs we are moving toward a matriarchy), the position of the man is superior; he is frequently given credit for an achievement that has been inspired by a woman whose practical nature and intuition have seen the need for such achievement. This is particularly true of the many inventions connected with the home and designed to lighten the burden of daily chores. I daresay the invention of the washing-machine had its inception in the mind of some imaginative woman with lots of children and laundry. And I'll venture the opinion that the inventor of the can opener, could he be traced, either was, or was inspired by, a modern-minded housewife. No doubt it is the mechanical-minded man, with creative and practical vision combined, who develops the original idea fostered in woman's need.

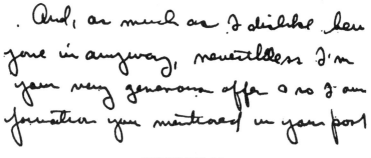

SPECIMEN 80

Specimen 80 is an example of a woman who possesses masculine logic. Her logical reasoning shows in the consistently connected letters. Because of the inner conflict caused by her masculine logic and feminine emotion, there is an indecisiveness in the weak *t* bars. It can be said that she feels with her mind, that all her emotional reactions are rationalized.

SPECIMEN 81

Specimen 81 is an essentially masculine hand and executed by a man. In the vertical angle the prevalence of reason over emotion is expressed. Yet on occasion he gets a flash of intuition ("nevertheless"), which he sets about tracing to its logical source.

SPECIMEN 82

Specimen 82, written by a man, shows a feminine, or intuitive, approach to everything. He sees many angles of a situation at the same time. Notice the breaks between letters all through the writing. He is forever jumping to conclusions, and his thinking processes are accelerated; but he is slow to act, not certain whether or not to trust his intuition, shown by a lack of self-confidence in the weak *t* bars. Incidentally, this person is not in robust health, which shows in the breaks in the letters themselves and in the extremely light, varying pen pressure.

SPECIMEN 83

Specimen 83 is expressive of the typically feminine woman. She is spontaneous, animated, gregarious, enthusiastic. She acts quickly and in accordance with her emotional impulses, which guide her, receives occasional flashes of intuition (see words "magazine" and "signature") that let her sense the direction she is taking. In the writing is seen alertness, curiosity, a receptive mind that can absorb knowledge from actual experience without needing formal education.

Feminine Traits

To understand the traits we attribute to woman, we must first consider her needs. (I speak here of the feminine woman pursuing her natural goal.) To foster her strongest instinct, the maternal, she must be economically secure. She is therefore more practical than man, through running the household and (later) rearing the children. The maternal instinct gives her first an interest in the bodily welfare of the children. And this interest she extends to her husband as well, since her maternalism embraces him also.

She is, through this instinct, more possessive than men; and this possessiveness, when aggravated through fear of loss or when denied expression or fulfillment, creates in her a natural suspicion. Watch the dog or cat who is nursing her young. She is suspicious of anyone who comes near them during this period. The human mother, unfortunately, may carry the possessiveness beyond the nursing stage.

The maternal woman's need to accomplish a hundred little tasks during the course of her day provides her with a natural executive ability. Catering to the needs of husband and children—perhaps taking care of one sick child, getting the others ready for school, preparing their meals, mending clothes—she can still find time to minister to a needy neighbor in an emergency. She is absorbed by her natural duties, and to give attention to such variety of details as her daily responsibilities demand, she must develop versatility. This trait is not essential to the man who goes to his specialized job, knows what it involves, and adheres to its demands, but it is almost a must in women.

Because women are motivated in their thinking by their emotions, they are more spontaneous and subjective than men. Few women really enjoy something they cannot do spontaneously. Spontaneity is usually the outstanding feature in a specimen written by a feminine woman, and will be accompanied by signs of a maternal instinct, often possessiveness (where this appears there are usually signs of suspiciousness also), versatility, and a predominance of emotion over reason.

More often than not the writing will be speedily executed and leaning to the right. When the angle is vertical, the formations are likely to be extremely rounded, and the writing will be quite large. Horizontal finals will be long and pen pressure heavy or medium heavy.

Mental Make-Up

Women, often forced to make decisions quickly, rely greatly upon intuition. It is this reasoning instinct that warns them of impending danger, and in acting quickly they do not take time to evaluate the cause of the danger. In a similar situation, a man would be more apt to take time for reflection, to figure out the cause, but woman's practical nature demands that she do something about it. She is, then, more active than contemplative. She is possessive because her practical reasoning is colored by her emotional need. She needs the man for both economic and emotional security, and is ready to suspect any object or circumstance that threatens to deprive her of him.

Not always capable of understanding a man's abstract reasoning, the feminine woman is apt to approach what she does not understand with an element of suspicion. Because, biologically, her risk and responsibility are greater than man's, she has a natural caution that she employs in pursuit of her pleasures. She is more naturally on her guard than is man and does not possess his occasional recklessness. (There are exceptions, of course.)

Yet frequently what we refer to as woman's intuition is equally strong in men. It lends a richness to man's vision. His logic and reason enable him to understand the form and structure of things in the universe; intuition gives him an insight into their face and spirit.

To a woman, intuition is a necessity for dealing with her problems; in a man it is an endowment. Man could not achieve greatness without intuition; woman, in her function as a woman, would be crippled without it.

Dominant Ambitions

The dominant ambition of the feminine woman is to excel as ruler in her own home (occasionally to inspire the envy of other women), primarily because to do so means to achieve the greatest assurance of security. Should she be endowed with imagination and a keen intelligence, she can make an art of her pursuit. Her children will then be the creations she seeks to perfect. And by encouraging them to engage in constructive endeavors, she caters to her own desire for achievement and to their mental and emotional development at the same time.

The independent feminine woman (I mean here economically independent of men), in choosing a career or goal that brings her into contact with the outside world, finds expression, often sublimation, for her maternal instinct in the very goal she chooses. Such women are usually of a social nature, and the creative instinct, if frustrated, may turn into a desire to reform (rebuild or recreate) others: If she cannot create a world in her own home, she will seek to perfect human beings in the outside world. And so we have the women who institute reform movements, who hold top positions at orphanages, special schools, nurseries. The same trait in men may lead them to choose such goals as the clergy; these men have a strong admixture of the feminine.

Combination of Masculine and Feminine Traits

Intuition raised to its highest level and seen in a man's handwriting may be called inspiration. When at its peak in a woman, it has been referred to as chronic suspicion.

The woman whose emotions are essentially feminine, but whose mind is capable of logical reasoning, is bound to be rather complex. She has a conflict between what her emotions demand of her and what her mind criticizes in these demands. She will have a combination of feminine spontaneity and masculine directness. She will be able to understand the reactions of both men and women. And if mature, she is usually decisive and forceful in personality, and she pursues a definite objective. (Also she may sometimes be mildly schizophrenic.)

These women pursue goals that foster a maternal instinct, but their approach to this goal is often masculine. We find them as physicians, artists and writers, and occasionally as musicians. In the scientific world, the most famous is Mme. Curie.

Dangers de la misère qui s'étend
pas suite du manque de récoltes,
manque de vivres,
Peste bovine, commerce interrompu
de fic... et les ravages de la
variole qui est partout! nous
étions si préoccupés, si déchirés par
la souffrance plus intense de Paris
et du reste de la France, que nous
ne pensions plus à nous mêmes.
nous respirons en pensant que
vous allez recevoir des vivres et que
les bombes ne tomberont plus
sur vous. j'eusse volontiers payé
ce soulagement pour les autres, de
ma propre vie, on ne tient plus
à la vie! mais je ne suis pas
de ceux qui font bon marché de celle
des autres, je n'ai pas le fanatisme
de la guerre, — espérons qu'ce soit
le sentiment du grand nombre
et que nous obtiendrons des
conditions équitables = quelle
bonne lettre vous m'avez écrite!
nous vous en sommes reconnaissant
et nous vous embrassons tous,
revenez nous voir
aussitôt que vous pourrez!   G Sand

They are the ones whose experiences mellow their thinking, and in whom there is often a combination of feminine practicality and masculine romanticism. George Sand comes within this category, as her journal will disclose. In the volume *The Intimate Journal of George Sand* by Marie Jenny Howe, George Sand's letters to her *masculine self* include an expression of her interest in character as disclosed in the handwriting of people who interested her. She collected handwriting specimens.

In Specimen 84 we find this combination: a masculine mind with many feminine traits. It was written by George Sand, famous as a writer and as Chopin's mistress. That she was cool, at times unfeeling and detached, is revealed in the vertical angle of her handwriting. Here we see signs of culture, a quick sharp mind, and an intuition that gave her many insights ahead of her time. Indeed she had many modern ideas regarding the emancipation of women, even to divorcing her husband—unusual in her day. She referred to her masculine self, with whom she communicated, as Dr. Piffoël.

The handwriting reveals enthusiasm in the *t* bars, which seem to fly off the right of the stem. There is also a measure of self-discipline expressed in the way the *t* bars often bow, but this she applied more to her work than to her emotional peregrinations. She seemed usually to be aware of what she was doing, and she was self-contained and didn't always care what other people thought of her.

Her signature, seemingly modest in the small capitals, shows emphasis and personal magnetism in the swirl at the end. As a woman, she was intense, impressionable, very responsive; as a writer, she was observant, critical, keenly perceptive, and interested in the lives of other people. Independence is shown in both the writing angle and small angular letter forms, yet there is an emotional dependency shown in a combination of factors too subtle for brief analysis. She had periods when she functioned completely as a woman; then there were periods of work when she intellectualized her emotions in a detached, cool, and unperturbed way. Sometimes the two sides of her nature fused, resulting in the confusion and dramatization of her role as a woman.

In the handwriting of Willa Cather (which appears in another section of this book) we see some similarities in angle, letter forms, and spacing, and we know that her intellectual approach was essentially masculine.

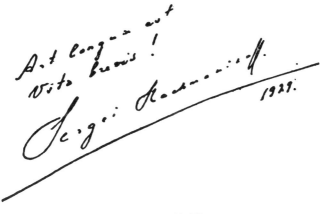

SPECIMEN 85

The inspirational hand, where all the letters are disconnected (often seen in the handwriting of poets), is admirably illustrated by that of Sergei Rachmaninoff. Here the rising lines depict vision and great optimism. The consistent rhythm and his acute responsiveness to harmony, nuances of sound, and delicacy of color affected his attitude toward life itself. If you had judged him from his face, you might not have guessed his handwriting would be so light in pen pressure, for his features were anything but delicate! Yet here is a man with unusual sensitivity, sensuousness raised to the highest spiritual level. Gentleness, kindness, paternalism, are all revealed in the one capital letter *A*. His prodigious memory often set off associations that caused him to vibrate inwardly to tunes remembered from childhood. The underscored signature tells us he had feelings of inadequacy which were hidden under a façade of dignity, seen in the capital letters. The *S* resembles a clef somewhat, and the long straight line shows a capacity for hard work. Essentially a creative man, to some he may have seemed out of this world, just as his handwriting is in a class by itself. So much intuition could only be found in a human being we might describe as being in tune with the Infinite.

The masculine creative temperament does not exist without the feminine adjunct of intuition. We see signs of it in the handwriting of men from every walk of life; they are the ones with keener perception, insight, and creativity. Women are endowed with it by nature, and those who make an art of their roles as women use it instinctively. Those who are attracted to men of creative temperament often have an inner urge to do something creative outside their natural status as mothers. "Women take pride in inspiring the creations of the artist. That is their share of masculinity," wrote the great Viennese psychologist Dr. Wilhelm Stekel.

IX

Great Men and Women

*"...I had yet to learn that genius whether
it lives in a hermit's cell or spends itself
outside, is always solitary, repressed,
suffering and misunderstood."*
        —GEORGE SAND

Neurotics and Greatness

MOST MEN AND WOMEN HAVE ACHIEVED GREATNESS
through attempting to compensate for an inferiority complex. We
have only to read their biographies to know this is so. The same
holds true of our contemporaries who give promise of immortality
through their unusual achievements.

To understand the motivating force that impels these special
individuals, we must know something about their intimate lives,
their suffering, deficiencies, innate beliefs, and drives. Their handwriting provides important clues to these, as well as to the common
denominators that place them in the category of the great. The
genius is often repressed, suffering and lonely, feeling more intensely
the *weltschmerz* that besets the outside world; many of them have a
need to make some contribution to better the world.

Dostoevski, a morbid neurotic, always in sympathy with the suffering of others, had a profound understanding of the neurotic on
all levels, and Freud admits that he learned a great deal from Dostoevski with regard to human behavior. He was an epileptic, and
in his autobiographical novel, *The Idiot*, he gives a vivid description
of his sensory reactions a few moments before an epileptic seizure.
In that moment, he relates, the entire world seemed to have become
illuminated with an inner light, his senses quickened to an almost

149

unbearable pitch, and then the light went out. After one of these it seemed as if all the tension that had been building in him over a period of time was discharged, and he was able to work, writing compulsively, as if his life depended on it. And it did in a sense, for he had to earn money to pay his gambling debts, which were forever hanging over his head.

Emotional ardor—as his handwriting expresses it—intuition, and conflicting wills were all part of his neurotic pattern. As in the handwriting of most neurotics, the pen pressure was uneven, ranging from a sensuous heaviness to a spiritual lightness. There was the sign of altruism which gave evidence of his masochism, and the speed with which he wrote his novels was revealed in the rhythm of his handwriting.

There is often some evidence of confusion and contradiction in the neurotic's handwriting. A variety of *t* bars show not one will but many, in conflict with each other. There are always signs of compulsiveness, and in some instances it is hard to draw the line between compulsion and dedication.

In those neurotics who are able to emerge from their mass of confusion for long periods when the creative urge drives them, we see in the handwriting definite signs of order in clear spacing between lines and words, along with artistic or mental signs. Those who have produced some achievements will show the signs of self-discipline in the strong bowed *t* bar. Without this discipline, nothing of any consequence can be achieved. The undisciplined person is usually neurotic in one way or another, although he may have considerable talent. He is the one who suffers most, for his creative urge is often blocked and his energy absorbed by neurotic drives.

There are always indications of sensuousness, intuition, and sensitivity in the neurotic's handwriting, and because he is more aware and imaginative than the so-called normal person, the neurotic's impressions are intensified and sharper. The adjusted neurotic is the person who can record, through his particular medium, those impressions that have left an indelible mark on his psyche from early childhood. Other people who are sensitive and impressionable, though not so creative or neurotic, usually become affected in one way or another by the achievements of the creative individual. The person who listens to music, who reads poetry, who goes to art museums and galleries is in this category, and his handwriting will reveal his appreciation of such things.

Perhaps the neurotic whose creative instinct is dominant will express himself without knowing why he does so. It is his inner force, unhampered by the restrictions placed on the outer man, that impels him to perform; he may even do so in defiance of the "civilized" limits he imposes on himself. If through such expression he contributes something beautiful or beneficial to the world, he possesses the elements of greatness. In the handwriting of both recognized and potential geniuses there are invariably signs of altruism, with its many and varying connotations. Even though an individual's striving may be for ego gratification, when his achievements have the power to affect our civilization constructively and for its ultimate advancement, the sign of altruism will be present in the handwriting.

The genius, simply by having lived and produced something to enrich the world, has bettered humanity in some way. Emerson associated greatness with kindness. It is this kindness, this sympathy, frequently taking the form of empathy, that I refer to as altruism. It is expressed in handwriting in the rightward turn of the return of the downstroke on the *y* and often in the *g*. This letter formation reveals an instinct to give, to make a contribution. The degree to which one follows this impulse and what form it takes should be considered. There are people who give to buy love, and people who give advisedly—with a string attached—and this sort of giving will show in other signs in the handwriting. Philanthropists have it with relation to material giving. Lincoln's humanitarian attitude toward the underdog, the downtrodden, revealed itself in this letter formation all through his handwriting.

Beethoven, Genius of Music

It does not matter in what language a specimen is written; energy, intuition, and imagination are all traits that will be revealed in handwriting of any language.

The first thing we notice in Beethoven's handwriting is the rapidity with which it was written. This shows a terrific energetic drive

Beethoven

SPECIMEN 86

and a quick, perceptive mind with antennae. When the mind works so rapidly as to make it difficult for the hand to record the thoughts, we are bound to have illegibility, as here. The writing is small, showing his powers of concentration. Some downstrokes are single strokes, often found in the handwriting of mathematicians, and we know that Beethoven was the master of counterpoint. The *t* bar (look closely and you will see it in the third line from the bottom)

above the stem of the letter indicates a vivid imagination and a perfectionist. Uneven pen pressure shows not only temperament but
also temper, and his signature shows positive force in the final stroke,
made with persistence and telling us of his compulsiveness and determination.

Napoleon

The following three specimens, written by Napoleon, were
penned at different times in his career:

Napoleon—1804—When He First Became Emperor

SPECIMEN 87 (ENLARGED THREE TIMES)

The first specimen (87) shows unquestionable forcefulness and
power. The heavy pen pressure (increased probably by the use of a
quill pen) reveals his sensuality, and the hook at the very end of the
underscore reveals tenacity of purpose. Illegible formations indicate

Napoleon—1814—From Elba

SPECIMEN 87A (ENLARGED THREE TIMES)

a quick mind that was never an open book to others. The underscored signature is the main clue to his inferiority complex, coupled with his striving for power to compensate for it. The tendency of the basic line to droop tells us he was not a happy man and was subject to moods of depression. A schizoid personality, isolated and lonely since childhood, introverted and somewhat morbid, he had far to go to achieve the high goals he set up, as shown in the high reach of the capital *N*.

Ten years later, at the height of his power and fully aware of his importance, Napoleon signed only his initials. Even these mirror a forceful personality at whose depths were a residue of anger and the determination to conquer at any price. The two capitals—illegible yet outstanding for their obvious brutal force—and the ferocious underscore speak for themselves. They might be compared to a violent storm at its height.

Napoleon—1815—After His Defeat

SPECIMEN 87B (ENLARGED THREE TIMES)

The signature here is less bombastic than in previous specimens, almost modest by comparison. Less ferocity, more reflection in small writing, and obvious unhappiness in the downward slant all show some withdrawal into himself. The emotions are quieted down, and the introversion is more marked.

Fyodor Dostoevski

In the handwriting of the great Russian writer Dostoevski we notice in the pen pressure a combination of lightness and occasional darkening, denoting a person who had great sensitivity and experienced periods of emotional stress and tension. Much depended upon

Fyodor Dostoevski

SPECIMEN 88

his varying moods. The writing is done quickly, with the compulsive tempo evident in the handwriting of most geniuses. It is small, showing powers of concentration; has intuitive breaks between letters; is well-organized on the page, and it tells us that despite his moods he could discipline himself to turn out a large amount of work. There are two capital *D*'s here—the first tightly closed with a loop, showing his reserve and tendency to be secretive; the other open at the top, meaning openheartedness and the kind of orality that impelled him to tell all. Contradictory? Indeed, for so much depended upon his feelings, whether his energy was at a high pitch and words spilled out, or whether he was holding himself in check, covering up his tracks when he had gotten himself into debt by gambling. (He was almost as compulsive about gambling as about writing, and suffered much deprivation because of it.)

The Greek *d*, the sign of culture; the literary *g*; signs of altruism in the last word, fifth line—all are clues to the instinctive writer. He had an intense interest in the lives of other people, sharing their suffering with an empathy that amounted to masochism. The underscore in his signature, made with a flourish, tells us of his need to feel important because of a deep-rooted inferiority complex. As an epi-

Josef Stalin

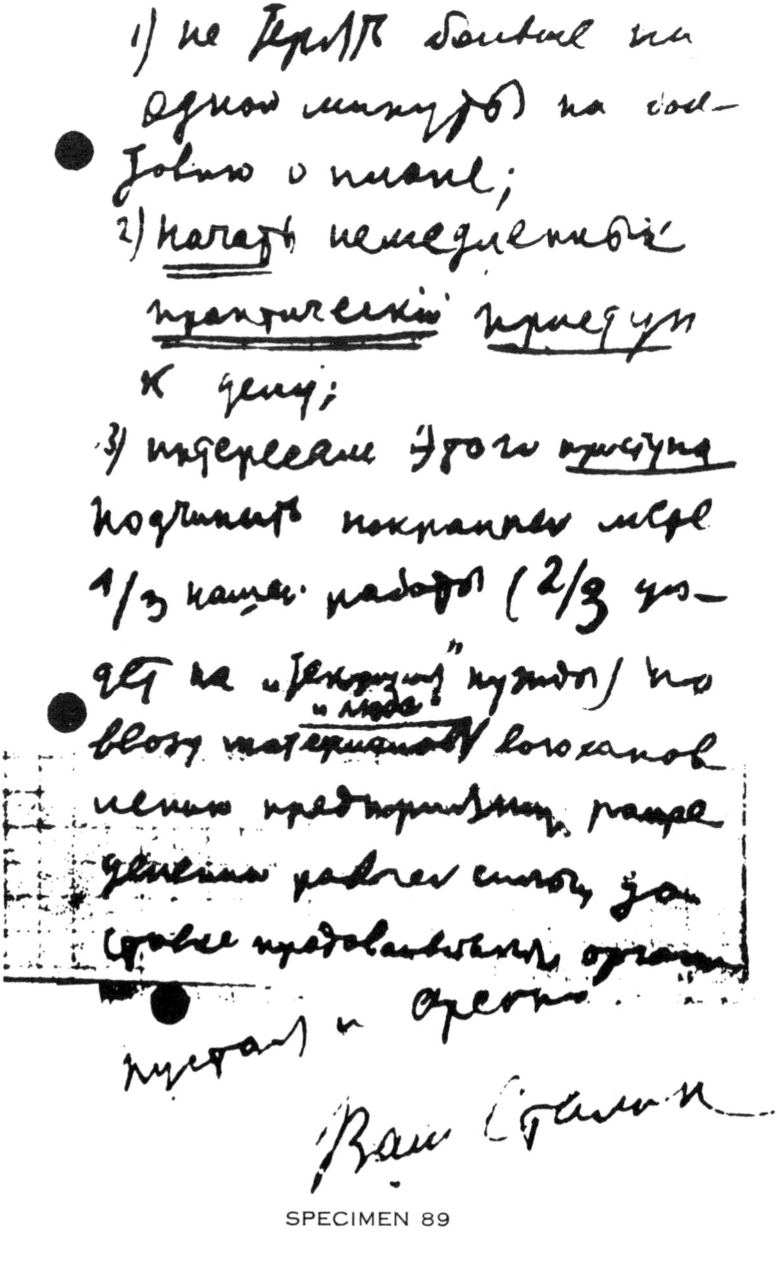

SPECIMEN 89

leptic, he had fallow periods when he could not work, when frustrations and repressed anger resulted in a seizure.

His preoccupation with violence in human beings derived from the violence he had witnessed in childhood. He was an outstanding psychiatrist without degree or formal training (though his father was a doctor).

Josef Stalin

This is a different kind of Russian, more primitive, a Georgian. Here the first thing we notice is the muddy pressure, which gives us a clue to innate brutality, despite the altruistic signs in the handwriting (second, sixth, and tenth lines). Although Stalin's goal seemed to be for the betterment of his own people, he took brutal measures to achieve it. He was intellectually keen, emotionally very intense, often unreasonable in his obsessiveness; and in his drive for power he was ready to sacrifice the lives of others to achieve his end. We see a spiritual sign that shows a measure of self-discipline—it originally led him to study for the priesthood, but his lust for power overcame his higher motives. The angle is both vertical and moderately to the right, showing he could do some things deliberately, whereas whatever involved his emotions brought out more spontaneity and sentiment.

Stalin's love for his daughter Svetlana aroused in him a strong possessiveness and generosity, even while his devotion to the Soviet Union brought out a cruelty—for which he seems better known than for his acts of kindness.

Albert Schweitzer

Although the pen pressure is fairly heavy, showing a person of intense feeling, the angle of the writing is vertical, telling us he held his emotions in check while he thought things out with some deliberation. Yet the *t* bar flying off the stem (second word) reveals enthusiasm; the extended line in the fourth word shows his curiosity and drive; the squared-off *g* reveals an obstinacy that prevented him from giving up when the odds were against him. His strong, firm *t* bars

Albert Schweitzer

SPECIMEN 90

in a well-spaced specimen show a determination to keep his house in order even when there was chaos around him. Small capital letters reveal his modesty; the consistent rhythm shows his responsiveness to music; and constructed (printed) capitals in the body of the writing show he could formulate ideas that he carried out independently.

His interest in the underdog, the helpless ones, is seen in the simplified version of the protective, paternalistic *A*—found in the handwriting of Abraham Lincoln and Poe, as well as in any handwriting where the writer is impelled to help those weaker than himself. Schweitzer's regard for all living things has its clue in this one simple letter formation. He was not a man many people could get close to, but when he did form an attachment it was deep and lasting.

G. B. S.

Most of the time, as in this specimen of George Bernard Shaw, he signed merely his initials, G.B.S., and with an underscore that negated itself to some extent by going right through the initials. A contradiction, indeed, for as sure of himself as he felt, he had doubts about his importance, and these, even if unconsciously, canceled out feelings of superiority. (In a deeper sense, I believe, this canceling out had a relation to Shaw's asceticism.)

George Bernard Shaw

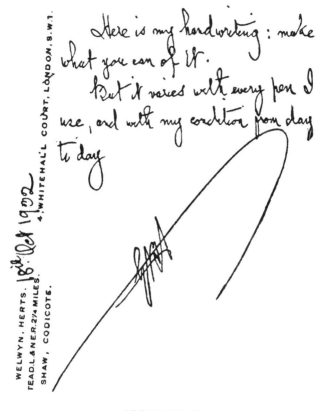

SPECIMEN 91

The vertical angle shows a measure of reserve: He looked at life realistically instead of coloring it with frothy sentimentality. His drive was inconsistent; anyone using such concerted energy to make this underscore had a capacity for hard work, but there was a hitch. He had difficulty getting started; notice the several *t* bars that do not cross, with merely a hook on the end. He had many wills, and we see the flying *t* bar away from the stem, which indicates enthusiasm and a tendency for the writer to be ahead of himself. Long, full lower loops are an indication of his interest in the material world, and money meant a great deal to him. Spacing is fairly good, though one lower loop ran into the line below (first two lines), an indication of self-centeredness. Anyone making such an exaggerated underscore could hardly be called a shrinking violet; but the personality was complex, which partly accounted for his handwriting varying "with my condition from day to day," as he wrote. Humor (in the roundness and curves) is indicated, and the open capital *O* in "Oct" tells us he had a capacity for frankness, even some open-heartedness, which was modified by the vertical angle, showing restraint.

Sigmund Freud (Age 26)

In Specimen 92 Freud was a young man courting his "sweet darling girl," and the very first capital letter we see is the old-fashioned *M*, telling us of his mid-Victorian ideas. The upper loops are high, which indicate his idealism and the high goals he set for himself; signs of energy and drive are revealed in the animated rhythm. Changing moods are seen in the uplift of the basic line, even while the drooping of the last word in the sixth line gives an indication of his moods of depression and doubt. Many of the words are broken up, disclosing intuition, and the angularity of the writing is a clue to his keen intellect and perception. The small, well-controlled specimen indicates his capacity for concentrated, disciplined work and for research. Sometimes a *t* bar does not go through the stem (as in the seventh line from the bottom), and here we have an interesting clue to Freud's emotional dependency—his neurosis (mother attachment), which led him to develop his theory of the Oedipal complex. That *t* bar is also a clue to his own repressions and inhibitions and his preoccupation with the past (his own and his patients'), and was a forerunner to developing the theory that in a person's childhood could be found the reasons for his adult behavior. Close examination will reveal the sign of altruism; he often felt the martyr (when he was criticized because of his Jewishness), and experienced the masochistic trends he analyzed so well in others. Angularity here is typically Germanic, and there are signs of the kind of compulsiveness we associate with genius.

Sigmund Freud

Jacob Freud
WIEN.

Wien, den 15 Juni 1882

My sweet darling girl

SPECIMEN 92

Freud at age 72

SPECIMEN 92A

Specimen 92A was written when Freud was in a serious state of illness and decay. We see similarities between the two specimens, in the angular forms and the leaning to the right; the hooks at the ends of words reveal he still had tenacity: he hung onto life despite the hopelessness of his malady. He was sick, angry, and confused, and even more self-centered. Yet his curiosity still remained, and with the end in sight he began to explore those occult fields he had earlier negated. His signature, still large and legible, is nevertheless made with a small capital *F*, and we wonder if this was a sign of his complete disrespect for authority in general, or whether Hitler evoked this sign. The whip end in his name is a sure sign of anger and attendant sadism.

If we had seen this handwriting without knowing who wrote it we might have considered the writer insane, but we know that a fine line often separates genius from insanity.

Willa Cather

One of the outstanding American writers is Willa Cather. And here, in a vertical writing that shows her calm, detached, masculine approach, we see all the signs of genius. The drive that impelled her to write persistently—though she started at 37; the consistent *t* bars above the stem that indicate her vivid imagination, spirit of adventure, and reaching for the unattainable (in other words, perfection); the altruistic formations throughout the letter—all combine to give us the major clue to her facile pen. Strange that her left-hand margin narrows with each line. This tells us that though her aesthetic sense was strong, there was a practical side to her nature that caught up with her desire to splurge. She was a person in whom reason prevailed over emotion and was therefore not particularly spontaneous. She once told me that a story had to be in her mind a long time before it took shape and she could write it. She disciplined herself with the deliberateness with which she kept her mental house in order—just as her handwriting is well spaced on the page—and she knew beforehand what her theme was to be and how she would work it out. She had the entire design outlined in her mind ahead of time, and then the words flowed. There was something of the hermit about her, though she had many friends. She observed her characters much as an analyst would, without sentimentality.

Willa Cather

[handwritten letter, signed] Willa Cather

SPECIMEN 93 (REDUCED TWO-THIRDS)

W. Somerset Maugham

In a previous chapter that deals with the inferiority complex and compensations I referred to the well-known writer W. Somerset Maugham, whose handwriting appears here. Mr. Maugham had a

W. Somerset Maugham

His love had tarried for a moment &
migrant bird that happens on a ship &
ocean and for a little while folds its
tired wings .

W. Somerset Maugham

SPECIMEN 94

speech defect earlier in his life, and to compensate for it he wrote prolifically. His handwriting shows some drive in the long *t* bars and the speedy rhythm, which also reveals a quick mind; there are signs of culture, a vivid imagination, innate talent. His facile pen was motivated by an inner urge that drove him compulsively, and he had the self-discipline to concentrate when necessary. As with all great writers, to quote Dr. J. H. Robinson in his *Humanizing of Knowledge*, "Writing is produced by having pains rather than taking them," but it does demand hard work, as any writer will tell you.

The tempo of Mr. Maugham's handwriting is slightly nervous, augmented by periods of tension. The mind races ahead of the pen, and this sometimes causes difficulty in coordinating the two. He makes the literary *g*; in the word "had," the mental formation of the *h* shows mental clarity and literary facility. Intuition is seen in a few breaks between letters ("for" and "fold"). His *t* crossings vary, some stems uncrossed, others heavily or wavily crossed—the last showing humor. This, in combination with tapering formations, as in the words "ocean" and "moment," indicates subtlety. The angle and pen pressure belong primarily to the extrovert, although these are modified by the mental formations, which show introvert leanings.

The inferiority complex, seen in varying pen pressure, alerts us to look for his compensation, which is shown in the high, simple capitals (without ornamentation) larger than the rest of the writing. Imagination is revealed in high *i* dottings with *t* bars above the stem, as in the word "white," third line. The constructed small *s* in "ship," generous spacing between words, and good margins, all show Mr. Maugham's aesthetic sense. (Wide spacing between words has the neurotic connotation, incidentally, of paranoid trends.) The wavering basic line tells us of varying moods, and in his rounded capital *M* is a clue to gentleness, tempered only by angularity and tent-shaped *i* dots, which point to critical perception.

Mr. Maugham was as facile with his pen as he would have liked to be in his speech had he not been frustrated by the very defect that resulted in his literary achievements.

Edna St. Vincent Millay

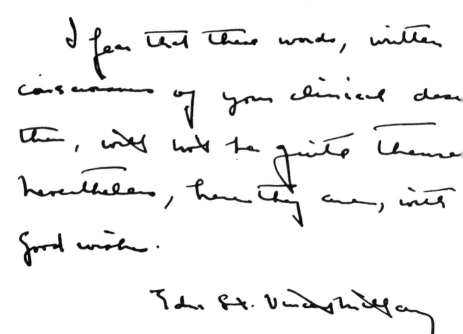

SPECIMEN 95

Edna St. Vincent Millay

The poet who wrote "My candle burns at both ends,/It will not last the night" was an introvert. Highly imaginative—and living in a world of fantasy, as shown in her consistently high *t* bars above the stem of the letter—she also had drive and tenacity of purpose (hooks at the end of *t* bars). She had a flair for the dramatic, seen in the lower loop in "quite," and used words to paint pictures, as an artist uses colors. She gave the impression of being cold, aloof, and undemonstrative, but her intuition was always working, and she sensed more in people and situations than was evident on the surface. She was detached in her attitude toward the world—the observer who saw and felt and then translated her impressions into poetry. She also wrote plays in a more or less sophisticated manner, for she was a realist who could see life with a cold, uncompromising eye. Some of the strokes in her words dwindle and diminish, telling us that there was much about her personal life she did not readily reveal, unless she did so obliquely in her writings. Signs of introversion are indicated by backward strokes in her signature. (They also appear in "will not.") There is a hint of the altruistic formation in the *y* in her name; a longer specimen would probably corroborate this. Indeed, she made her contribution to literature; and in her personal life, too, she had periods of generous giving because her instinct impelled her to do so.

Albert Einstein

The small, microscopic writing, light in pen pressure, and the simple capitals and legibly formed letters combine to express the unostentatious, scholarly Professor Einstein. Excellent powers of concentration in the very small writing tell us that he often looked at life as if through a microscope. The simple capital *A* in his name (simplified version of the protective formation) indicates his paternal gentleness, his concern for the underdog, while *t* bars above the stem show the imagination of the dreamer reaching deep into his intellect for answers to seemingly unanswerable questions. The *i* dots are meticulously placed above the letter, showing an excellent

Albert Einstein

Sehr geehrte Frau Olyanova!

Ich hätte Ihre Bitte gewiss früher erfüllt, wenn Ihre Briefe nicht in der Fülle ihrer Geschwister aus meinem Blickfeld verschwunden wären. Denn Graphologie hat mich stets interessiert, wenn ich mich auch nie systematisch dafür interessiert habe, ich mache es mit Schriften wie mit Gesichtern, ich urteile instinktiv.
Hochachtungsvoll
A. Einstein.

SPECIMEN 96

memory. Consistent rhythm (perhaps not so dynamic as that of Beethoven) shows his delicate touch in wielding not only the pen but also the violin. The bowed *t* bar above the stem in his signature tells us of a spiritual quality, his desire to make a contribution that might make the world a better place to live in. Unfortunately, because of his share in the creation of the atom bomb he suffered guilt feelings that pursued him to the end of his life. All the signs in his writing tell us that this man never lost the human touch, despite his preoccupation with math and abstractions beyond the understanding of most men of his day.

Amelia Earhart

The spirit of adventure that sent Amelia Earhart into the air is seen in the flying *t* bar above the stem through much of her hand-

PACIFIC SOLO

The take-off is general regarded as the most ? part of the flight. I can Try as well as I am a lift the heavy load fu rough field. If I do a good job it will because the plane an

Amelia Earhart

SPECIMEN 97

writing. When it flies away from the stem, to the right, the connotation is enthusiasm. She had a quick mind and followed plans with action; her capital *T* tells us she could formulate ideas, and her curiosity (some horizontal final strokes) impelled her to make investigations. She was a social, gentle woman, protective toward those weaker than herself (the capital *A* in her name); she must have been a good social worker, though it is probable that such work failed to satisfy her adventurous spirit. Something of the little girl remained in her, as shown in the *t* bar that does not go through the stem in "take-off." She still clung to memories of her past and was enacting a pattern of rejection associated with it, though she tried to compensate for those things she lacked earlier. She was generous—many small *o*'s are open at the top; she was adaptable and literary—the *g* made like an 8; she had periods of anxiety (she was especially anxious at the time this was written, before her Pacific solo), and this is shown in her going over the word "lift." (In any handwriting, the impulse to do this shows anxiety.)

In her intellectual approach, there was something masculine about Miss Earhart. She had the foresight and courage to invade a field regarded as being for men only. Yet emotionally she was entirely .feminine, with the yielding, gentle, passive qualities attributed to such women.

Thomas Wolfe

Here certainly is the dynamic energy we associate with genius (although not everyone with such energy has genius). Tenacious— see the large hook in the word "Trust" and realize this gives us the major clue to his persistence, his hanging on relentlessly to the bitter end. It speaks also of his compulsive ardor (we see it again in the capital *T* in his signature). His quick, impressionable, perceptive mind absorbed impressions like a sponge. Because of his sensuousness, he felt sharply everything that appealed to his senses and wrote of this is in his books. (Remember the odors described in *Look Homeward, Angel?*) He wrote his manuscripts in longhand, with something resembling fury, and it was hard for his hand to keep up with his thoughts—as shown here. Look at the way he ended the word

Thomas Wolfe

& he said   "Decidedly." I
asked him what changes and
revisions he thought should be
made & he said he did not
know that there were any —
it is simply not the kind of
Trust Company.   Place de la
Concorde, Paris.

   With love, & the very
best wishes to all,
     Tom Wolfe

SPECIMEN 98

"simply." It is a gesture of impatience and is not without sadism, and yet in the broader sense he had a great deal of patience, inspired by dreams of what he wanted to accomplish. He had a sense of the dramatic, a vivid imagination, robust physical appetites; but he was also extremely sensitive and perceptive, yet somewhat subjective and self-involved. His books are, most of them, biographical, yet there was much about his past he preferred to block out, as shown in *i*'s that are not dotted. His memory was more sensory than factual, and although he had a sense of humor, it often took on the color of ridicule. He was an angry man, not always good-tempered (see the pen pressure in the *k* in "know"). He made his contributions despite himself, driven by an urge bordering on genius. The signs of an immense talent are also here—in printed small letters, in mental formations, in good spacing between words and letters. But the writing also looks somewhat disturbed, though it was the kind of disturbance belonging to a person rarin' to go.

Dr. Alfred Adler

Dr. Adler, whose theories embraced the "will to power" psychology, wrote a sensitive light hand with small letter formations, showing his fine powers of concentration and intellectual penetration. Intuition and judgment gave him the keen insight into human motives for which he is famous. The simplicity of his entire handwriting is synonymous with his greatness. Yet the writing, although done quickly, seems lacking in physical robustness, and it was not long after this specimen was written that he died in Scotland of a heart attack.

It was Dr. Adler who developed the theory of the individual striving for superiority as compensation for an inferiority complex, and he took what might be called the common sense approach. He was a gentle, kind man whose personality had a healing quality. He was a born scholar, deeply concerned with the causes of human behavior. Material things were of little interest to him. His handwriting is influenced by foreign formations, for he received his training under German influence; yet it is essentially legible, just as his own style

Dr. Alfred Adler

SPECIMEN 99

of life (his phrase) was unpretentious, sympathetic, and humane. Patience and optimism are revealed in the rising lines and rounded letter formations. We also see the literary *g* and the Greek *d*, the signs of the writer. His book *What Life Should Mean to You* reads more like a novel than a scientific book on psychology and is the compilation of a series of lectures he gave in New York City. (It is of great assistance to students of graphology.)

Jakob Wassermann

The author of the classic *The World's Illusion*, which was suppressed in the 1920's because of its frankness, wrote a tiny microscopic hand. Extreme introversion is revealed here, despite the slight leaning to the right, and the pen pressure, although essentially light, darkens occasionally. So we have a person whose feelings and sensations varied and are a clue to his neurotic temperament; the closeness of his letter forms, coupled with angularity, tells us that he packed a great many impressions into a mind that was like a scientific labora-

Jakob Wassermann

SPECIMEN 100

tory. Although he was rather undemonstrative, he felt deeply the intense suffering of other people, and this is reflected in his fictional characters' behavior. He depicted every human emotion from the highest nobility to the lowest degeneracy in the book mentioned.

Mr. Wassermann was an introspective, critical, exacting individual whose greatest pleasure came from thinking. Although his signature has no underscore, it is somewhat larger than the rest of the writing; this tells us he had an awareness of his importance, though he did not allow it to influence his behavior. He was seclusive and much more the observer of life than the participant.

William James

Outstanding as a philosopher and psychologist, William James was also an artist, physician, and educator; his handwriting reveals his enormous talent and versatility. Above all, he was a great human being, and we see the signs of this in consistent altruistic formations. There are signs of culture, a capacity for concentration when he was not restless—for he had great self-discipline, shown throughout the specimen in the firmly bowed *t* bar. Emotionally, he was not always consistent, as he was subject to moods; there were times when he had to have a change of scene, and he traveled extensively. His keen, incisive mind, accelerated by intuition, was always alert to happenings around him, and he had a genius for seeing through a person's superficial aspects to the deep inner core.

William James was ahead of his time in his researches, showing a great interest in psychical research, for he had the quality of open-

William James

**95 IRVING ST.
CAMBRIDGE.** *March 19. 09*

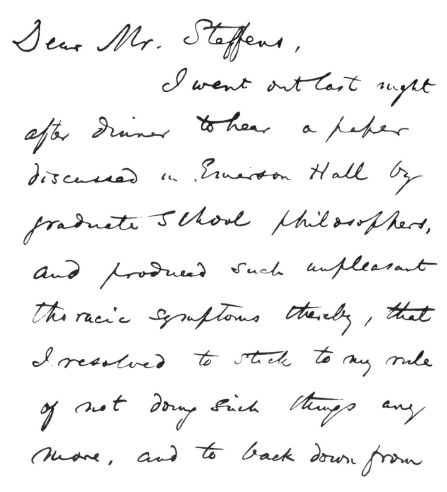

Dear Mr. Steffens,

I went out last night after dinner to hear a paper discussed in Emerson Hall by graduate School philosophers, and produced such unpleasant thoracic symptoms thereby, that I resolved to stick to my rule of not doing such things any more, and to back down from

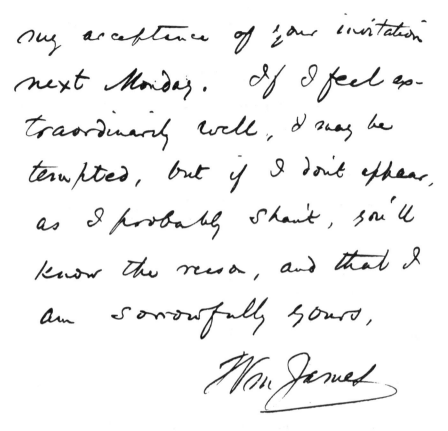

my acceptance of your invitation next Monday. If I feel extraordinarily well, I may be tempted, but if I don't appear, as I probably shan't, you'll know the reason, and that I am sorrowfully yours,

Wm James

SPECIMEN 101 (CONT.)

mindedness that refused to deny the validity of anything the human mind could conceive. He had originality, noticeable in some original letter formations, a sense of humor, an empathy for suffering humanity; he made many friends in many walks of life, and although critical in his observations, he could be kind, gentle, tolerant, and reasonable. Though modern in many of his ideas, he wrote an old-fashioned capital *M* with all its implications of protective paternalism. It was a clue to his interest in classicism and in a world of cultural tradition, from which he drew much to stimulate him. This letter to Lincoln Steffens was written the year before he died and shows signs of failing health.

St. Teresa of Avila

SPECIMEN 102

St. Teresa of Avila

Even a glance at this specimen written in Spanish discloses a vig-
orous, intensely emotional, purposeful and dominant, extroverted
individual. St. Teresa knew what she wanted and brooked no refusal
in getting it. Her large, heavy-pressure writing, leaning moderately
to the right, expresses a person who was guided largely by her emotions, though she exerted a demanding self-discipline to keep them
under control. She was a born executive and had many original ideas
which she put into practice, fighting any opposition and doing it with

clarity of thought and organization. We see signs here of intuition in the numerous breaks between letters, and some of her *t* bars slant downward, showing some aggressiveness. But this was tempered by tenderheartedness, and she was capable of pouring oil on waters which she herself had stirred up in order to find out what was causing trouble.

It was she who originated the phrase "the dark night of the soul," for she had periods of spiritual dryness during which she felt a separation from God. For the religious person, this is indescribable torture, so imagine the depths of despair into which it might have thrown a saint!

Her ideas were clear, as shown in the spacing, and she was resolute in judgment, not wavering once a decision was made. Emotionally turbulent, she was a woman of strong sexual drives; she had a great struggle with herself on this level, but she sublimated her passion into her activities, which she approached with unusual fervor. (We see this same kind of intensity in the handwriting of some actresses, and indeed there was something of the actress in this outstanding saint.) She had a lively imagination, as well as common sense; a superb administrator, this unique woman was many-sided, essentially a dynamo who made her mark in the religious world.

St. Francis of Assisi

Consistent breaks in words, especially where the specimen is printed, is the sign of the poet. In the instance of St. Francis, we have all the signs of the great poet. He was capable of original ideas that sprang from an inventive intelligence, and he had a strong leaning toward art. This could have been in the area of design. To him, the song of a bird, the gurgling of a stream, the sound of the wind were sources of inspiration. He lyricized his impressions in the "Canticles of Creatures," which could easily have been put to music. (It is not known, but it is not unlikely that he designed the monk's habit he wore, especially since he showed a concern with appearances. This derives more from an aesthetic quality than from a concern with superficialities.)

Altruism, for which he is largely remembered, is evident in the

St. Francis of Assisi

SPECIMEN 103

formation of the *y* and in the letter *g* (last word, third line) and throughout the specimen. This was also predicated upon a desire to give orders, for he had a decisive will that he liked to exert over others. It was his humility that impelled him to found a mendicant order, but he was nevertheless governed a good deal by ambition. So many forceful strokes in his writing tell us of his decisiveness, but the pen pressure varies from heavy to light, which means he could be gentle and considerate of others. There were also conflicting emotions, and he could be practical, even though his intuition (which was inspirational) lifted him from his earthly moorings.

St. Thomas Aquinas

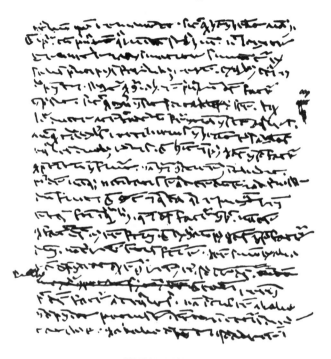

SPECIMEN 104

St. Thomas Aquinas

The small vertical handwriting of St. Thomas Aquinas could easily belong to a scientist, and in this field he could have excelled. He could also have been successful in musical composition because of his natural bent for mathematics. (This is the counterpoint recognized in the works of Bach and Beethoven.) Original letter formations appear all through the writing, and although the underlying emotional force is dynamic (seen in the pen pressure), he was a detached, seemingly cold and isolated human being who sought solitude. No one, except perhaps his Confessor, knew how he felt.

A complex architectural structure characterizes the writing, which tells us his mind built up theories that he then set out to prove to allay his own doubts.

We see in the entire specimen a methodical well-ordered intellect tempered by the changes in pen pressure, an indication that he struggled with both emotions and sex, which he learned to sublimate. Yet the writing is done with speed and signs of keen intuition. Essentially a scholar, he could move from one problem to another with unusual mental agility. He was concerned primarily with reducing everything to an intellectual problem, and his powers of analysis reach a peak where nothing is left to imagination or speculation but is expressed in clear, unmistakable, concise terms. The angle leans to the left, and this tells us he withdrew from anything that might threaten to disturb his quietude. He was an isolate, reticent and laconic. Extremely critical of any subject he dealt with, he was also self-critical and somewhat masochistic in the demands he made upon himself. His humor sometimes took the form of wit with a sharp cruel edge. But the wall he built up around him prevented others from getting close to him. His firmness and patience made him something of a solid rock, yet he suffered greatly inside, but did so in silence.

Emily Dickinson

Here we see the instinctive poet, immediately recognized by the consistent breaks throughout the specimen, showing the inspirational hand. (We saw it in the handwriting of Rachmaninoff, Specimen 85.) Here the writing leans to the right and tells us of the poet's warmth and sensibility; the vivid imagination, evident in the *t* bars above the stem of letters—almost as though they were flying heavenward—give the major clue to her rich world of fantasy. There is kindness, an almost childlike responsiveness, in the rounded formations; a hairline sensitivity in the light pen pressure, and an openheartedness shown in the capital *D*, open at the top.

The rhythm is consistent, and if we imitate the writing we will see that it was done quickly, the mind working with almost lightning

Emily Dickinson

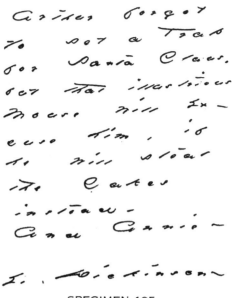

SPECIMEN 105

speed. Formations are without ornamentation—simple and legible. There is humor, a kind of whimsy, shown in the *i* dots that are parts of circles. And the spacing between lines and words is generous, showing clarity of thought and instinctive aestheticism.

However, we must also notice the *t* bar that does not go through the stem of the letter—in "forgot," "to," "set," and "but"—and because there are several of this kind, we have to conclude that the famous poet was repressed and suffering, the badge of genius. She made adjustments to her spinster life, but she went through periods of loneliness and introspection, having vivid memory associations of the past that inspired many of her poems. She could empathize with others who were soul-sick because of her own inner longings, and it is not unlikely that some of her best known poems had their inspiration in a nostalgia for the things in life she dreamed of but never realized.

X

Outstanding Personalities on the Contemporary Scene

> *The heights by great men reached and kept*
> *Were not attained by sudden flight,*
> *But they, while their companions slept,*
> *Were toiling upward in the night.*
> —LONGFELLOW

In THE HOME AND RELATED FIELDS OR IN AREAS TO do with children there is no doubt that women excel. The more objective, detached, masculine woman who can project her energies outward toward worldly attainment has a better chance of achieving greatness. Thus, only the woman with a generous admixture of masculinity has the capacity to become great in some field of endeavor outside the home.

The example of Willa Cather (Specimen 85) is proof of this; but consider the handwriting of St. Teresa of Avila (Specimen 102), a feminine woman. Where do we draw the line? Miss Cather's handwriting showed a generous share of masculinity in her intellectual approach, with an ability to view people and situations abstractly. St. Teresa, although more subjectively feminine, nevertheless possessed the aggressiveness usually associated with masculinity, and she ventured into fields that in her day were looked upon with awe by many.

In history, women who have been regarded as great have become so through an accident of royal birth. Catherine the Great, essentially masculine in many of her attitudes and even her tactics, is perhaps an exception. Her desire to rule with a dominant masculine force had its origin in a childhood inferiority complex. She was born to a superficial mother who had wanted a boy and who did not hide her disappointment. Catherine, determined to show that her mother was unjust, developed a rebelliousness that led to her later achievements. Because of her desire to prove to her mother that being a girl was no detriment to greatness, she strove for the high position she finally attained. The striving may have been unconscious, but it motivated her, and in the end she overcompensated for her inferiority complex.

There has been—and perhaps still is—too much sex-consciousness in most women to permit them to detach themselves completely from their sex drives and to achieve goals where sex does not play a dominant part. Throughout history women have used their sex as a means of achieving recognition, though not in creative fields. Such recognition has been in woman's own sphere, for it is in the art of love-fulfillment (including the art of flattery), catering to the whims of their monarch lovers, that they have excelled. Consider Ninon de Lenclos, who won her fame through the role she carried off so successfully—that of mistress to Louis XIV. She was a woman of exceptional wit and physical beauty, and she used these attributes as a means to a typically feminine end—getting her man. What's more, she was in her fifties at the time!

This kind of sex-consciousness does not, as a rule, exist among men, and their perspective is not colored by their sexuality when they strive for a nonsexual objective. There are exceptions, of course, men whose sexual inferiority and frustration have been reflected in their work, whose brushes and pens have been dipped in sanguine colors.

With the exception of Madame Curie, we know of no really great and famous woman scientists. Even she took time out to raise a family. She was always her husband's inspiring factor, and her dedication impelled her to continue his work after his death. This was *her* share of masculinity. We know of no outstanding doctors among American women today. Russia, however, has a plethora of women doctors, and some of them might well become famous. Our medical schools are admitting more women than formerly (most U.S. medical schools previously excluded all women), and perhaps a famous diagnostician or surgeon may emerge in time.

As yet there is no record of a woman composer in a class with

Beethoven, Mozart or Bach. Yet all the great composers had a strong admixture of the feminine in their natures. Among interpreters of music, however—pianists, violinists, singers—many women have gained recognition. And there are great women performers in ballet and in modern dance, as well as on the dramatic stage. But in all these women there is a mixture of the masculine. The dancer is perhaps an exception, as for the most part her sex impulses are sublimated. (Many ballet dancers have the same sign in handwriting—the *t* bar above the stem of the letter—as aviators, for just as the dancer leaps upward with her body, the flier does so with his plane.)

OUTSTANDING WOMEN—CONTEMPORARY

Jacqueline Kennedy

I should have known that it was asking too much to dream that I might have grown old with him.

SPECIMEN 106

Jacqueline Kennedy

Written during her period of grief, the handwriting of the wife of the late President shows the effects of emotional shock in the uneven basic line and the varying angles, both vertical and back-hand; the striving to achieve some control and equilibrium (in the last line of this specimen). The handwriting itself discloses a person of talent in the printed formations (small *s*). She has a lively, per-ceptive intelligence, a great deal of intuition, an excellent memory. The rising *t* bars tell us of aspirations, imagination, a striving for per-fection. The uneven pen pressure shows emotions that are in a state of tension and flux (understandable at this time), although for the most part Mrs. Kennedy is a woman of poise, charm (as is so often found in this kind of vertical writer), and strong artistic leanings. The specimen is well organized in its spacing and margins. Although the rhythm here is obviously disturbed, there is evidence of musical tastes, as well as literary ability, which she could put to use if suffi-ciently encouraged.

The signature, written after the sharp edge of grief had worn off slightly, shows better coordination, gracefulness of line and form, the sign of good judgment in the *y*. We see a woman who has the strength of character to face life's vicissitudes and to emerge even stronger because of them.

Kim Stanley

No fancy flourishes exist in this simple, clearly written specimen of one of today's outstanding American actresses. There is a slight leaning to the right, showing warmth, but for the main part her emotions are disciplined, so that she does not use the broad technique of a Barrymore. Instead, she is more the realistic actress who is always believable in her role, an actress who, though the dramatic instinct impels her (as shown in the broad, swinging lower loops), does not overact. She has a keen intelligence (shown in angular formations), an avid curiosity (indicated in the horizontal lines at the ends of words, noticeable in "Olyanova"), and literary tastes (seen in the *g* in "delighted").

Her talent shows in the printed capital *S*'s; she is openhearted and often frank, seen in the open capital *D*; her intuition is revealed in some breaks between letters (mostly in the salutation), and there is also evidence of clear, logical thinking in the many words where the letters are connected. While there is evidence of good judgment, the compulsiveness of the dedicated artist is apparent in the formation of the *y*, repeated many times. She has a break in the lower formation of the *y* in the word "Sincerely," which, in graphological terms, suggests a physical disability of the lower limbs. Playing the part of Freud's first patient (in *The Far Country*), whose legs were para-

Kim Stanley

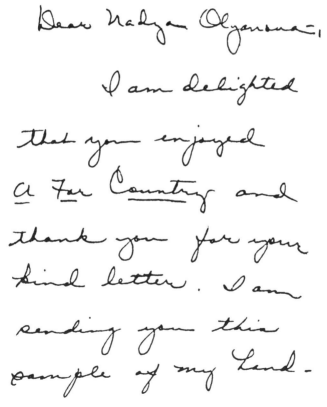

SPECIMEN 107

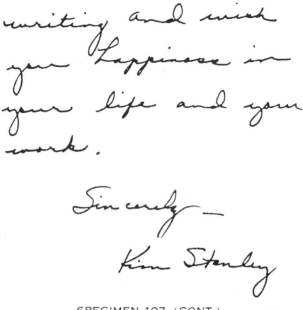

SPECIMEN 107 (CONT.)

lyzed, Miss Stanley actually took on the malady of the character she was portraying, and it was so real to her that it showed up in her handwriting!

Bette Davis

The dynamic energy of the creative artist shows in the speed with which the specimen was written, and discloses intuition in the many breaks in words. Enthusiasm and optimism are seen in the rising lines and flying *t* bars, short and even curt, as Miss Davis can sometimes be. Added to this, there is a capacity for frankness in the open capital *D* in her name (and the *O* in mine), and the angularity tells us of her intensity, along with her striving for perfection and exactness in creating whatever character she is portraying.

There are signs of good judgment in practical matters and the use of common sense, but the emotions are so intense that there are times when they overwhelm her and allow neurotic behavior to take over. She manages, always, to regain her equilibrium, for she is a

Bette Davis

20ᵗʰ *November* 1939

My dear Nadya Olganova,

How kind of you! I do appreciate the spirit which prompted you to write me, & only hope my performances may continue to please!

Sincerely
Bette Davis

SPECIMEN 108

woman with good resilience, as well as keen insights, originality, and a sense of humor. Her aesthetic demands are great, as shown in the margins and spacing, and the squared-off lower loop in "performances" tells us she has a consummate obstinacy that will not permit her to admit defeat even when faced with it. The rightward angle means she is outgoing, capable of showing the intensity she often feels; but there is also a hint of subtlety, for she senses when she must tone down her expression, and she does this within a framework of poise, reserve, and studied movement. There is no doubt that Miss Davis has achieved a measure of greatness in her chosen field; that she cares about what her audiences think of her has contributed to her continued popularity.

Helen Gurley Brown

Sensitive, restless, impressionable, and obviously talented, the author of *Sex and the Single Girl* has a handwriting that shows a person of lively spirits, a great deal of optimism, and a measure of compulsiveness. She does things quickly; sometimes undertakes so many things that the day seems too short to accomplish them all. But she is a woman of warmth and generosity, apt to become impatient with little things, yet capable of showing great fortitude in the face of a real crisis. She is either quite logical (as many of her connected letters in words show) or very intuitive (as the broken-up word "two" indicates). She is imaginative, yet can be practical, as shown in the cautious (closed) formations. She has a rich world of fantasy, seen in the many high upper loops, yet some upper loops that are slightly above the middle zone reveal her practicality.

A many-sided person with a number of contradictions (as lack of uniformity in small letters shows), she nevertheless can organize her thinking to accomplish many things. At present she is the editor of *Cosmopolitan.* Although her interests are many and varied, her chief one is people. In dealing with them, her sense of humor is usually apparent—as it is in her handwriting in the *i* dots, the rising terminals, and in the over-all demeanor. She is cooperative and capable of sharing, and she still retains something of the little girl that can brighten up at the promise of a new adventure. She can be gracious, permissive, and at times persistent, and despite her success she still has a measure of modesty (see the small capital *I* in the fourth line).

Her signature reveals, however, that she is obviously striving for continued recognition. The signature was written at a different time, obviously with a different pen, and shows a robust quality and concern with the sex drive (as seen in the lower loops). It is understandable that she should have written a book on sex. At heart she is really conventional, but there is enough of the rebel in her to wish to

Helen Gurley Brown

Satisfying, memorable episode
two persons' lives, Even
things end sadly, a party
arely says (nor, il believe, il
thinks) he would have given
anything for the whole thing

Helen Gurley Brown

SPECIMEN 109

change some things. With such a volatile personality, there is no likelihood of anything remaining static around her for any length of time.

Dr. Miriam Lincoln

SPECIMEN 110

Dr. Miriam Lincoln

Outstanding as a physician and author of the book *You'll Live Through It* (which deals with the menopause in women), Dr. Lincoln shows the energetic drive that is characteristic of women of achievement. Her handwriting is small, which tells us of her excellent powers of concentration and capacity for doing research. It leans moderately to the right, indicating that she is responsive and sympathetic, capable of expressing her feelings within a framework of reserve. And we see the beginning stroke of altruism in the first *y* in "My," telling us that her bent is in that direction. The *t* bar above the stem in several words, most noticeable in "through" and "that," reveals her spirit of adventure. In such an intellectual hand this would indicate adventures of the psyche; signs of intuition in the breaks in words show she has insight, which is one reason she is an excellent diagnostician.

Dr. Lincoln is modest, as seen in her modest, simple capitals; her perceptions are sharp and critical (as the tent-shaped *i* dot reveals in her last name). As in all very small writing, the introversion in the nature is evident, telling us that she spends much of her time thinking things through carefully and analytically, then goes into action when the need arises. Her intellectual ability is more masculine than feminine, for there is a capacity for objective reasoning; but where we see mild confusion—where the *Y* of "You'll" runs into the line below—it is evidence of occasional subjectivity, which we have come to believe is a feminine way of reasoning. So she has both—the ability to understand women because she is one and sometimes reasons as they do, and the analytical, critical mind—in all a perceptive, purposeful, cooperative woman.

Katharine Cornell

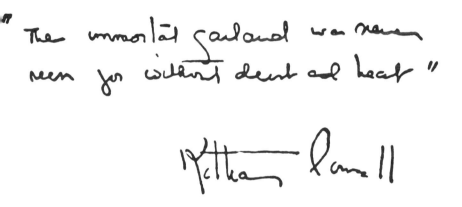

SPECIMEN 111 (REDUCED ONE-FIFTH)

Katharine Cornell

Here we have the introvert, unusual among stage people. Withal, there is a show of energy, enthusiasm, and animation in some *t* bars, and in others there is the kind of acute sensitivity (in the hook instead of a *t* bar) that prevents her from taking the initiative if she feels someone might be hurt by her actions. There are the signs of the artist; talent (printed capitals); intuition (breaks between letters); clear spacing between lines and words indicate clarity of thought, augmented by the mental formation of *h* in "heat." The long *t* bar in her signature—and notice there is no underscore—tells use of her tenacious drive when her heart is in what she is doing, a compulsiveness characteristic of the great and dedicated person.

Miss Cornell's first name ends in dwindling formations, which means there is much about herself she prefers not to reveal. She is gentle and kind, as many rounded formations reveal, but there are not many people with whom she is close. Although there still remains in her an element of timidity, it is compensated for by her ability to appear calm, self-possessed, and poised in front of other people, whether on the stage or off.

Alice Neel

Described in *Art Magazine* as "probably one of the greatest portraitists of our day," Alice Neel has all the signs in her handwriting to bear this out. She has the compulsive drive of the creative artist, as shown in her long *t* bars, some of them with hooks on the end, and a vivid imagination, disclosed in the *t* bars consistently above the stem, which derives from her childhood world of fantasy. Although she is left-handed, her writing leans to the right; a combination of roundness, angularity, and altruistic formations shows her preoccupation with people. Her insights are keener than average, and she paints the souls of humans. Her curiosity is insatiable, as shown in the elongated finals at the ends of words, most noticeable in the word "the" in the third line, in "love," and in her signature.

Her portraits are not slick, romanticized likenesses of her sitters, but reveal instead all the anxiety and hostility that is implicit in the insecurity of our age. She has been described as a curator of souls, and in those high *t* bars that reach for the unattainable, we see her striving for added dimension in the human equation, in which she succeeds so admirably. Above all, she is not afraid to be human, and the easy rightward flow of her writing shows this. The specimen is well spaced on the page; margins and spacing between words are wide; and her viewpoint, expressed in these, is one of tolerance, understanding, and empathy.

Alice Neel

Feb. 8 '68

Dear Nadya; ——

I was so glad
To see you at the
Gallery yesterday. The
pictures in the show
were all done in the
last two years. ——
I'm enclosing the
two handwritings.

Love

Alice Neel

SPECIMEN 112

Geraldine Page

It is comparatively easy to approach the handwriting of one of the best actresses on the American stage today from an over-all angle. For even a glance at it tells us that here is a person of energy, determination, and will power, whose nature is generous, expansive, and intensely emotional. There are signs of enthusiasm and tenacity of purpose (in hooks on *t* bars and terminals) all through the writing. It speaks to us of a frank, outgoing individual who is keenly

Geraldine Page

SPECIMEN 113

us all work so hard
& bring this theatre
into being.

My gratitude!

Geraldine Page

P. S. You honor me with
your request

SPECIMEN 113 (CONT.)

intelligent, although her emotions dominate most decisions; she has a vivid imagination which is often held in leash by her self-discipline. However, hers is a rich fantasy world that spills over into her world of reality (as seen in the lower loops that run into the line below), so that when she is acting out a character in a play, she is that character. Sometimes one thought trips over another, as shown in her formation of the word "to" in the third and tenth lines, but for the most part she is keenly perceptive, and her thoughts are never static or sterile, since they are imbued with intense warmth and meaning, as is everything she does.

A spiritual quality, the desire for perfection so prevalent in many great artists, is shown in the high *t* bars, especially noticeable in the word "with" in the P.S. There is so much here that can be described, but I will merely say that Miss Page has many of the elements of genius, mainly her compulsive drive, and that she cares about other people. She is healthy, robust, and enjoys living, often infecting others with her *joie de vivre*.

Ingrid Bergman

SPECIMEN 114

Ingrid Bergman

Gentle, sensitive, responsive, we see in the handwriting of Ingrid Bergman outstanding talent in her printed capitals and small letters, in the intuition, and in the original way she makes the capitals in her name. She is, however, caught up in a world of fantasy many times, and becomes passive as well as introspective. Energy is evident in the even pen pressure and the ending stroke of her last name, but there are also many signs of indecision and self-doubt, and she needs —and responds to—encouragement. Her energy drive is inconsistent, yet when given an assignment she is overconscientious, mainly because she is somewhat lacking in confidence.

But here is a human being who has a sense of justice, as shown in the many angular formations; any form of injustice causes her to identify with the person put upon. She is simple, unaffected, spontaneous, although there is a measure of reserve, and she has great dignity, as seen in her original and large capitals. There is also a capacity for firmness and relentlessness as shown in that stroke on the *d* in her first name. When she has made a decision, there is no turning back. Her difficulty is in making up her mind, and the indecision that follows causes anxiety and inner tension. There are some unsolved problems deep within her or she would not write the form of *t* bar that does not go through the stem, but she is optimistic, intellectually honest, and anxious to do what is right. Because of her altruism, any decision she makes will be to the advantage of those she loves and who share her life. Notice the altruistic formation of the letter *g* in her last name. She is struggling to overcome her masochistic trend, is capable of self-sacrifice, but has enough common sense to counterbalance this and ultimately to come to terms with herself.

Florynce R. Kennedy

An outstanding, articulate civil rights attorney, Florynce Kennedy, in her handwriting, shows the vitality, optimism, and vivid imagination that make her unique. The roundness, coupled with some angularity, shows a keen mind in a nature that is kind, warm, friendly, and pliable. The *i* circle dot is a clue to her uniqueness, and her high upper loops reveal her idealism. The writing is connected, which shows she uses logical reasoning to such an extent that even when she gets a flash of intuition, she doesn't trust it, seeking always to back it up with facts and evidence. But her vivid imagination,

Florynce R. Kennedy

SPECIMEN 115

seen in the flying *t* bars above the stems, augments her vision, gives her foresight and a spirit of adventure. This also tells us she is a perfectionist, reaching out for the unattainable, and corroborates our findings wherein she strives for betterment, not just for herself but for others too, for she is essentially a person with a strong social conscience.

Her humor shows in the wavy strokes, frequently in the *t* bar itself; her keen business sense, in the small *b*'s that are tightly closed, tells us she is cautious and signs nothing until she has read the small print. She has a rich world of fantasy in which she lived as a child, but she can face reality when necessary, and we therefore see an individual of strength and purpose who has common sense and is cooperative. She is extremely sensitive to the needs of others and has a strong sense of justice, which probably led her into the practice of law. She is deeply spiritual, self-disciplined, and often compulsive in her pursuits.

Jeane L. Dixon

SPECIMEN 116

Jeane L. Dixon

Something of a childlike scrawl characterizes the beginning of this specimen by the clairvoyant who has foretold many events in Washington, including the death of President Kennedy. It is puzzling to observe the lack of intuition through the entire handwriting of Mrs. Dixon, although there is a rising lilt to some of her endings, disclosing a striving for spiritual attainment. She is not in any sense an original thinker, and as a person with great respect for authority, she is very likely to repeat what those she admires say. She is outgoing and enjoys being with people, especially when (according to her large capitals) she can be the center of the stage.

Her signature, on the other hand, has many intuitive breaks in it, and this says that she has a natural gift of above-average insight (call it E.S.P. or clairvoyance); but it is not consistent, for it comes into conflict with a mind that concerns itself with life's material advantages.

Though the expansiveness of her writing gives the impression that she tells all, there is much she prefers to withhold, as seen in the lack of clarity in the last name of her signature. There is evidence of a dichotomy in the character, considering that the body of her writing is at variance with the signature. There are constructive formations in the signature that show a talent not fully developed because of a measure of intolerance and a limiting superstition.

OUTSTANDING MEN—CONTEMPORARY

During periods of world turmoil, personalities emerge to champion one cause or another. In their zeal, they make promises that give hope to nations looking for leadership, but in their handwriting are major clues as to whether or not they are sincere about keeping their promises. On the following pages are handwriting specimens of some of the men in the public eye, and we can learn why they attract us or repel us or leave us indifferent.

We have also selected the handwriting of men in other fields: writers, musicians, an actor, a well-known psychiatrist, a bishop, and we shall see why these individuals are outstanding, some even unforgettable. In all of them is found a common denominator: a desire to be useful to the greatest extent possible. The great psychologist Dr. Alfred Adler equated genius with the extent of man's usefulness. In analyzing the handwriting of these exceptional personalities, we shall try to understand each man's individual capacity for his productive relationship to the world.

In each of these men there exists a kind of vitality that gives rise to his productivity, whatever his field might be. Whether he goes down in history or lives in posterity is not easy to discern during his lifetime. But in each one there is a spark of genius, which may in time burst into flame and light up (or burn up) the world.

Eugene McCarthy

Where you are confronted with so large a writing as that of Senator McCarthy, you may be sure that he is expansive and concerned with larger issues. Although some of his words taper, as in

Eugene McCarthy

Dear Nayda,

This may not be an adequate sampling of my writing — or perhaps it should be on a sub-

SPECIMEN 117

SPECIMEN 117 (CONT.)

"substantive," this is a sign of his ability to be diplomatic rather than evasive. He is sensitive, gentle, and permissive to some extent, but he can also be firm when convinced he is on the side of right. In feeling, he is introverted; in thinking, extroverted. This causes some inner conflict. The angle, though vertical, showing a measure of reserve, when combined with such large writing tells us he can be a good listener; he is concerned with the welfare of others and takes into account the needs of the man in the street. The *y* in the word "my" is an altruistic formation, and the breaks between letters, showing intuition, tell us he has insight into more than the externals of a situation.

He has been described as an intellectual, but this is not essentially the handwriting of a hidebound one. The emotions are much more in evidence, although they are held in check by a mind that first sees the large picture and approaches it deductively; but he can break down an issue into its component parts and reason inductively as well. He is constructive and capable, imaginative and idealistic; slow to make a decision unless certain in his own mind as to where it will lead, and resolute in fulfilling promises—which he would not make unless certain he could keep them. We see here also a sense of drama, coupled with a literary faculty; he sees himself as a character in a play in which he has a leading role, but he considers the other parts equally important. He has infinitely more ability than he gives himself credit for, and in a crisis he would show strength tempered with humaneness.

General James M. Gavin

SPECIMEN 118

General James M. Gavin

We are confronted here with a man of a keen intelligence, great drive, and sensitivity; one who is somewhat visionary in his ideals (as shown in the very high upper loops, which are wide open). The long lower loops, which sometimes go through letters in the line below, tell us that General Gavin has a rich world of fantasy, some of which spills over into the world of reality. Thus he dreams of the perfect world in which he might have a leading part. And for this he has many capabilities. Important among them is intuition, which gives him insight into people and situations; the ability to be articulate in expressing ideas, both in writing and conversation; and a kind of optimism (in rising lines) that gives lift to his thoughts and hope to his spirit. Most noticeable are the lower loops, which are exaggerated and rhythmic, and they characterize something unusual in him so that we know why he has been described as a maverick. He dares to depart from the strict conformity of his position, to express ideas that are novel and unusual yet that fall within a constructive framework. And these same loops tell us he is attracted to that which is novel, unusual, and exotic mainly because there is some of that in himself. A sense of humor is shown, as are open-mindedness, generosity, and versatility. We see him as a man who would lend something colorful, dramatic, and emphatic to anything he gave his energy to. His intuition is not apt to mislead him, as it is balanced by good judgment and foresight; therefore we can trust his first impressions, for sooner or later they become justified.

Robert F. Kennedy

SPECIMEN 119

Robert F. Kennedy

Obvious in the handwriting of the late Senator Robert F. Kennedy is its angularity, the indication of his keen, penetrating mind, relentless in seeking the correct answers to prevailing questions. Accelerated by intuition, he often saw through situations (the motives of other people, too), but he had sufficient reserve so that he did not always reveal what he might have been thinking. When he did, it was apt to be to the point and without fear of contradiction. If he contradicted himself after a period of time, it was because his judgment told him it was expedient to do so; and in being blunt at times, he showed an element of fearlessness. His *t* bars are firm and they vary in thickness, showing determination that varied in intensity, but he also had a good share of self-discipline. There were times when he did what he might not have particularly enjoyed doing, merely as a means to a constructive end from which (he reasoned) many people might benefit.

Although he had a retentive memory for facts and figures, there is evidence (in the omission of some *i* dots) that he also had some blind spots. These relate to the unconscious level, telling us there were some experiences in his past he preferred to block out, probably because of the pain they engendered. He could be exacting, efficient in undertakings, firm in conviction, very intense in feeling—which he did not readily show. The wide spaces between words, coupled with well-spaced lines on the page, give us a clue to an element of wariness, derived from caution, which caused him to become suspicious frequently. He therefore battened down his hatches against possible storms and sailed through them with outward calm, even though he may have felt an inner turbulence. Very few people really knew what he was feeling, and he told them only what he thought they should know.

Ronald Reagan

This specimen was written in the early 1940's by the man who is now governor of California. From Ronald Reagan's handwriting we

Ronald Reagan

SPECIMEN 120

Governor, State of California

SPECIMEN 120A

see that he is genial and not deeply emotional, and for the latter reason unable to deal with human suffering in the abstract. It is the writing of a provincial person, essentially the small-town boy who is likely to become confused by large issues, who would avoid change because it represents a threat to him by upsetting the even tenor of his ways. He has a spirit of adventure, however, which is the clue to his ambition (see the *t* bar above the stem in the word "everything"); but even this operates within a limited framework, and he found expression for it in the roles he played rather than in life itself. There is little insight; there are no intuition breaks in the writing except one in the word "Christmas" and one in his first name, and he would not trust a hunch because of fear that it might mislead him and threaten his security. The one *t* bar that slants down shows a capacity for defending himself when he is under fire, but for the most part he is apt to avoid dissension. He can be blunt if challenged, as revealed in the blunt ending of the *d* on his first name, but the roundness of his letter forms tells us he is boyish and pliable and can be influenced by someone whose authority he respects.

The second signature, written recently, shows one major change: The angle has become vertical, including a development of aloofness with a desire to think things through before acting. But in the main he has not changed very much in these many years. By the same token, he takes the conservative position because he is fearful of any form of change. He has a way of closing his eyes to ugly problems so that for him they do not exist.

John V. Lindsay

Mayor Lindsay's handwriting is characterized by an energetic drive, for the rhythm is as quick as his active mind. The latter is accelerated by intuition, shown in the many breaks in words; the vertical angle shows a prevalence in many instances of reason over emotion, but it is nevertheless the writing of a deeply emotional individual who feels deeply and has a capacity to empathize with other people. There seems to be a slight disturbance in the rhythm, but then this was written after a rigorous campaign and his nerves were obviously ragged. Despite his capacity for articulation, there is the kind of *d* in the word "deep" and in his last name that tells us he can be petulant, poker-faced, and noncommittal when he deems it expedient. But he is generous when his emotions become involved, constructive, versatile, and extremely sensitive. He has overcome some of his earlier weaknesses, as revealed in the firm, almost bowed *t* bar in the word "with," and he has a built-in strength to cope with the rigors of his office. He can be critical in his observations (see the perfect tent formation of the *i* dot in the word "City"), yet he has a good sense of humor, as well as an instinct for the dramatic; this last is indicated in the final lower loop in his signature.

Taking the *gestalt*—the entire specimen as a whole—we see something unusual about the writing; and close examination points up mental formations, as well as the literary *g*, which show his tastes, ability, and adaptability. Thus, we are confronted with a person of

John V. Lindsay

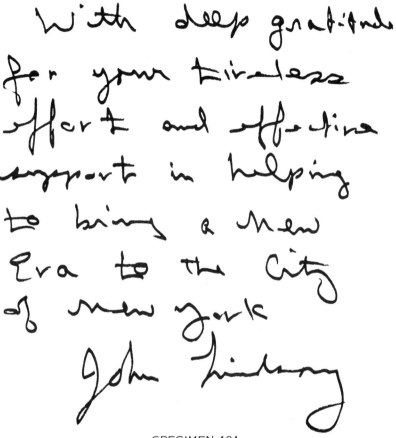

SPECIMEN 121

unusual abilities who could go far because of ambition and vision. He has the charm so often found in those whose handwriting is vertical, and the artistic appreciation of one whose emotional and intellectual house must be in order for him to be happy.

Charles de Gaulle

Signs of mental acuity are here in the small, angular writing of General de Gaulle. There are signs of assertiveness, independence,

Charles de Gaulle

SPECIMEN 122

and determination in his short, blunt finals. His memory is prodigious, as seen in the way his *i*'s are dotted directly above the letter. And there are the signs of ambition and optimism in the ascending lines, especially noticeable in his signature. Signs of brusqueness and tenacity (hooks at the end of strokes) are here; he does not give up once he is in pursuit of something.

The signature, larger than the rest of the writing, tells us he is autocratic, apparent in the individualistic position he often takes. The plunging downstroke on the capital *C* in his name shows his obstinacy. What is unusual in the signature is the dot made after it. Few people place a period after their names but those who do may as well be saying: "I have said it and that is the end of all arguments." It has a finality about it. There is, however, another meaning of this heavy period after his name: It shows caution, secretiveness, and a measure of suspicion, and in a manner of speaking is a divider between himself and his enemies. The last stroke before the final period is a mark of his persistence and also reveals his own image of himself —which is one of importance. This is a man to be reckoned with, and there are signs that, to some extent, he lives in a world of private meanings, giving us a clue to his neurosis.

Norman Thomas

Vertical, with accompanying angularity, the handwriting of Norman Thomas shows a capacity for clear and logical reasoning with occasional flashes of intuition, and we deduce from this combination a person who both thinks and feels and who has a sense of direction. The simplicity of his capital *S* in "Sincerely," coupled with the single downstroke of the *y*, tells us he can formulate ideas that are simple

Norman Thomas

SPECIMEN 123

and judicious, designed for those of simple understanding to grasp. Open small *a*'s that tell us of his ability to articulate also show generosity where his emotions become involved. But despite his capacity for deep feeling (shown in the pen pressure), his sense of humor (in the wavy *t* bar in "with") often tempered his feelings and enabled him to see the funny side of even serious issues.

From the way some letters at the end of words grow larger, as in "your," "yours," and the last *s* on his name, we know he can be outspoken and direct; this gives us a clue to his fearlessness, based on his having the courage of his convictions. There is a waviness in the rhythm, which indicates a nervous sensitivity arising from inner tension that finds release in expostulating ideas. And in the way the signature is written—the names are connected and made with a continuous stroke—we see the signs of the leader, the executive who can connect not only thoughts but ideas as well. The noticeable ending stroke on his last name tells of his capacity to deal with details, some of which make him impatient. With larger issues there is more than average patience, optimism, and hope.

J. W. Fulbright

The clarity with which this specimen was written shows a forthright, clear-thinking person who is articulate and who does not waste words in expressing what he is thinking. He is essentially logical and can handle facts and figures; there are also signs of intuition in breaks between letters in the words "study" and "handwriting," and we

J. W. Fulbright

J. W. FULBRIGHT
CHAIRMAN

United States Senate

COMMITTEE ON FOREIGN RELATIONS

Graphology is the study of handwriting.

J. W. Fulbright

SPECIMEN 124

conclude that Senator Fulbright has insight into more than the externals of a situation. The high *i* dots show imagination and the ability to plan ahead, corroborated by the well-spaced specimen on the page. His long lower loops, made firmly and rhythmically, tell us he can deal with the material exigencies of life and also reveal an instinct for the dramatic. His heavy pen pressure shows consistency, as does the rest of the writing, and the firm *t* bars show a man of self-control and purpose. He can be firm and abrupt in situations where such an approach seems best, as shown in the ending downstroke on his last name; and the large capitals written in a conventional manner tell us he can deal with ideas that concern the conventional man.

However, a puzzling element appears in his signature where the *l* in the last name is a mere upward stroke resembling an angular *i* —almost as if he prefers being realistic about situations that concern him to setting up an unrealizable ideal. It relates to something deep within him to which he may never have come fully to terms, but it has no relation to his integrity and honesty as a human being. His humor is evident in the *i* dot resembling part of a circle in the word "handwriting," high though it is; and the closed small *b* in his last name tells us he can be cautious where serious expenditures are concerned. The broad *r* in "Graphology" discloses a strong visual sense and concern with appearances, not in a superficial sense, but in the broader one, where he looks beneath the surface.

Leopold Stokowski

SPECIMEN 125

Leopold Stokowski

The handwriting of Leopold Stokowski, long an outstanding conductor, looks like an original design. The squared-off formations reveal an exacting quality that is part of his pattern of aiming for perfection. The *t* bar flying away from the stem of the letter is an indication of his enthusiasm, although the vertical angle tempers this to an extent, and the large writing is evidence of his expansiveness as well as his extroversion.

Many of the letters are printed, and, as in the handwriting of many poets, we see here the feeling for cadence and rhythm, as well as the inspirational quality that springs from keen intuition.

A hook on the upper stroke of the first letter in his last name, as well as the last stroke rising in the air, so to speak, gives us a clue to his tenacity of purpose and his compulsiveness in the pursuit of perfection in his work. This kind of signature needs no underscore to signify the importance the writer attributes to himself; it is unusual and original, with a high point that reaches into the clouds that Phoenix embraces. The evenness of the pen pressure, with occasional darker strokes, shows his sensitivity to light and shade which he translates into sound. He is in a class by himself as a conductor and an original, unusual man.

Truman Capote

Dear miss Clyanova —

Thank you for your letter.
my handwriting varies according to my
mood — when I am in a hurry it is
very large. But this is fairly Typical.
Sincerely
Truman Capote

SPECIMEN 126

Truman Capote

There is a great deal of the poet in Truman Capote, shown in the broken-up writing and the printed letter forms and the way the whole is framed on the page. Such light pen pressure tells us of his acute sensitivity; small writing shows powers of concentration; high *i* dots show a vivid imagination, corroborated by *t* bars above the stem. Simple, gentle, and almost childlike in some respects, he has an immense reserve (vertical angle), and although he may enjoy many people, there are few—if any—who can get really close to him. Obviously, there was a lack of closeness in his early childhood, and he developed a pattern of isolation during his formative years. There is a great need to be loved, appreciated, and approved of, for the signature is larger than the rest of the writing and it says, in effect: "Please notice me."

That he is capable of tenacious endeavor shows in the hook on the end of the *t* in his last name. He is a person of varying moods, and he tells us his handwriting is very large when he is in a hurry. Naturally it would be, for when his energies are unleashed he does things on a larger scale than when he is concentrating. The bowed *t* bar above the stem in the words "this" and "typical" discloses a quality of mysticism that satisfies some deep religious murmuring.

Gore Vidal

SPECIMEN 127

Gore Vidal

Originality, quickness of perception, and lively spirits are all seen at a glance in the handwriting of Gore Vidal, the well-known author and playwright. His capacity for clear, logical reasoning is indicated in connected letters in words—all of them except the word "of." Here the break tells us he gets flashes of intuition that sometimes take the form of suspicion—which is usually justified. (Suspicion is indicated here in the unusually wide spacing between words, as if the person stops to look around in answer to an intuitive prompting.)

He can be generous—shown in the open formation of his small *o*'s —especially when his emotions become involved. He has a leaning toward people and can deal with all comers, as revealed in the right-ward slant of the writing, although there is some reserve in the almost upright capital *I*. So he can be friendly without always becoming intimate, for there is much about himself he does not reveal. His underscored signature, besides giving evidence of a positive, magnetic personality, tells us of an inferiority complex that had its seat in early conditioning. But there is a blunt fearlessness that characterizes him, and he is intellectually honest. Certainly the signature is written with original formations, showing he is capable of original and independent thinking.

Melvyn Douglas

A man who is guided mostly by his emotions, actor Melvyn Douglas is, nevertheless, a person of a keen, critical intelligence whose writing shows mental formations, coupled with all the signs of unusual talent. His ideals are so high as to be visionary (shown in high upper loops). The pen pressure is medium heavy and tells us he is intensely emotional, with a sensuousness to form, color, and music. Imagination is indicated in the high *t* crossings, most of them firm and made with either a hook on the end or a continued stroke, which shows his capacity for hard work, along with the compulsiveness of the creative artist. The rising lines on the sheet are a clue to his optimism and moments of great exhilaration, but by the same token he can experience periods of depression. The large writing tells of his expansiveness; a hint of altruism is in the *y* in the word

Melvyn Douglas

SPECIMEN 128

"only." Letter formations are not particularly uniform—some are large, others small—but in so dynamic an individual we must not expect consistency, even though he would be consistent in his loyalties.

There is a special significance in this kind of capital *M*, where the last upper stroke is higher than the other two. It shows a man who can assert himself when least expected, who has a desire to be in a position of significance or authority. Essentially, it is a clue to neurotic overtones, usually found in individuals of outstanding ability in some areas.

Pete Seeger

Dear Nadya Olyanova —

I have a lousy handwriting, many of our typewriter generation school taught me to print first, I gradually joined some letters. daughter has a good script, though ancestors would be proud of her.

Best wishes —

Pete Seeger

SPECIMEN 129

Pete Seeger

In the handwriting of folk singer Pete Seeger, we see more than just the musician. He is intellectually keen, versatile, and creative, showing such signs in the capital *I* made with a single stroke, in the Greek *d*, and in printed letter formations. He is a gentle person, as revealed in the light pen pressure and the roundness; and his intuition (in the breaks between letters) shows he gains quick insight into other people and situations.

The consistent rhythm all through the writing is the clue to his responsiveness to rhythm, harmony, poetry, for at heart there is something of the poet in him. And his *i* dots, which are parts of circles, tell us he has a sense of humor and that he can appreciate the subtlety of humor others may miss. There is a somewhat spiritual aspect in the writing not easily explained in a few words, seen in the bowed *t* bars above the stem of the letter (indicating imagination) in the word "ancestors." Although there is a capacity for hard work, at times even a compulsiveness, there are also signs of thought and reflection in the spacing between words. The way the two *o*'s in "school" are tied up tells of caution he has developed, probably as a protective measure, but by and large there is warmth, simplicity, and spontaneity which he expresses in his folk music.

Karl A. Menninger, M.D.

SPECIMEN 130

Karl A. Menninger, M.D.

At first glance, Dr. Menninger's handwriting could be placed in the category of the artist, for it reveals many of the letter forms, varying pen pressure, intuition, and originality we find in artistic hands. (I have always believed that medicine is more of an art than a science—as many handwritings of medical men show, especially those of surgeons.) However, in this specimen we see the scientific bent, too—in angular formations and small, though various-sized, letter forms; and the vertical angle shows a prevalence of reason over emotion. Dr. Menninger is a keen observer, which is revealed not only in his handwriting but also in his books.

To Dr. Menninger, human beings are entities to be observed impersonally, scientifically, and with detachment. His sense of humor can be caustic and critical, as seen in tent-shaped *i* dots; and in the word "handwritings" there is an absence of *i* dots, which tells us he is somewhat absent-minded; on the unconscious level there are some things he blocks out, perhaps because they are too painful. Although very sensitive, he does not make a ready display of his feelings, and despite his friendliness he manages to keep a distance between himself and others, preventing an easy intimacy. Further, he is a man of decided opinions, with a strong elemental force—shown in the blunt downstroke on the word "my" and in the heavy downstrokes in his name, where the nib of the pen widens. This could be construed as a form of sadism, but it is clothed in subtlety—the iron fist in the velvet glove. A tendency of the signature to rise shows he has an optimism fostered in vision and foresight, but it comes into conflict with a mind that approaches new issues with curiosity and doubt, despite his desire to be open-minded. In his approach to most people he can be formal and aloof, yet there is a need for warmth and closeness which he may have felt were lacking in his early life.

He is still in there pitching, performing experiments, and observing the human equation in its various aspects.

Horace W B. Donegan

The handwriting of the Episcopal Bishop of New York City is that of an intellectual—though the rightward angle shows his interest

Horace W. B. Donegan

P.S. As you Bishop I ask you to send a gift
to this major charitable agency of our
Diocese this Christmas. It is very much needed,
& Your personal participation will make
a great difference in the lives of those
whom we seek to serve.

SPECIMEN 131

in people, and altruistic formations reveal a concern with their welfare. He has the signs of culture and literary ability, and powers of concentration are seen in the small writing; long *t* bars indicate a capacity for hard work, determination, and will power. His capacity for clear logical reasoning is apparent, and there are signs of intuition in the occasional breaks in words: Thus he could take a short cut to a conclusion, guided by his good judgment. Here is a man with great self-discipline, yet he understands those who lack it (among other things). He not only theorizes the Christian concept, but acts in accordance with it, and he is well suited to his high position, with his evident ability for spiritual leadership.

Added to his many other abilities, he is a good administrator; this does not lessen his desire to lead his flock toward a fuller, better existence. The underscored signature tells us of his dominent personality; it is also the sign of the dramatic instinct which is so often found in the handwriting of clergymen and other public figures.

Richard M. Nixon

Monday, Dec 13.

Dear John
When Pat & I returned from Georgia Sunday I tried to reach you but found you had already left for Great Falls.

Certainly no one could have done more to make a mother proud and happy than you did.

Pat and I want you to know our prayers are with you in these sad hours —

Dick

Richard M. Nixon

The unusually large capital *D*, the long, firm *t* bars all through
the writing, and the long horizontal final on the word *had* show the
consistent drive and ambition of an individual who is very sure of
himself. His literal-mindedness is expressed in connected letters in
words, showing his essential use of logic. There are some intuitive
breaks in the writing: the word *Great* in the first paragraph and the
word *certainly* in the second; he is, however, too cautious to trust
his intuition when he does get an occasional flash of it. The spacing
between the words is often meager; his factual approach is often
narrowed down within a provincial framework. He can be firm and
rigid in holding to some of his opinions (see the abrupt finals in *Pat*
and *want*). The return strokes on many of his *y*'s reveal compulsiveness, even though a few of them have the altruistic construction.
These tell us that he has a capacity for giving, albeit advisedly.

His attention to detail is revealed in an extra final stroke on the
word *Falls*. This is corroborated by carefully dotted *i*'s, showing a
retentive memory for factual detail. We see both roundness and
angularity in the writing, indicating more flexibility in the emotional
area than in the intellectual. There is inconsistency in the letter
forms—some are hardly visible, while others taper—which tells us
that he may not always reveal what he is thinking or planning. He
is a competent, single-tracked executive, on the side of the haves,
conservative in identifying with the have-nots. Obstacles do not
discourage him. They often act as a challenge to spur him on toward
realizing the ambition that gives him a drive for power.

XI

The Maladjusted

In men whom men pronounce as ill,
I find a lot of goodness still.
In men whom men pronounce divine,
I find a lot of sin and blot;
I hesitate to draw the line
Between the two—where God has not!
    —JOACHIM MILLER

Neurotics and Will Power

THE NEUROTIC DIFFERS FROM THE HEALTHY, WELL-adjusted individual in that the adjusted man directs his collective energies to achieve the goals he sets up for himself, whereas the neurotic cannot do this. The reason he cannot is that his will is divided: he has not one will but many, all coming into conflict with each other. He is, as a result, indecisive, not knowing what it is he wants, for often he desires the unattainable. This is because he lives, for the most part, in fantasy. It is the same fantasy world into which he retreated as a child, and since the child in him remains (making unreasonable demands of him), he is unable to meet the demands of an adult world. He cannot readily adjust to an ordered society with the necessary self-discipline, and he becomes rebellious when he thinks he must conform. He then feels thwarted and frustrated, and develops a neurosis through which he consciously or unconsciously expresses his rebellion. He wants to eat his cake and have it too.

Because the primitive urges in the neurotic are so close to his so-called civilized instincts, the conscious and unconscious drives are brought into closer relation to each other, and a conflict arises as to which will gain the upper hand, the child or the adult. The neurotic who is able to function with a measure of common sense, who is cooperative in his relations with other people, and who fills a useful niche is already somewhat adjusted. But the neurotic who is without discipline, who lives in fantasy, and who seeks some form of escape from reality is in trouble. Neurotics tend to be more sensitive than non-neurotics; therefore their emotional reactions are intensified, and they think of themselves as unique, misunderstood, and sometimes mistreated. The neurotic is essentially a very angry person who feels the world does not accept him, but all too often he lacks the insight to realize why he is unacceptable. He wants to be loved even when he is most unlovable; he can be critical of the faults in others that he himself possesses; and he may be unable to communicate with others, for he sometimes lives in a world of private meanings.

Living in a world that is suffering from anxiety, most of us are more or less neurotic in this day and age. How neurotic we are is simply a matter of degree. And this degree is readily discerned in handwriting. The handwriting of neurotics is characterized by extremes and contradictions. There may be varying pen pressures in a single line of writing, ranging from extremely thick and heavy to extremely fine and spindly light, which shows instability and expresses both sensuality and spirituality. It is obvious such extremes should result in conflict. If the pressure is uniformly heavy or light, letter formations will be unusual, inverted or queer-looking, often disturbing to the eye. And already we have some clues to the neurotic personality. The *t* bar, which most obviously expresses the will of the writer, will vary from a short bar that does not go through the stem to a long bar with a hook on the end. (Often it will appear with other signs that indicate compulsiveness.) Some stems may be entirely uncrossed; some *t* bars will go through the stem from right to left and not return; in many instances the *t* bar will be above the stem, indicating a reaching for the unattainable—the perfectionist, the person not easily pleased.

The basic line may waver, indicating changing moods that go with instability, and the angles may vary from right to vertical to left in one specimen of writing. Usually there will be signs of talent or other compensatory factors in the handwriting of the neurotic who is making an effort to express himself constructively.

The neurotic whose energies are not tied up by his neurosis, and who can develop a measure of self-discipline in even one direction, can make unusual contributions to civilization. Where the neurosis absorbs his attention and energies, and where a desire for self-gratification becomes uppermost so he is unable to project his attention outside himself, the person is very sick. The condition may take another form and in an extreme case may result in complete withdrawal where all communication with the outside world is cut off. The connection between his inner (fantasy) world and the outer world (reality) is severed, and he lives in his fantasy world; we then refer to him as insane.

Handwritings of insane people vary, as do their particular kinds of mental illnesses. A great deal of research has already been done in this field by serious graphologists, but a great deal more remains to be done. Psychiatrists are, more than in former years, enlisting the aid of graphologists in making diagnoses; they submit patients' handwritings for analyses, and compare them with their own psychiatric findings. Graphology, for so long considered the stepchild of psychology in the United States, is finally finding a respectable place among the projective tools; it is being used by clinical psychologists in connection with Rorschach tests, T.A.T.'s (Thematic Apperception Tests), and others. A course in graphology is being offered in the New School in New York City, and experiments are being performed under scientific check in various universities.

To the alert eye of the expert graphologist, any form of neurosis, psychosis, or psychopathy is readily apparent in handwriting, though it is only through further research and cooperation with psychiatrists that the graphologist can discover the true nature of the illness. In European countries this has been going on for many years; in the United States it has had a good beginning, and the research continues.

The Alcoholic

In the alcoholic, in whose handwriting we find all the signs of the neurotic, we have a person who suffers from a compulsion neurosis. To understand what led him into a pattern of excessive drinking, we must look back to his childhood to learn what his conditioning influences were. Usually we will find an oversensitive child, orally deprived and experiencing rejection. There may be an over-protective mother and a strict father—sometimes a cold and un-loving mother—and the child is yanked in different directions, so he is not certain whether he is loved, approved of, or even wanted. Very early in his life he develops resentment toward parent domi-nation—and from then on he is rebellious against authority.

There are many types of alcoholics—from the extreme extrovert who makes a bid for attention by getting drunk and making a nui-sance of himself, to the extreme introvert who finds that the "magic liquid" loosens his inhibitions and lets him act more socially. There are common denominators in the handwriting of alcoholics no mat-ter what their temperament, and the same signs appear in the hand-writing of compulsive-obsessive neurotics. First, there is usually the sign of energy, more readily released when the alcoholic is in pursuit of his bottle. This misdirected drive, if applied to something con-structive, might result in unusual achievement. Since alcohol is a drug and a depressant, the excessive drinker under the influence will show signs of depression in his handwriting. Another common denomi-nator is the desire for perfection. The alcoholic is always reaching out for the unattainable (perfection), setting his goals so high that he is unable to attain them; and, feeling frustrated, he takes to the bottle.

Another strong factor in the alcoholic is guilt, which often over-whelms him and sends him scurrying for the bottle, ostensibly to drown such feelings; it doesn't always work. Guilt is shown in a number of signs, the most outstanding being the *t* bar that does not go through the stem of the letter. That he is rebellious and feels him-self an outcast shows in the same kind of weak *t* bar that slants down-ward and does not go through the stem. (Arrogant weakness.) The alcoholic, as well as most neurotics, uses a form of projection to cut the other fellow down to size. He projects his own feelings onto someone else because it alleviates his own sense of inadequacy. And alcoholics, although supersensitive to criticism, are usually extremely critical themselves, finding fault with little things, dramatizing situ-ations to make themselves appear important. They are all emotion-ally immature, self-centered, and dependent; they resent the very people on whom they are dependent, and their drinking is an expression of defiance. They are angry people and were often problem children who somewhere lost their way on the road to maturity.

Actually, the alcoholic is a soul-sick person, and in every alcoholic's handwriting there will be signs of a spiritual quality struggling for release. (We are not talking here of the psychotic whose drinking has resulted in the Korsakov psychosis, who has what may be described as "wet brain" and who is disorientated in time, for he is usually an institutional case.) We are concerned here with the alcoholic who can eventually adjust to reality, of whom there are many. And in examining their handwriting, we can discover signs of hope and a chance for recovery. Alcoholism, although a physical illness, is also a symptom of some deep inner disturbance that starts in childhood. Since to date there seems to be no valid cure, the next best thing is to cope with the symptom, and for this we have a number of symptom therapies, the most successful of which has been the fellowship of Alcoholics Anonymous.

In the following specimen we have an example of a woman alcoholic who made an adjustment to reality through Alcoholics Anonymous and has been "dry" for a number of years.

She was the first child in a family of two girls, with a cold selfish mother who was probably incapable of showing much love, so that from the very outset Mrs. G. did not feel a closeness to her mother. She was a solitary, sensitive, and impressionable little girl, reared by servants and given all the material comforts; but obviously there was a paucity of love. Her father was seldom at home, for his business required that he travel.

Mrs. G. says: "When he came home, he always brought a book for me, usually of fairy tales. I loved them." Already at age six, she was identifying with the fictional characters in the fairy tales. "I also found that I could play the piano by ear and started lessons which I continued for 30 years at least." Her piano was her closest companion at an early age. "I was chubby as a child and loved to eat" (she was feeding herself the love she did not get from her mother) "but it wasn't until I married that I got really fat" (235 pounds). "My sister and I were really brought up by servants. Father was out of town a lot and mother went somewhere every day

Recovered Alcoholic

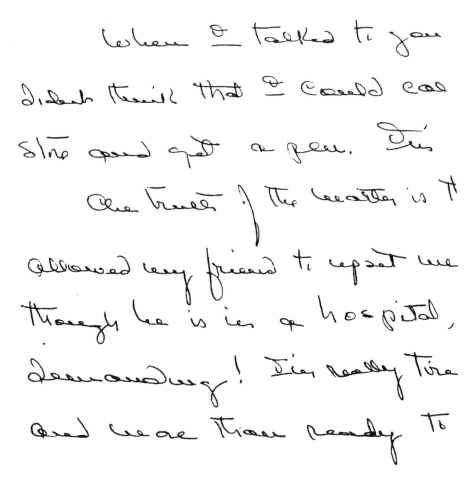

SPECIMEN 132

in a social way. I think of my childhood as being lonely, although I
did have a few friends at school." (She did not get close to anyone,
since she got no warmth or closeness in her formative years.)

"I was fourteen when I met my first husband, was extremely shy
but hid it with a very brusque manner. . . . At sixteen we eloped. . . .
Within a year I became pregnant and started to *eat and gain*." (The

orality manifesting itself is not unusual with an orally deprived child.) "When I was about 23, my sister was divorced and came to live with me and my husband." (The sister, also an alcoholic, still drinks.) "She had started drinking and I disapproved, but after she had lived with us for about a year I tried taking a drink. What a relief and release! I had always been so tense and ill at ease except when eating or reading. Now, here was almost an instant cure! At first, I drank only on weekends, but being extreme in everything it wasn't long before alcohol was practically *my life*. By the time I was 28 I was a full-fledged alcoholic. . . . Soon after this I got a divorce. There were physical symptoms, too, for my kidneys became affected and the doctor told me I would have to stop drinking for at least a year. I started to do this but was so miserable, it wasn't long before I was back on the merry-go-round again. I went to Florida where I met my second husband who was a heavy drinker. This suited me fine. My greatest ambition then was to 'drink like a lady' and I controlled it for a couple of months, but it wasn't long before I was drinking like anything but a lady! I had a recurring dream for years after I married. I dreamed that I was wandering in an old, abandoned house, very large, many rooms. It had once been very handsome and the furnishings were very costly, but now there was dust everywhere, the curtains hung in tatters. Sometimes some other people would be there but always people I didn't know. After I joined A.A. I stopped having it. . . ." (A simple dream, not difficult for even the amateur to analyze; house is symbolic.)

Mrs. G. had been hospitalized a number of times for her drinking, and every time she came out she swore she'd never touch the stuff again—but the compulsion was stronger than her strongest resolve. And, as she concludes: "I could not imagine my life without alcohol, but with the philosophy and fellowship of A.A. I found that answer and a new life, and although that was years ago I still try to practice these principles—the 12 steps in AA—in all my affairs."

We see in her handwriting the pattern of isolation she developed very early in her life in the left slant. Nevertheless, there is a roundness (turn the specimen upside down and it will be more obvious) that, coupled with some breadth, tells us of pliability and kindness. She has the sign of the perfectionist in the high *t* bars, especially noticeable in "matter" and "than" (in last line); some *t* bars slant downward, indicating assertiveness, and there are signs of intuition in the breaks between letters, which indicate her ability to see through situations and people. Although she enjoys being by herself, she also has a capacity for deep and lasting friendships. There are the signs of culture in the Greek *d* and literary *g*, pointing to her preoccupation with reading since childhood. The lines are well-spaced; so are margins and spaces between words; and there is evidence of talent in printed small letters (the *s*). The energetic drive is lessened, although she does have spurts of enthusiasm (shown in the *t* bar flying away from the stem in "store"), and rising lines indicate her optimism, which originally led her to seek help in A.A. Her capital *I* is unique and points to a mild form of eccentricity, but it also reveals some persistence, and this helped her to gain sobriety and sustain it.

In Specimen 133 we are confronted with the active but not deteriorated alcoholic—a man with energy and drive which he uses inconsistently, depending upon the direction in which his inner conflict leads him. It looks messy and is a mirror of his turbulent emotions. Yet there are good signs here that tell us that deep down this man can be kind, generous, and concerned with helping another person. (See the altruistic *y* in "discrepancy.") In this kind of hand, and knowing that the writer is a homosexual, we construe this same sign as one of masochism, that is, a form of self-punishment (which his alcoholism engenders to a point). Yet he has talent, and when he is sober he can be creative, for he also has imagination. The *t* bar above the stem in "qualities" is a clue to his perfectionism, which he probably applies to his work. But it is more than that: It shows his reaching up, even though he falls by the wayside in doing so. There are signs of persistence in the looped *t*'s; but you can see the depressive results of the drug he ingested in the falling over of the word on the second line and in the tendency of all the words to droop. There is no uniformity in the letter forms or the spacing or pen pressure. He is in a state of confusion and irrationality—the constructive tendencies are turned in a destructive direction, and the masochism expressed tells us that the direction is self-destruction.

Active Alcoholic

SPECIMEN 133

The Hippie

The common denominator of the hippie is immaturity and in many instances a regression to the infantile pattern of behavior. Their oral deprivation sometimes expresses itself in taking drugs, marijuana, LSD. They are the rejected, disinherited children who feel their parents do not understand them; they are afraid of life and herd together for safety. In most of their handwriting are signs or restlessness and the lack of self-discipline; they were the neglected and unloved children (or they felt neglected and unloved), and despite their "love-ins" few of them have a capacity for mature love. They are in rebellion against an older generation that, they feel, seeks to impose on them an authority they resent. Their ornamented garb is an attention-getting device. In many of them are the roots of the problem child. Among them are some who are talented but whose talents have not been sufficiently encouraged. Others are victims of broken homes or of parental cruelty. Many hippies are simply successors to the Beat Generation, but there are some people who are hippies by temperament, though they are older. All of them fall within the category of the so-called Bohemian; that is perhaps why a large number of them live in the East Village in New York City, or in the Haight-Asbury section of San Francisco, or in other sections of the country where the artistic temperament finds freedom of expression. They speak of being free, not realizing that freedom itself is a responsibility. That segment that can assume responsibility has its fling, leaves the subculture of the hippie environment and returns to a more conventional life.

Teenage Hippie

SPECIMEN 134

This handwriting of a so-called hippie shows the child plainly in the very rounded formations, coupled with the weak *t* bars that do not (or barely) go through the stem. But there is hope for her making a practical adjustment, since she has a desire to study beauty culture; some day, and with the proper encouragement and help, she could succeed. The circle *i* dot tells us that she considers herself different; it also means she could develop manual deftness, as she has a natural bent in this direction. The vertical angle expresses signs of passivity and isolation, forced on her by elements in her environment. Yet she can also be outgoing and responsive when she senses she is on friendly soil. (The unfriendly soil is her home environment in which a stepfather subjected her to physical cruelty and threatened to shoot her in the back!)

She is 18, yet there is something old-fashioned in her outlook (a contradiction perhaps), shown in the protective *A* in "And," and in her relationship with another hippie, a boy her own age, she is maternal and permissive. There are hopeful signs in her handwriting that she has enough determination to extricate herself from the mess she is in. But she needs help from someone she can trust, someone who will show her the kindness she did not have in her home environment.

The following Specimen 135 is written by what can only be described as an adult hippie. She is in her 50's and not without an element of maturity, but she is a wanderer who has something of the gypsy philosophy: She lives one day at a time, and when the going gets rough she uses her training as a registered nurse to smooth out the economic wrinkles. Despite signs of a weak will and a lack of discipline in some areas, she retains a tenacity (in the hook at the end of the words "my" and "buy") that tells us she hangs on to life—which she feels is a drama in which she plays her particular role. Her nurse's training is her ace in the hole, but she is a person without roots, a female version of the bindlestiff who goes through life with his pack on his back and takes lodging where he may. A history of her early environment would give us clues to the influences that formed her character. If she were of this generation, she would probably be a constructive factor among the lost children. The kind of *t* bar that appears in the word "postage" (there are others like it in the full specimen not shown here) tells us definitely that following the line of least resistance is a habit of long standing.

Adult Hippie

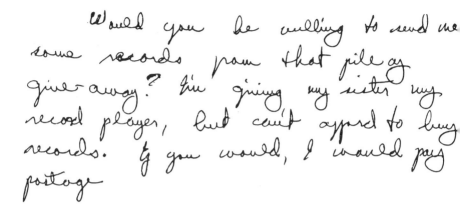

The Drug Addict

This was written under the influence of heroin. The writer is in control of his faculties up to the point where the fear of the effects of the drug wearing off causes him to become anxious, depressed, and suspicious. He is—as are all addicts, whether the addiction be alcohol or heroin—a very angry young man, as is seen in the dark endings of *t* bars, as well as in the uneven pen pressure. The latter is the clue to emotional instability. In the vertical angle we see a person who plans deliberately rather than one who rushes impulsively into ventures. There is something of the child in him—the orally deprived child—noticeable in the rounded formations; he is above average in intelligence, as some of his mental formations reveal (in the *h*'s and the *b*'s, where the first stroke is unlooped). He dissimulates (shown in the word "dream," fourth line, fourth word), and like most addicts is almost incapable of telling the truth. He has lots of energy and drive (he is 23), but his energies lead in a self-destructive direction. He has difficulty staying on a straight line in his writing, just as in life. Yet there are hopeful signs: He has a strong will, which, if redirected, could result in his being constructive. Despite all the disturbances revealed in this specimen, there is still a desire for order,

Drug Addict (under influence)

This morning I bought a hundred
of heroin. Then I preceded to t
otis Moss.

I had a dream this afternoon as
up here It was so good I could
the whole set up. I was in
business big time. I gave my br
a job for the winter driving
I built a nice garage up on th
a couple of new trucks. Making
money. new car the works. Felt
I think nice thoughts but do n
to ~~sacrifice~~ the time and effort

SPECIMEN 136

Drug Addict (not under influence)

SPECIMEN 137

Drug Addict (under hypnosis)

SPECIMEN 137A

as shown in the spacing of the lines on the page; this, however, tells us there is method to his madness.

The above specimens are the result of a controlled experiment with a drug addict: 137 was written without the influence of the drug, while the person was trying to kick the habit cold turkey; 137A was written while under hypnosis. The patient was a doctor whose intense emotions led him into taking drugs to allay his anxieties. He finally reached the point where life became untenable, and being a fighter (as the downstrokes of the *t* bar show consistently in Specimen 137A), he made up his mind to submit to any form of therapy that would cure him. As this was before the days of Methadon, he chose hypnosis as a way of finding some relief from his intense suffering.

Specimen 137 is a striking example of terrible depression and anger, and yet it shows determination to put up a fight. It reads: "Don't lose confidence in me, stand by me till I get this Drug out of me."

Under hypnosis, he is freed from the overwhelming craving, and his writing (137A) takes on a brighter aspect, almost a euphoric optimism. It reads: "Am Happy I am going to be well so we can make [money] & cure people."

Here the aggressiveness shown in the first specimen is dissipated and replaced by hope, shown not only in the uplift of the basic line but also by the sign of control revealed in the kind of *t* bar in the word "to." The sign of altruism shown in both specimens, though it also points to his masochism and self-destructiveness, takes on a positive meaning in his desire to "cure people." Later history revealed that he made a comeback and concentrated on the cure of other drug addicts.

The following two specimens were written by a young woman, not a drug addict, but one who experimented with one of the hallucinogenic, consciousness-expanding drugs.

Under the influence of the drug (138), the handwriting expanded, showing a broadening of vision as she "turned on"; but she seemed still to be in control, as the *t* bars remained firm. The caution remained intact, as seen in the closed *a*'s and *o*'s, but inhibitions were somewhat released—shown in angles that vary slightly from vertical to rightward. Senses are sharpened, as is inner awareness, but something happened to the will, albeit slightly, as shown in the formation of the letter *t* in "than" (second line) and in the last word, "this." Her habit pattern was slightly disturbed, for normally she crosses her *t*'s with firmness and determination. But in this specimen, as in the one following, there is an absence of *i* dots, and this gives us a clue to blind spots on the unconscious level, whether she is function-

Hallucinogenic Drug (under influence)

ations to people we love (+ ove) finds us — more than inal correllative noises, more prospect of discussing this

SPECIMEN 138

Next Day—Without the Drug

for the future growth of international look towards the day when outer be used for territorial observation.

SPECIMEN 138A

ing normally or abnormally while under the influence of a drug.

Returning to normalcy the next day (138A), she is now a person of well-ordered mind, well disciplined and capable of clear thinking; but there are signs of repressions and inhibitions which often made her feel imprisoned. She sought release from her imprisonment and found it in a measure of emotional expansion, where her instinctive altruism (the *g* in "discussing") gave her a greater feeling of love for her fellowman.

Timothy Leary

The hairline sensitivity of the prophet of the "turn on, tune in" cult shows at once in the light pen pressure of his handwriting. But its outstanding feature speaks of a keen intellect that has been sub-

Timothy Leary

Enclosed is one of the 6 missing chapters for EX-STATIC ESSAYS. The original is just being submitted for magazine publication.

The 5 remaining fugitive manues. are in New York and I'll assemble them on Feb 6th when we arrive in N.Y.C.

This — is Chapter 14

Peace and good wishes

[signature]

dued. The nature is essentially gentle, as shown in many rounded formations; there is obvious talent in the printed capitals and some small letters. The capital *T* in his signature "Tim" is unique, an expression of his unique personality. But the energy seems vitiated. We see instead a lethargy in the rhythm, corroborated by weak, ineffectual *t* bars. The bowed *t* bars—and there are several, though even these lack real force—tell us of his spirituality; Mr. Leary is cogent and rational when he talks of raising yourself to a higher level of consciousness, for he has done this himself.

A definite lack of robustness characterizes the writing, showing physical symptoms of poor health, as letter forms lack force despite their clarity. Some words taper, showing consideration and tact. The small *b* is tightly closed, indicating caution; and this, combined with such wide spacing between words, gives us the clue to paranoid trends. He seems to be living in a fog. Too much intimacy on the part of others arouses his suspicion; he prefers to keep his distance, and few, if any, develop a real closeness to him despite his friendliness. The high *i* dots and *t* bars—weak as they are—nevertheless point to delusional thinking, to a person with Messianic goal. (This is most likely a redirecting of beliefs inculcated in him during his formative years.)

Many *i*'s are not dotted and *t*'s not crossed. This combination tells us he isn't always "with it" where reality is concerned. He draws blanks, so to speak, is often absent-minded, prefers not to remember things related to his past which might be painful. Yet here is an imaginative, extremely intuitive man, more concerned with real values than with material possessions. His sincerity is unquestioned in his belief that life could be better through the use of psychedelic drugs. But his handwriting is a poor testimonial to this, for it reveals a man whose starch has been taken out, whose talents are not being fully put to use. His intuition sometimes is inspirational, an indication that at heart Dr. Leary is really something of a poet.

The Homosexual

The homosexual, more sinned against than sinning, is the product of his early environment and, in some cases, the victim of a glandular imbalance. There is a division of opinion about the physical components that result in homosexuality. Many homosexuals are extremely talented, and many make contributions to the arts. A few may look like caricatures of women, but they are the extroverts who call attention to themselves by their mannerisms, dress and unconventional behavior. There are, however, a large number—the vast majority—who function successfully in the heterosexual society, in the face of widespread hostility and medieval laws that treat them as criminals. The adjusted homosexual who accepts his way of life is no threat to society, and those who are critical of him might do well to examine the reasons for their hostility to a way of life that in no way interferes with their own.

To be sure, we may find in the handwriting of homosexuals negative traits—viciousness, envy, greed—but these are traits found in heterosexuals as well, often to a greater degree. At the root of the homosexual's attitude is anger, but we find this expressed in the handwriting of fairly well-adjusted people, as well as in that of neurotics. The fact that the homosexual is not accepted by society is a good reason for his anger—but it goes deeper than that. In his early childhood there was a controlling mother and usually a weak father with whom the boy could not identify; the seed of anger begins there. As a small boy, he is usually more sensitive than the average child, and may be tormented and harassed by the school bully, so already we see good reasons for his rebelliousness and in many instances his turning inward.

The common denominators of the homosexual, as they appear in handwriting, are signs of narcissism, masochism, and emotional immaturity. Many are still children concerned (as children are) with their own bodies; this results in narcissism. Others, with common sense, often marry in order to wear the coat of respectability, and eventually adjust to a heterosexual relationship. Some choose to enter a monastery, which offers a solution to their sexual problems and allows them to sublimate their sex drives in a religious vocation. Homosexuality has been with us for a long time and there is some hope for its acceptance in this enlightened age with the advent of the Mattachine Society.

Following are two specimens of homosexuals: one a man, the other a woman.

Specimen 140 belongs to a very talented dress designer whose en-

Homosexual (male, active)

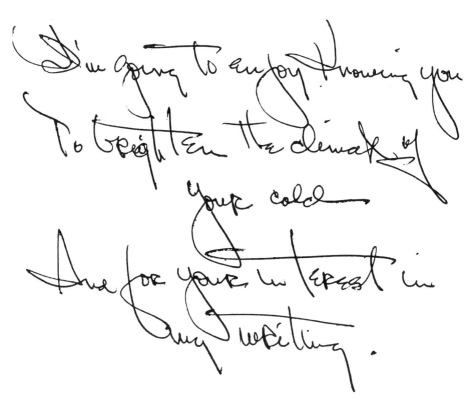

SPECIMEN 140

ergetic drive is shown in the long *t* bars with hooks on the end that tell us he is compulsive. The long, swinging lower loops that run into the line below tell us of his strong dramatic instinct, as well as a strong desire for material possessions. These show also that his fantasies spill over into his world of reality, and he often lives in fantasy. He often expects from others what they are unable to give, and although he makes lavish gestures, he himself is rather cautious and self-centered. His own comfort comes first, and his narcissism is so apparent as to make it overwhelming. (This is seen clearly in his signature, which for obvious reasons is not shown here.) His defensiveness shows in the downstroke of the *t* bar in the second "to." The formation of the two letters in the words "going" (where the *g* and *o* run together) and "your" (where the *y* and *o* are intertwined) tells us of his secretiveness, and the printed small letters *s* and *r* show his sense of design. He has intuition, which, in a hand with so much exaggeration, takes the form of suspicion and shows paranoid trends; and although the angle of the writing is vertical, with a slight tendency to lean left, this is no introvert. He is the exception to the rule concerning vertical writers, for he is very much the showman, the exhibitionist, making a bid for attention in various ways—and one of them is by showing his physique. Blunt ending strokes, as in the word "interest," show his obstinacy as well as his anger; but he is not without a sense of humor, seen in the *i* dots and other curved variations throughout the writing. So here we have the common denominators of the homosexual: narcissism; emotional immaturity, in rounded, often childlike curves; defensiveness in the *t* described; and masochism, shown in the rightward turn of the downstroke on *g* and *y*. In a different kind of hand this stroke would mean altruism, but since there are distortions in this writing, the sign has a different meaning. In catering to his self-centeredness, he would make a small gesture of generosity—he would throw a minnow to catch a whale.

Homosexual (female, reconstructed)

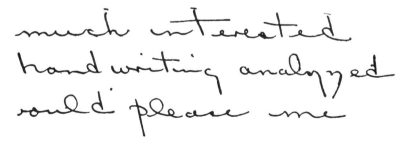

SPECIMEN 141

Here, in Specimen 141 (a woman), is what might be called a reconstructed homosexual. The outstanding sign of her departure from the norm is in the way she writes her *d*'s consistently. It is an inverted letter form, the opposite of what she was taught in school. She is reserved, yet, as seen in the breadth of the writing, not withdrawn. She can be friendly without becoming really intimate with others. She has drive and determination, and therefore keeps herself in control; her head rules, rather than her emotions.

The intuitive faculty, seen in the breaks between letters, shows a capacity for gaining insight, not only into others but into herself as well. After several years of psychoanalysis she made the decision to abandon her homosexual existence and take up a heterosexual life. She is now married and the mother of two children, and in the roundness of her writing we can see she is a kind, attentive mother who rears her children with common sense and judgment.

The original sign of flexibility so apparent here in a lack of rigid forms is what led her into seeking help for her problem and responding to it. She has made a good adjustment and is much happier, better balanced, and more constructive than before. Some formations look artistic; she has been teaching art to children and enjoying it.

The Suicide

From the records of the New York City Medical Examiner's office I have secured the handwriting of a man who committed suicide. The record states: Depression because of business reverses. The man was found dead in a bathtub. The following note (in part) was what he left behind. Notice how the lines droop, showing a depression amounting to hopelessness.

Essentially, this man was very neurotic, lived very much in fantasy, as shown in the *t* bar above the stem in the word "last." Other *t* bars do not go through the stem and reveal his indecision, lack of self-confidence, and preoccupation with the past. It is also the sign of emotional immaturity. He was, despite the slight rightward angle, very much the introvert, turning inward, riddled with guilt and anxiety, and unable to face reality. The records further revealed that he got drunk before the final act, for even this took a kind of courage he did not have. There was no fight in him, though there are signs

Suicide (last letter)

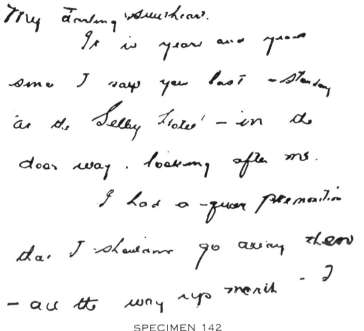

SPECIMEN 142

that in some situations he could exert some will power. But his masochism, shown in the rightward turn of the downstroke on the *y* in "way," eventually led him to kill himself. He was suffering from soul-sickness and had lost contact with the deep inner core of his being. Even the words hang over, showing that the depression was deep and of long duration. It was not an impulsive act, and his business reserves were a cover-up for deeper causes. The premonition he mentions means he had often thought about suicide, and his intuition told him that this is the way he would close the books.

Marilyn Monroe

Specimen 143 is the handwriting of Marilyn Monroe, who ostensibly committed suicide. From her handwriting, which shows none of the signs of the suicide, we can only conclude that her death was an accident. For here we see a love of life, a heightening

Marilyn Monroe

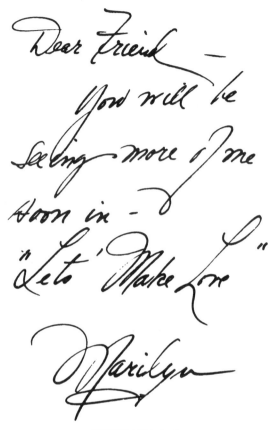

SPEC...EN 143

of the energies on the least provocation, and certain visionary ideals that she realized in her position in show business.

It is true that there were mild paranoid trends in her make-up, but no more than would be found in anyone in her position at the top —after starting at the bottom. The rightward flow tells us she had an absolute need for human companionship, and could be generous with those who showed her love. There are signs of talent, of a dramatic instinct, of a desire to be outstanding—in the form of the capital *M*, as well as in the underscore. Though large, the writing does not show much expansiveness, and despite her desire to give, this was attended by fears of being hurt if she did. She could be rigid and unyielding in some instances, as shown in the angular formation of the *s* in "soon" and in the short finals. Nevertheless, she could make a generous gesture, as the long final in "Friend" shows; but essentially Marilyn was a child with a longing for something she never had, and she sometimes despaired of ever finding it. Her last gesture would appear to be one lacking in judgment rather than a deliberate taking of her life, for she was compulsive, and in following a compulsion she overdid what might have been a temporary escape from reality.

Richard Speck (brain damage)

1-13-67

I understand Dr. Ziporyn is writing a book about me. I am glad he is doing this, because he is the only person who knows anything about me. I want the world to know what I am really like, and I feel he is the one who can tell about me.

Richard F Speck

SPECIMEN 144

Richard Speck

What would cause a boy who is known to neighbors, friends and schoolmates as a "well-mannered, good boy" to commit a heinous crime, seemingly without any previous overt actions on his part and not premeditated? Psychiatrists have puzzled over this, although deep analysis might point up such possibility to the astute analyst. Yet Whitman, the young man who shot down so many people from the tower in Texas, warned his psychiatrist that this is what he was about to do. What seemed like fantasy turned out to be reality.

In the case of Richard Speck, there were no warning signals set up, and he was not in analysis, although his history showed instability and unpredictability and might have given clues to later actions.

I have obtained from Speck's psychiatrist, Dr. Marvin Ziporyn, permission to use Speck's handwriting to show the signs of the brain damage that, in effect, was directly responsible for his crime. It reveals at first glance the roundness we see in the handwriting of children, and to the uninitiated eye it may appear harmless. But on close observation, signs come to light that tell us a great deal about his attitudes, his style of life, and indications of brain damage.

The ineffectual downslanting *t* bars which do not go through the stem are evidence of his arrogant weakness and disclose repressed anger which was released under the influence of alcohol. Words written close together tell us he lived in a narrow, caulked-in world of private meanings which he permitted no one to enter. Thus, lines of communication with the outside world were nil, and in a sense he was the world. The scratching out of words was his way of struggling mentally for self-expression—as a physical cripple might have difficulty walking—and this is further shown in a combination of a distorted ego (see the way he makes his capital *I*'s) and a difficulty in clarifying his thoughts (shown in the fourth line "I want"). The rhythm of the writing is slow, and the specimen is painfully executed. This type of *y*, which curls under in "Ziporyn," "only," "really," has come to be recognized as being prevalent in the handwriting of the juvenile delinquent. Notice that the word "Dr." is written with a small *d* instead of a capital; this is usually construed as a lack of respect for authority, something ingrained from early childhood.

Actually he is the child—rebellious, angry, obstinate, and hypersensitive. The rising lines show a kind of optimism that approaches euphoria, a belief that he could accomplish anything he set out to do —although this was in fantasy. In reality, he is timid, self-conscious, fearful, lacking self-confidence. The omission of letters in words— characteristic of brain damage—is evident in the first word of the fourth line; then the mind does a double-take trying to express the thought—"anying thing" when he wanted to write "anything." We see this twist again in the words meant to be "I am." The combination of the broad *r*, as in "Ziporyn" and "really," and an amazingly retentive memory (in the carefully dotted *i*'s) reveals his almost photographic memory for recalling what he has seen. But there are no signs of insight; the letters are all connected, and he therefore reasons in his own laborious way, with a self-centered logic of his own and with a method akin to madness not generally observed by the outside world. Nor does he have any conception of the enormity of his crime, for to him it was tantamount to a child shooting down so many clay pigeons. That he chose women as his victims shows his hostility toward his mother, developed very early in his life. The book *Born to Raise Hell* by Dr. Marvin Ziporyn* reveals a great deal that corroborates our graphological findings.

Walter Tjunin

At age 17 Walter had already been in a reformatory, and it was not long after his release that he committed the crime that made headlines: killing a 15-year-old girl to whom he was attracted. It gave him a release for pent-up frustration and anger, abnormally directed because of brain damage. His history revealed that he had been dropped as a child, although the parents were not aware of the extent of the damage. But in his handwriting here, the signs are obvious. He is more aggressive than is Speck, for his *t* bars are strong and tend downward, accompanied by the squared-off formation of the *y*, which is usually the sign of aggressiveness. But the actual brain damage is indicated in the omission of letters in words ("abut" instead of "about," whereas in "hade" we have an added letter). See how the word "visit" is spelled—in two places an *i* is omitted; and there are many other errors.

Here also the tempo of the writing is slow and laborious, similar to Speck's. Rounded formations belong, again, to the child: the angry one whose unconscious hostility toward his mother caused him to murder a girl to whom he was attracted. There were no outward signs of his unpredictability, although the crippling effects of the brain damage would, naturally, place him in this category. And here, too—as with Speck—there is a logic of his own: the letters in words are all connected and reveal no insight into himself or others. The pen pressure is uneven and reveals his emotional instability. He starts writing at a vertical angle; thus he appears self-contained at first, until

---

* Grove Press, New York, 1967.

Walter Tjunin (brain damage)

Dear Mom + Dad

. I hope when you receive this
letter you are in the best of health.
And don't worry abut me I'm
doing fime. I was glad to .
see you when you came to
vist me. And eventhing is
fine heard. And thanks for
the Chess set and the candy
too. Well I hade a good time
when you and other pople
came to vist me. And I received
a letter from the girl that I
have told you about. And I
hope you wrote a letter to
Mr. Cohen. about me going
down this week end. Well I
guess I wrote enouth for
now

You Son
Walter

SPECIMEN 145

the conflict raging within him finds extreme expression—and without the use of outer stimuli. He is a seething volcano that erupted.

The following specimen is unidentified; it belongs to an adult with a different type of brain damage.

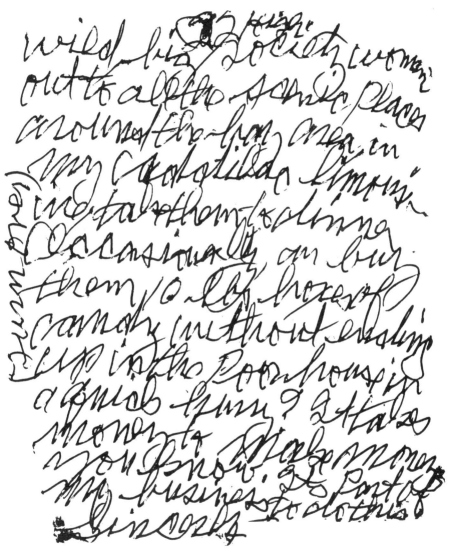

SPECIMEN 146

He was kicked by a horse in later life (not childhood) and this disturbed the physical brain. The early psychological overtones of hostility and feelings of rejection are absent, and the man actually tries to function despite his confusion, and he does so sporadically when not in great pain. There is an attempt—valiant, to be sure—to be cooperative, social, generous, and he exerts as much self-discipline as is possible considering the damaged machinery he has to work with. There is no lack of energy here; the man is motivated in his actions by feelings most of the time, although he does have brief periods of lucidity.

Cushioned in early life by love and a closeness to his mother, he has developed into a warm, expansive individual, capable of coping with the vicissitudes of life and even capable of functioning constructively —as far as his crippled brain will allow. His ego has remained intact, and although there are signs of neurosis, there is also an ability to make adjustments. The disturbed rhythm, evident all through the writing, tells us of his faulty motor faculties, but because of a will to hurdle obstacles (shown in the *t* bar in "society" in the first line) we have a man who has overcome great trials and thus has a built-in strength.

Mary Fallon (mouth writing)

SPECIMEN 147

Mary Fallon

As a result of a fall, when Mary was about 20, she injured her spine, which caused paralysis, and lay on her back for twenty-five years in a city hospital on Welfare Island. Her body had finally atrophied after numbness set in, and all she could use was her head. Being artistic, she asked the woman who attended her for many years to put a brush between her teeth, and with this she learned to paint on sheer fabrics which were stretched for her on a frame.

Her writing, done with the paintbrush, proves that no matter what a person writes with—hands, feet, or mouth—the character, disposition, and innate talents will be revealed. (The unretouched specimen is reduced to one-third its original size.)

The roundness of the letter forms show her childlike, credulous nature, untouched and unembittered by her misfortune. Although her confinement prevented contact with the outside world, she was always pleasant and cheerful, communicating with patients in neighboring beds and beloved by the attendants in the hospital. The good spacing and margins are clues to an instinctive love of order and beauty, and point to artistic potentialities. *T* bars show her fortitude and, coupled with carefully dotted *i*'s, reveal her attention to detail. The rhythm is disturbed and lacking in coordination, but the entire specimen shows infinite patience, and the capitals reveal an ego that remained intact. Because of her ability to cooperate, her desire to communicate and to make her contribution, to give of herself to the fullest she was able, she made a remarkable adjustment in her circumscribed world.

Forrest Layman

Similarly, Specimen 148 was executed by the toes of an armless man in a circus. I asked him if he could do it, and here is the result. The muscular coordination is better here than in the writing of Mary Fallon, and there is a lilt to his wavy *t* bar that tells us he has humor and flair. The rising lines show his optimism and cheerfulness. Flourishes on capital letters indicate a measure of personal vanity, developed as a compensation for his physical deficiency, and it has given him the drive to support himself in the most useful way he thought

Forrest Layman (foot writing)

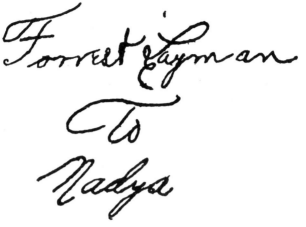

SPECIMEN 148

he could. There are evidences of showmanship and extroversion, and in his arrangement of the words—few as they are—we see an artistic bent. There is one break in his last name, but even this one is a clue to his quickness of perception: He can sense how people react to him. Here, too, is the spirit of cooperation—he did not hesitate to write for me—which helped him adjust to a life without arms. The chances are that even if he had arms, he would have sought a career in connection with show business.

Lee Harvey Oswald

All the indications of the schizoid (split) personality with paranoid trends are seen in the variations, distortions, and contradictions of the alleged assassin of President Kennedy. The lines veer upward, which tells us of his periods of euphoria when he felt that nothing was impossible for him to accomplish. He could not keep at this high pitch for long, and then depression set in, and his anger resulted in sadism likely to be directed at someone who could not defend himself (his wife was often the target of his cruelty).

The gross fluctuations in letters (notice the difference between the word "that" in the second line and "of" in the last line) indicate emo-

Lee Harvey Oswald

Гостиница „МЕТРОПОЛЬ"
г. Москва

I Lee Horey Oswald do hereby request that my present citizenship in the United States of America, be revoked.

I have entered the Soviet Union for the express purpose of applying for citizenship in the Soviet Union, through the means of naturalization

I affirm that my allegiance is to the union of Soviet Socialist Republics.

SPECIMEN 149

tional instability, corroborated by changes in pen pressure, inconsistent rhythm, and a variety of *t* bars, many of them weak and not going through the stem. He could be compulsive at certain times, as shown in a few long *t* bars ("naturalization"), though his drive took a destructive direction because of his fierce anger. The dropped letters in "applying," with the exaggerated *y* running into the line below, and the instability of the line direction show wide mood swings, great self-concern, and confusion amounting to distortion. Gross enlargement of the final letter on some words indicates a dangerous impulsiveness and a tendency to act out fantasies. The omission of capital letters ("America" is written with a small *a*) shows either awe of or complete disrespect for authority. His name shows signs of distorted grandiosity in the first line of the specimen, and even more so in the final signature. The ego is generally weak and is coupled with an uncoordinated middle zone in a stringy light-pressure hand. This is commonly seen in FBI "wanted" posters. Sadistic fantasies (shown in the whiplash *t* bar in "through"—sixth line) tell us of the likelihood of explosive and violent acting-out of fantasies in a grandiose and megalomaniac fashion. The action may not be planned but rather done on impulse.

Oswald was fiercely jealous of the man he allegedly assassinated, envisioning himself in a ruling position. With such a distorted self-image as his signature reveals, it is reasonable to suppose that he could be adamant in setting himself against a world he never made.

Transvestite

SPECIMEN 150

Transvestite

Here is an example of the complete hermit—a man who wanted to be everything to himself, both man and woman. During the greater part of the year, he was the robust, healthy male with a letter in crew, an avid student with a scientific mind who could concentrate as a scientist might in a laboratory. He was, however, antisocial and made few friends.

During his vacations he lived in a cabin in the woods by himself, wore women's clothes made to fit him (he was over six feet), and played the role of a woman. He was not homosexual, merely egocentric and determined to live in his own world of private meanings in which he had no communication with the outside world.

His history revealed that he was an only child and indulged by both parents. His father wanted him to be a real hundred-percent boy; his mother dressed him in girl's clothes and let his hair grow in curls. To please each of them he assumed both roles. Since he is still enacting this schizoid pattern, he has carried it into his adulthood, deriving neurotic satisfaction from his own private and untrammeled world. What others think is not important to him, for to him they are so many microbes, as they would be in his microscopic vision. If this writing can be seen under a magnifying glass, signs of indecision, emotional immaturity, dwindling formations will come to light; and in all these we see the individual who does not reveal his real self to the world, which, for him, doesn't exist, since he is still living in fantasy. The well-spaced specimen, showing some degree of order, is what really saves him from going over the borderline into insanity.

Petit Mal

Although this handwriting looks disturbed (no doubt the 16-year-old boy who wrote it is disturbed), there is still a certain pattern to the writing, which looks like a design. He is interested in designing and can, out of all the confusion, make unusual designs of both simple and complicated mechanisms. He is fascinated by airplanes and knows a lot about them. (He asked to be permitted to design draperies for his aunt.)

The underlying cause of the apparent disturbance here is a brain malfunction which resulted in a petit mal. As a child he had difficulty speaking and even now is rather slow in articulating. But if the handwriting is observed closely, we see signs of a strong desire to help himself in the many bowed *t* bars. And although the writing looks cryptic, it is not illegible, and the words are readily discerned. There are, of course, signs of immaturity, which is to be expected in

Petit Mal

SPECIMEN 151

a boy of 16; but he makes an effort to be social and friendly, although his difficulty in communicating because of the physical defect makes him supersensitive and selective.

The broad *r* all through the writing is an important clue to his strong visual aptitude, important in any form of art (and in graphology), and despite his apparent departure from the norm, there is no reason why this boy could not make adjustments and ultimately be able to function successfully.

Senile Dementia

Although this woman, suffering from senile dementia, has moments of lucidity, the deterioration that has set in is aptly revealed in her disturbed-looking handwriting. We see the angles going in different directions—left, right, vertical; *t* bars vary—some show persistence; others are peculiarly formed. The basic line varies, too, go-

Senile Dementia

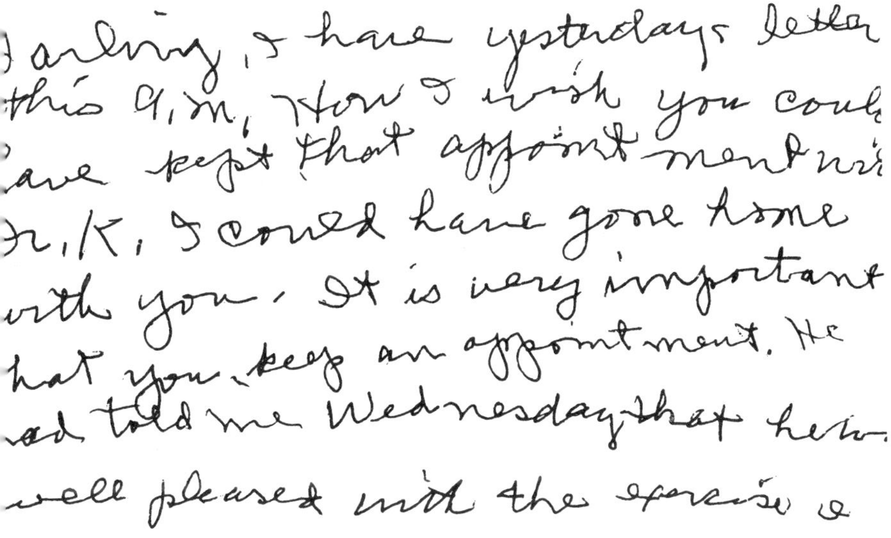

[handwritten specimen]

Darling, I have yesterdays letter this a.m. How I wish you could have kept that appointment with Dr. K. I could have gone home with you. It is very important hat you keep an appointment. He ad told me Wednesday that he... well pleased with the exercise a

SPECIMEN 152

ing up and down, showing moods that can change within a few minutes. Roundness is a clue to emotional regression to childhood, and at other times she becomes demanding and her writing becomes angular. The capital *I* varies also, from large to small, from leaning toward the left to being upright and ragged, which shows the evident deterioration. There is no uniformity of either capitals or small letters. She really does not know what she is doing most of the time. The controls are down and she needs custodial care, which she is getting in a mental institution.

Hysteria

The neurotic woman suffering from hysteria neurosis often finds escape from responsibilities (imposed on her by society) in physical symptoms. The origin of this type of neurosis is in the maladjustment

Hysteria

SPECIMEN 153

of the individual's sex life. Not all hysterics are in hospitals, for their cases may not be that extreme, but we have seen instances of women laughing wildly one minute and then soon afterward bursting into tears. Usually hysteria is the result of sexual repression where the individual finds no normal outlet for the sexual drive. (The word "hysteria" has its origin in the Greek word *hysta*, which means womb, and the legend has it that at certain times the womb became detached from its moorings and wandered around inside the body, causing outward signs of disturbance.)

For the most part, this ailment occurs in people of extroverted personality, and the handwriting will then reveal signs of emotional intensity with those of repression. The *t* bars will vary, as will the pen pressure. The hysterical person will be given to fits of activity when the sexual energy finds release or is sublimated, and this may readily show in tenacity hooks on *t* bars and other horizontal strokes. The same person will also have periods of inertia and complain of general exhaustion, which could be traced to frustrated sexual energy.

The hysterical female (men suffer from it too, though not to the same extent), feeling that her sex desires are being thwarted because of the conventional demands imposed upon her, may in protest break the rules and express herself by overindulgence or promiscuity. Should there occur a prolonged continence, due perhaps to fears of pregnancy or lack of opportunity, the unused, frustrated sex energy will express itself in fits of hysteria, especially when the imagination has full play and when there is a sympathetic audience.

The handwriting in Specimen 153 is one type of hysteric—a woman who can function as long as her energy keeps moving and she is active, but will retire to her room and in the privacy of it go through fits of weeping without really knowing why she does so. Tears can be a welcome release and have a temporary healing effect, but they are no solution to the problem of hysteria. The only solution is a normal, healthy sex life. This woman has been a widow for many years, and because of notions as to what men want of her, which she is unwilling to give (an attitude common to many women), she remains frustrated and takes out her frustrations in quarrels with others The writing is fairly large and shows extroversion, and she has momentary enthusiasms which take the edge off her tensions. But she can keep controlled only to a certain point, and then there is an outburst that can be described as orgiastic and resembles a volcanic eruption. (Wilhelm Reich expounds on this in his book *The Function of the Orgasm*.)

In this handwriting, there is compulsiveness and a desire to dominate situations; difficulty in cooperating, unless she can have the upper hand; strong sex impulses held in restraint. Although not a clinical case, she falls into this category, but is saved from reaching an extreme because of a preoccupation with religion—in which she finds some sublimation for her sex drive.

Heart Disease

In the handwriting of a person whose heart is physically affected to a point where it also affects the viewpoint, goals and vitality, there is one definite sign that reveals this. It is the broken or ragged upper loop. One such loop in a specimen may have little significance, may be the result of the pen scratching on the paper. But a repetition of such loops is a sign that something is radically wrong with the person making them. It may seem strange that this should occur in the very formation, the upper loop, which has been referred to graphologically as "the avenue of emotion." But there is evidently some motor connection between the hand and the heart, and as the hand records impressions in handwriting, this is the area that shows a malfunctioning, much as the encephalograph might show of the brain.

We speak of our hearts being broken when disappointment in love overwhelms us, or through the loss of a loved one. Yet this broken loop has no direct connection with the sentimental heartbreak, although the latter may be a contribution to it. It is essentially physical. The break or ragged formation registers in the pulse while the individual is writing and transfers itself to the paper through the hand wielding the pen. An occasional broken loop in a specimen of handwriting may hint of a defective heart where there is nervousness and it occasionally misses a beat. If such a sign is accompanied by other signs of devitalization and lack of energy, it is time for the graphologist to sound a warning. When we hear of a person dropping dead of a heart attack, the person himself may not have been aware of his bad heart. Yet his handwriting would have disclosed the symptoms, if examined when the person first complained, or if there was a history of high blood pressure or hypertension.

When all or most of the loops are broken or ragged, and the basic line sags on the page, and the pen pressure is light or feathery, we are confronted with an advanced case of heart disease, with other possible complications. Usually such a patient is already under treatment. Specimens 154 and 154A are examples of advanced cases with complications. The persons find that any action saps what little vitality they have. In cases of coronary thrombosis, an attack may come on very suddenly, although it is likely that the life of the victim was long fraught with tension, which aggravated the heart. In the handwriting of such patients there may be signs of good health, so that it takes the discerning eye of the graphologist to discover where the weakness exists. (Much research is yet to be done in this area, so that to date there is nothing clearly definitive in graphological data.)

Advanced Heart Disease (female patient)

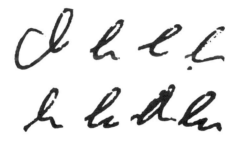

much but I would like to have some-thing to look forward

SPECIMEN 154

Heart Disease
(Male victim, taken from his last letter)

SPECIMEN 154A

Tuberculosis

In instances of tuberculosis, as in other chest ailments such as asthma or emphysema where the lungs are in some way affected, the handwriting is characterized by a tendency of the basic line to swing on the paper in a semicircular manner. The characteristic tendency of such patients to be optimistic is what causes the lines to rise, yet the expenditure of energy the optimism takes results in a lessening of energy. This is what causes the lines to swing downward toward the end. There will also be signs of inertia and lack of drive in weak *t* bars. The patient has no sustaining ambition despite the cheerfulness. Sometimes the advanced tubercular patient will get a spurt of ambition and make lavish plans, as if hanging on to life. A strong heart may keep him alive even after a lung has been collapsed through treatment, and the handwriting may show the person's difficulty in breathing by a spasmodic rhythm, while the pen pressure will be both light and dark, as though streaks of light enter his dark world, giving him hope for recovery.

Sex desires are often augmented through denial and may become apparent in the tendency of the pen pressure to become dark in lower loops or in other signs expressing sensuality. It is understandable that when someone is hanging on to life that the sex desires should become heightened, considering that sex is the primal instinct for perpetuation. We often see startling signs of life in a tubercular patient's writing if he is well enough to write, almost like a candle guttering into flame before it goes out.

The following specimen written in a foreign language (Yiddish), from right to left, shows something of this semicircular swing. The writer had a predisposition to tuberculosis and great difficulty in breathing. The small writing and light pen pressure tell us of his acute sensitivity, introversion, and powers of concentration. The rhythm is

Tuberculosis

SPECIMEN 155

consistent, for here was a man with definite musical talent, added to which he was a good mathematician. We are concerned here with the delicate health of the writer, and we see occasional darkening of the pen pressure when he was optimistic and felt hopeful; but in the end his malady overtook him, for this was written before the advent of the miracle drug which might have lengthened his life.

It should be mentioned that concerted research has been conducted by a dedicated graphologist, Alfred Kanfer, who after many years of examining handwriting of cancer patients has been given a grant to continue his researches at the Strang Clinic in New York City. It is hoped that his efforts will encourage other serious graphologists to conduct controlled experiments in cooperation with doctors, scientists, and psychiatrists, as well as with the police department (in connection with drug addiction), so that the world might be further enriched by their findings.

The Hunchback

If you are one of those people who sees pictures in handwriting, as Rafael Schermann* did in Germany some years ago, the semicircular swing (as far as the basic line is concerned) of the hunchback's handwriting will give you a clue that here is a person who is different in some way. (The hump is semicircular.) In him, the chest apparatus is naturally affected and apt to function abnormally. We see the same semicircular swing in the writing of the tubercular patient, the tendency of the lines to rise, revealing characteristic optimism; but the more lift the spirits have, the less is the energy—thus the tendency of the lines to come down toward the end of the line. In this specimen, there are signs of both inertia and periods of activity; some *t* bars are short and do not go through the stem, whereas others do, and in fact are strong and bowed. The short lower loops in a hand that appears to belong to a robust person (because of the pen pressure) tell us the writer does not indulge in physical

* A book about Rafael Schermann was called *Secrets of Handwriting* (1937, London, Rider and Co., translated by Prince S. Lubomirski). He was more a clairvoyant than a graphologist; he saw events that took place or were about to happen, in handwriting in the shape of guns, etc. The book was used by the police department in the solution of crimes.

The Hunchback

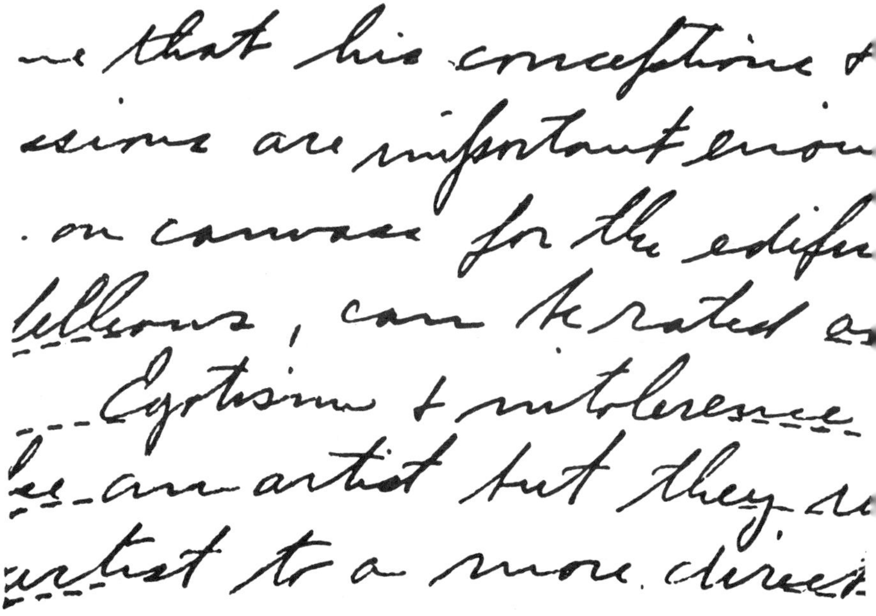
that his conceptions
are important enou
on canvas for the edifi
can be rated as
Egotism & intolerance
an artist but they
artist to a more direct

SPECIMEN 156

activity to any great extent. Sensuality is evident in pen pressure that has a pasty look, but it is transferred to the level of sensuousness because of signs of imagination in the high upper loops and high *i* dots.

Constructive (printed) formations show artistic ability. The person finds sublimation for his sexual urges (frustrated to a degree because of his malformation) in an art form. The speed with which the writing is done tells us he has a facility for expression, can express himself in writing as well as in conversation, is versatile, and has a sense of humor. This individual paints and writes poetry and art criticism.

The rightward angle reveals his outgoingness and his sentimentality, which manifests itself in his painting and poetry. His sex drive is sublimated in his painting, and he derives a substitute release in painting beautiful, romantic nudes.

PART TWO

How to Analyze Your

Own Handwriting

Oh wad some power the giftie gie us
To see oursel's as others see us!
It wad frae monie a blunder free us,
And foolish notion.
—ROBERT BURNS

For the student of graphology, it is important to realize that there are empirical rules to be followed when analyzing handwriting. These were established many years ago by the precursors of this study. There are exceptions that will become apparent after some experience, but the beginner would do well to stick by the rules. If a sign in handwriting puzzles you, don't guess; better to not say anything than to draw a wrong conclusion.

The *gestalt* approach—analyzing the total personality—should be left to the experts who have had thorough grounding in psychology which gives them insights into why a person writes as he does. To the experienced, discerning eye of the expert, often the first glance at a specimen of handwriting tells him in what category the writer belongs. Even the beginner may look at it and feel intuitively that there is something unusual, different, or disturbed about the writer. But it is wise not to trust your intuition—though it will help you later on, after you have become more expert; as a beginner don't take chances. Try to forget what you *think* you know about the person whose writing you are about to analyze. You might discover your estimate of him is wrong, and his handwriting might reveal traits you never suspected.

In the following pages are bare outlines, clues to what has formed the character of the individual, but conclusions are not always definitive and may have to be modified or qualified by conflicting signs in the handwriting specimen. You may be dealing with a symptom without realizing it, rather than a definite cause. Be cautious. Try not to make a statement unless reasonably certain. Novices can make harmful mistakes. The serious graphologists of long practice realize their limitations and make no claims that cannot be supported.

271

They may even consult with a colleague for another opinion, just as doctors do.

There is still a great deal about the working of the mind yet to be explored. Handwriting is mindwriting, and it will give you a composite picture of how the mind works and what effect the emotions have on it. Bear in mind, too, that human beings are dynamic—not static—creatures, and there are often imponderables in handwriting that challenge even the expert.

If a sign appears only occasionally in a handwriting, it reveals a tendency. If it appears often, it shows a habit. And where it is fairly consistent all through a specimen, we regard it as an integral part of the character structure.

Usually signs in a handwriting corroborate each other. Look for corroborating signs before drawing a conclusion. If you see a sign of weakness, as in an ineffectual *t* bar, this does not mean the person is a weakling. It may be just a clue to some weakness or neurotic tendency. You may see in the same handwriting the strong, forceful *t* bar, depicting determination and tenacity of purpose. How are you going to explain this apparent contradiction of procrastination and energetic drive? Well, the person might put things off till the last minute, then complete whatever has to be done by driving himself tenaciously. Many of us do this, and many handwritings show occasional signs of procrastination. Most of us are often confronted with chores we don't like to do for which we make excuses. It is only when a person's habit pattern is one of procrastination and indecision that we know we are dealing with something pathological.

Be careful how you use the words "always" and "never." Few human beings are that consistent. It is a mistake to judge from just one sign—for instance, to state that a person is jealous because she makes one incurve. It is tantamount to judging a person by the shape of his nose, or the glint in his eyes, or by a single mannerism. Strokes and curves are clues, not certainties. You must balance the plus signs against the minus signs before reaching a conclusion. That is what constitutes analysis.

Graphology is not a game, though a number of people consider it fun to analyze handwriting at a social gathering. Everyone wants to know more about himself, and graphology is one means of finding out. And it draws people to you, even if you are only an amateur practitioner. But be sure not to don the mantle of authority unless, after many years of practice, you earn it. It's a long hard road, but it has many rewards.

Estimate Correctly*

Pen Pressure—whether heavy, medium heavy, light, feathery light, muddy or pasty-looking, uneven (light and dark). Relates to sensuousness, sensuality, sensitivity.

Angle of Inclination—whether left-slanted, vertical, rightward, varying angles. Relates to introversion, extroversion, combination of both, showing the person's approach to life.

Size of Writing—whether small, tiny, large, medium large, varying. Relates to concentration, inability to concentrate, tendency to generalize or specialize. Also concerns generosity, expansiveness, stinginess.

T *Bars*—whether high, above the stem, on the stem, weak, strong, looped, wavy, hooked, downward, upward, through the stem, bowed. Relates to will power (or *won't* power), volition, initiative, determination, energetic drive, self-confidence or lack of it, conscious striving or lack of it, inertia.

I *Dots*—whether high above or close to the letter, wavy, tent-shaped, a circle, to the left or the right of the letter, omitted. Considered in combination with *t* bars and other letter forms such as the upper loop, it shows imagination or lack of it, humor, critical faculty, exactness with detail. Relates to mental pattern, perception.

* The text of a specimen should not be considered when making an analysis. It may have been copied or dictated, not written spontaneously. The spontaneously written specimen lends itself best to deductive analysis. There are exceptions where the text has to be considered, where what is written corroborates graphological findings in instances where pathological evidence is a factor. This need not concern the beginner.

Small Letters—whether simple, with flourishes, ornamented, printed, original-looking (different from style taught in school), cultured, illiterate, clear, dwindling, straggling, rounded, or angular. Relates to the pattern of the mind: whether broad, narrow, cautious, secretive, talkative (oral), reticent.

Capital Letters—whether simple, ornamented, with flourishes, printed, original, very large, dignified, small and modest, distorted. Relates to taste, pride, egotism, vanity, conceit, inferiority compensation. The capital *I* has a special significance, for it reveals the ego and the individual's self-image.

Upper Loops—whether tall, unusually tall, short, wide, compressed, without initial stroke, firm, ragged, broken. Relates to upper zone, to ideals, emotionalism, repression, mental clarity; where the letter is broken or ragged it shows a heart condition.

Lower Loops—whether long and wide, greatly exaggerated and running into the line below, short and ineffectual, without return stroke (descending in single stroke), turning to the right on the downstroke, hooked, lancelike, blunt, a loop within a loop. Relates to lower zone, to materialism, physical vitality, sexual drive, amount of energy expended, judgment and mathematical ability, persistence, aggressiveness, obstinacy.

Zones—three: upper, middle, lower. Relates to goals and how approached; whether visionary, practical, compulsive, and (where the loops of the upper line run into the line below) the extent to which the writer's dreams spill over into his world of reality.

Basic Line—whether ascending, descending, wavy and uneven (disturbed). Relates to spirits and moods, attitudes, feelings; tells if the person is optimistic, pessimistic, skeptical, cynical, buoyant, cheerful, ambitious; if downward, relates to depression, morbidity, unhappiness, hopelessness, or lack of physical vitality.

Connecting Strokes—whether consecutive or broken, connecting words, entirely disconnected writing. Relates to manner of thinking process, whether logical, intuitive, literal-minded, pedantic, didactic.

Terminals—whether long, short, blunt, lancelike, curved downward, rising gracefully upward, elongated horizontal with hook.

Relates to attitudes derived from emotions; to curiosity, possessiveness, mental and emotional receptivity, generosity, reticence;
whether opinionated, sadistic, domineering or amenable to reason;
to type of disposition.

Roundness and Angularity—whether rounded top and bottom; angular top and rounded bottom; consistent roundness. Relates to
disposition: whether gentle, flexible, immature, kind, naive, yielding, submissive. *Angularity* relates to: being exacting, efficient,
unyielding, intolerant, brutish, inflexible, unresponsive, righteous,
exaggerated sense of justice, controlling and uncooperative.

Uniformity—whether letters are all of the same clarity; whether
larger at end of words; mere slurs, dwindling, tapering, growing
indistinguishable at end of words. Relates to honesty, impetuous-
ness, impulsive outbursts; or diplomacy, finesse, tact, shrewdness,
dissimulativeness, deviousness, dishonesty.

Legibility and Illegibility—may be considered with uniformity.

Margins and Spacing—whether (on left side) wide, narrow, or
totally lacking; starting wide and narrowing; uniformly wide, or
absent; whether spacing is obvious between words or words run
together, where lower formations run into the line below. Margins relate to aesthetic quality, determining if practical considerations are predominant. Spacing relates to breadth of mind,
tolerance or intolerance, reflection, clarity of thought or mud-
dled thinking.

Signatures—whether underscored, larger or smaller than the body
of the specimen; whether manufactured, consciously developed,
or spontaneous. Relates to individual marks of importance, personality, whether magnetic, forceful, unique, positive, or negative.

Combination of Signs—consider type of person according to interests; predominance of strong signs over weak (or vice versa);
natural demands—whether physical, mental, artistic, aesthetic;
whether strong *t* bars are predominant over weak ones, showing a
conscious striving; whether weak and ineffectual *t* bars predominate, showing habit of procrastination, indecision, neurotic overtones. Take *t* bars, *i* dots, upper loops into account (upper zone);
middle zone for adjustment to reality and common sense; lower

zone (below the   rests, physical
prowess, primitive i

*Take into considera   ate whether he
is heading toward attainment of that goal. Constructive signs, coupled
with those denoting strength, place him on the plus side.* Predominance of weaknesses, *despite constructive signs, places him on the
minus side, showing he is not expressing himself fully, probably because of energy tie-up due to neurotic trends.*

Pen Pressure

THE TYPE OF PEN a person chooses is important,
for from this choice the graphologist immediately gets a clue to the
pen pressure. Those who like a fine pen will produce light writing,
showing unusual sensitivity. This will be borne out in many factors
in the handwriting, in letter formations and in graceful curves in
capital letters. Other signs may lessen or augment the degree of
sensitivity, but if the writing is essentially light, sometimes hairlike,
there is always a fundamental sensitivity.

When a stub pen (or broad nib) is preferred, it is usually because
the pen pressure is heavy. Ink can flow readily through the broad
nib. Should such a writer use a fine point, there is a chance of the
point bending, even breaking, perhaps scratching through and tear-
ing the paper. We can be certain that the heavy-pressure writer not
only has more physical energy and vitality than the light-pressure
writer, but also a greater sensuousness to forms, color, and music.
The heavy-pressure writer is essentially materialistic and earthy.
The extent of materialism, which direction it takes, and whether or
not it is coupled with an interest in people will be revealed in letter
formations.

The light-pressure writers, being less physical, will have more
interest in people and social activity. But this does not mean that

heavy-pressure writers lack such interest. In fact, their interest may be extremely intense and result in overwhelming possessiveness.

Many shades of pen pressure may appear in one specimen, making it difficult (especially for the beginner) to evaluate the actual degree or type of pressure, but examination of one person's handwriting, written over a period of time, will show the typical degree of pressure, which will be borne out by the person's interests or hobbies. Varying pen pressure at any time indicates a measure of emotional instability, but here it is important to look for other signs that corroborate this finding.

A person who appears robust may surprise you by writing a very light hand; this is where the danger arises from judging from appearances. A measure of natural robustness may be sublimated into mental activity, causing the writing to be lighter and smaller than expected. Where emotion is diluted by reason, an extremely emotional person may write a light hand. This is an exception, however, and all factors have to be taken into consideration.

All specimens to be analyzed should be written in ink. Pencil lead (and ball-point pen) is rounded and does not register certain important points that bear a direct relation to the senses. It is not as easy to make an analysis from a specimen written with a ball-point pen as with a fountain pen or a holder and pen point, but because of the ball-point's widespread use, we must do the best we can. Sometimes the graphologist must work with a specimen written in pencil. She can use her vast experience to recognize from other signs what kind of pen pressure the writer would have. Should heavy pencil marks show a tracery on the other side of the paper, we are sure the writer would have a heavy hand with pen and ink.

The extremely light writing that looks as if the pen hardly touched the paper will usually be accompanied by signs of spirituality and a lack of physical appetites and robustness, and no desire for material possessions. (See the handwriting of Rachmaninoff in Chapter IX, "Great Men and Women.") The original specimen was extremely light in pen pressure, yet on seeing this musical genius, with his coarse features, one would have sworn that his handwriting would be robust.

Thus, the pen pressure, indicating the physical make-up of the individual, usually gives us an immediate clue to his interests, but, as with Rachmaninoff, there are exceptions. (We expect almost anything from a genius!)

The physical type (heavy pressure) has an interest in things, concrete objects, work in which he uses physical energy; the social type (usually medium-heavy or light pressure) in people first and then in material things; people with extremely light pressure, in spiritual development and in helping others attain it too. Specimen 157 is a good example of very light pen pressure. The spiritual connotation is corroborated by the *t* bars bowed above the stem. The writer is intellectual and gentle (rounded formations); she has intuition, sound judgment, the ability to get down to essentials without wasting time, as shown in the single stroke of her capital *I*. As an advanced student of graphology, she prepared some amazing analyses.

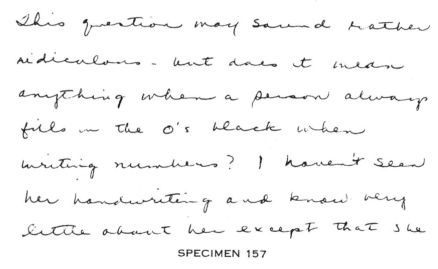

SPECIMEN 157

Angle of Inclination

This tells us in what direction the main interests lie. (See Chapter II, "Extroverts and Introverts.")

Size of Writing

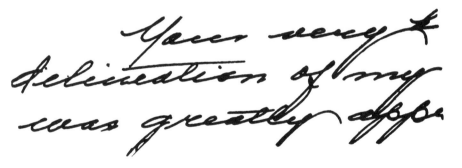

SPECIMEN 158

SPECIMEN 159

SPECIMEN 160

LARGE RIGHTWARD-FLOWING WRITING, where letter formations are open and there is good spacing between words, shows diversified interests. The writer finds it hard to concentrate on one thing at a time and tends to generalize. If the writing is extremely large, so that only two or three words appear on a line, we have signs of extravagance sometimes carried to a neurotic extreme. This is also an indication of extroversion and some forms of exhibitionism. The desire for activity is greater than for reflection, and material possessions mean a great deal. Possessions are vivified and reflect the personality of the owner. (Specimen 158.)

Medium-large writing (where there are angular formations and signs of good control) shows that the writer is able to concentrate best when under pressure. But the tendency here is also to generalize, rather than to get down to fundamentals, and there is a greater bent toward activity than reflection. These people are the doers rather than the thinkers. (Specimen 159.)

Small writing reveals power of concentration. The smaller the writing, the greater the power of concentration; it also tells us that the writer has something of the hermit in him, is greatly introverted, and in the extreme shows pathological tendencies. (See *Transvestite* specimen in Chapter XI.) If it's so small that it needs to be examined under a magnifying glass, we may have a mind that resembles a tightly wound buttonhole watch, which is apt to snap under pressure. These people derive more satisfaction from cerebrating than from activity. The energies go to the brain and everything is intellectualized. Emotions are drained of their intimate warmth and lose much of their value.

Diffused writing so large that the letter formations are distorted is a sign of a mind that does not think clearly. It often resembles a negative out of focus or a double exposure. In its extreme, it is the handwriting of a mentally disturbed person.

Specimen 160 is written by a person who can concentrate without being easily distracted; one whose mind and emotions are well coordinated, and who is capable of scientific research. There is enough breadth to the writing, along with intuition, to show an interest in people, but the engrossing interest is in literature, and the writer plans to become a professor at a university.

T Bars

1.

2.

3.

4.

5.

6.

7.

8.

9.

10.

11.

12.

CHART A

13.   14.   15.

16.   17.   18.

19.   20.   21.

CHART A (CONT.)

THE BAR of the letter *t* is one sure way will power and personal force are expressed in handwriting. Other horizontal strokes will usually corroborate the drive shown here, but essentially the *t* bar gives us the major clue. From the way the *t* bar is formed we can get some idea of the backbone or stamina of the individual, and in its various forms we can see to what degree the writer is either neurotic or well adjusted.

1. This is the sign of procrastination, although it has other implications. The person starts but does not follow through, just as the bar does not go through the stem of the letter. It implies weakness of will, lack of voltage behind the will power, indecisiveness, inability to make choices readily; a tendency to be fickle and capricious, to live in the past, and to be emotionally

immature and dependent; difficult to pin down, restless. When the sign appears often in a handwriting, the habit of procrastination points to neurotic trends bordering on the pathological and relates to strong guilt feelings in the writer.

2. Good control is shown in a strong balanced *t* bar. The person is conscientious, dependable, well balanced. Where it appears consistently, there is a meticulous attention to detail.

3. The bar running away from the stem shows enthusiasm, animation, nervous energy. The writer is ahead of himself, anxious to get something finished even before he starts. In a heavy-pressure angular hand, this stroke indicates a hasty temper.

4. The hook on the *t* bar (it will also appear in other strokes) shows tenacity of purpose; the person hangs on relentlessly, often compulsively, to the finish. It shows will power, determination, a capacity for hard work, often a measure of possessiveness. Here even the pen is loath to leave the paper.

5. Downward stroke of the *t* bar, the sign of the fighter (in a weak hand it indicates quarrelsomeness, shows aggressiveness, combativeness, often an opinionated, argumentative person who must have the last word; won't take no for an answer; defensive, chip-on-shoulder; the sign of the salesman. The writer must be in a controlling position to feel adequate. Where the downstroke of the stem goes below the basic line, we have a kind of controlled obstinacy that makes him difficult to reason with.

6. Slow but brutal temper, usually found in either heavy- or pasty-pressure writing. In the latter (pasty) the person may be dangerous and unpredictable. The *t* bar that becomes thicker resembles a club.

7. Wavy *t* bar, curved and fanciful, shows humor, good nature; often gracious and fun-loving; also shows ability to mimic.

8. Sarcastic, lancelike *t* bars show a sharp tongue; there's a tendency for the temper to flare up and die down quickly. (Other strokes in the same writing will corroborate this conclusion in lancelike finals and downstrokes on *y* and *g*.)

9. *T* bars rising upward on the stem (or even over it) show aspiration, imagination, ambition. In a vertical hand it often shows

elements of smugness, self-satisfaction, and social climbing.

10. The bow above the stem shows curbing of physical weaknesses through spiritual values; indicates imagination, mystical interests and tendencies. When this bow appears in a muddy or pasty hand even once, it shows an effort being made on the part of a sensual individual to overcome (or cope with) sensuality, to improve and better himself. Where the bow appears in the center of the stem, written firmly, it is a sign of good muscular coordination and self-discipline; it is often seen in the handwriting of surgeons, fliers, certain types of athletes.

11. The straight *t* bar above the stem shows imagination, a spirit of adventure, a tendency to reach out for the unattainable. It is also the sign of the perfectionist. In a heavy-pressure hand it shows desire for adventure involving physical activity; in a light-pressure hand it indicates an adventurous mentality impelled by curiosity to explore, to learn from experience. In a practical hand that also indicates good judgment, it is a sign of foresight and the ability to visualize and plan ahead.

12. Ineffectual *t* bars, lighter in pen pressure than the rest of the writing, show weak will; an inverted bow low on the stem shows a tendency to follow the line of least resistence. If the *t* bar is heavy and an inverted bow it shows willfulness: the writer does things the hard way, but considers it an easy way for him.

13. Looped *t* bars show persistence. When seen in combination with a star-shaped formation (angular), it shows a kind of persistent obstinacy. (In a neurotic hand it's a sign of paranoid trends, usually corroborated by other signs.)

14. Supersensitivity is shown in a type of star-shaped *t* formation that is weak and does not go through the stem. Here we have a combination of two indications: procrastination and indecision, coupled with repression. The second example shows a tendency to withdraw into fantasy and become unrealistic, a negative form of the signs described in 13.

15. Opposite of bow-shaped *t* bar (described in 12) showing willfulness, indulgence of sensual appetites, brutishness. When *t* bar ends in an additional looped stroke, the writer is eccentric.

16. Weakness and aggressiveness combine here in the downstroke that does not go through the stem. This is the sign of arrogant weakness, querulousness, defensiveness which sometimes takes the form of offensiveness; a fault-finding, petty nature (usually an attempt to compensate for an inferiority complex). A definite neurotic sign. The writer projects his weaknesses upon others, cuts them down to size. Often perverse and rebellious from childhood.

17. No *t* bar; shows a lack of initiative due to supersensitivity. It may appear in writing showing strength, but discloses weakness in some areas and difficulty in getting things started. Once the initial step is taken, the person may even become tenacious.

18. The persistent loop appearing above the stem of the letter indicates a persistence about personal habits; often found in the handwriting of people with idiosyncrasies in matters of appearance and personal surroundings rather than in their social relations. Mild eccentricity.

19. Hooks on beginning and end of *t* bars show an indomitable will, ambition, tenacity of purpose, determination, and a compulsive drive that often borders on the neurotic. The person must be doing something to allay anxiety. Cannot relinquish a task until it is finished, even though energies may be exhausted; often suffers from exhaustion as a result, but usually has good resiliency.

20. The return stroke going leftward through the stem without the hand being lifted from the paper shows a desire for protection. (It is the child going back—leftward—to the time when he felt protected, seeking to continue the pattern.) There is a tendency toward introversion (true of any strokes that lean leftward, even in the most extroverted hand). Often the writer is readily influenced by a will stronger than his own.

21. Variety of *t* bars in one specimen shows many wills. The writer falls into the neurotic category. There is usually conflict between what the mind dictates and what the emotions demand; often difficulty in making adjustments. Peculiar *t* bars made with double strokes or strangely curved, or where the stem looks like a broken back—all are signs of something odd or eccentric about the writer.

I *Dots*

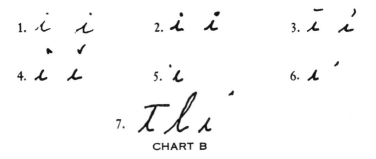

CHART B

WHEN THE *i* is continually undotted (in such instances we are apt to find many uncrossed *t*'s as well), we have the graphological indication of a poor memory. On the deeper levels, we see this as an expression of blind spots. The person blocks out certain memories of early experiences because they cause pain. On the conscious level, this takes the form of absent-mindedness.

1. Firmly dotted *i*'s exactly above the letter are a sign of a factual memory. The writer is careful of detail, as a rule. (*T*'s will usually be crossed firmly in the middle of the stem.)
2. In a heavy-pressure hand, the careful *i* dot tells us the writer is somewhat aggressive, exact about detail, and often lacks imagination. Other signs in the writing will substantiate this. The dot may appear club-shaped at times.
3. Wavy strokes for *i* dots, where the dot looks like part of a circle (referred to graphologically as "laughing mouths"), show a sense of humor and will be corroborated by other signs of humor in rising terminals.
4. Tent-shaped *i* dots indicate a critical faculty. Found in handwriting of people with keen minds, shown in angular letters and mental formations.
5. The *i* dot to the left of the letter shows caution.

6. The *i* dot to the right of the letter indicates enthusiasm and often accompanies *t* bars that fly in the same direction.
7. High strokes of any kind show imagination, and we often see them in the same handwriting in the *t*, *l*, and high *i* dot.

The circle *i* dot is usually found in the handwriting of people attracted to fads or who are manually dextrous—often designers.

When seen in a handwriting of varying angles and pen pressure—signs of emotional instability—we discover the writer is doing work that doesn't suit him. The circle *i* dot also shows an innate dislike for routine work and for mundane conventional forms. There is something in the person that rebels at the necessity for conforming. Often the circle *i* dot appears in vertical writing where many letters are printed, showing artistic potentiality, a feeling for design. When found in an ordinary copybook hand, it shows the desire to be different. It is a way of calling attention to oneself, and the fact is the writer is different in some respects.

These people making the circle *i* dot, though artistically inclined, are better suited to fields of adaptive or interpretive art than to the fine arts. It is, in fact, a sign of *artiness*. Much depends, however, upon other signs in the writing of the circle *i* dotter, for though it is an artificial manifestation, it gives us a clue to an inner rebelliousness of which the person himself may not be fully aware. The following specimen belongs to a furniture designer.

SPECIMEN 161

Very few people place a dot (period) after their signatures. When it is done (as by General de Gaulle) we have a person who regards what he says as the final word. Period. In one instance a forger gave himself away by this habit. Accustomed to placing a dot after his own signature, he followed the unconscious urge to do the same with the forged signature, placing it at the same distance from the last letter in both instances; this led to his indictment.

Small Letters

1. Open at the top shows generosity when the emotions are involved; in rightward-flowing hand shows loquaciousness and generosity.
2. Open at the bottom, when consistent shows dishonesty. (This is rare.) Such people are not interested in petty larceny, but will embezzle huge sums of money and are often not aware of their weakness. Usually found in handwriting that shows mathematical ability, and for this reason such writers get positions in banks, where the weakness finds the opportunity for expression.
3. Tightly closed with a loop shows caution; in vertical hand it shows a measure of secretiveness. In angular vertical hand it denotes cool, calculating caution.
4. Initial strokes show preoccupation with detail, and also indicate more impatience with details than with bigger problems because of the importance given the former. Such writers may make ending strokes, too.
5. Open lip of small *b*, found (although not always) in rounded writing, shows credulousness, a tendency to be gullible, trusting, without guile; the person is readily taken in, lacks sales resistance.
6. Tightly closed small *b*, often with a loop, reveals caution; usually found in handwriting of people with business ability, which will be corroborated by signs of good judgment and foresight.

1.

2.

3.

4.

5.

6.

7.

8.

9.

10.

11.

12.

13.

14.

15.

16.

17.

18.

19.

20.

man

21.

CHART C

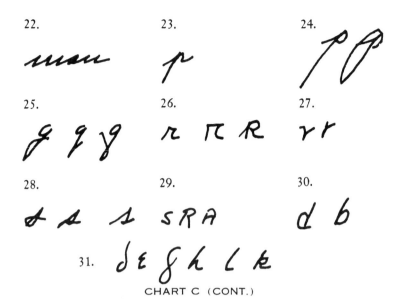

CHART C (CONT.)

7. Final stroke on letter *d* or *t* ending bluntly and below the basic line shows obstinacy, a controlling, domineering element in an opinionated, unyielding person. When the vertical stroke comes down on the same line, forming a single tall stroke without a loop, the person is dignified and capable of being sarcastic in a quiet and cutting way. The higher the vertical stroke, the more evidence of dignity.

8. Open space between up and down strokes in such letters as *d* and *t* has same significance, showing a taciturn, often poker-faced person; sometimes such spaces are found in the handwriting of inarticulate people.

9. The Greek *d* in any form shows culture or a desire for it; it is often accompanied by the Greek *e*. When the final stroke is wavy or curved, we have the sign of a pleasure-loving nature within refined limits. Found in handwriting showing literary leanings, in either tastes or ability.

10. When the loop is as pronounced on the *d* as in the stem of the *t*, we have the sign of a sensitive, even touchy nature. This may be found in a specimen where a *t* is uncrossed and looks like an *l*.

11. The Greek *e* shows refinement in a person who aims for cultural advancement. When it appears in a handwriting showing

another form of *e* it indicates versatility. (Any letter appearing in a variety of forms shows versatility.)

12. Small *e* closed up to look like *i*, usually found in an angular hand, is sign of mental keenness (often accompanied by Greek *e*) because writing is done quickly.

13. Elimination of strokes shows good practical judgment, common sense, ability to get to essentials without wasting time on unnecessary details.

14. Constructed, printed *f* shows artistic leanings or ability, as well as aesthetic sense; it is often found in writing with other printed, undecorated formations.

15. This squared-off lower loop (in *y* or *g*) reveals aggressiveness and obstinacy: The writer does not give up without a struggle. Shows a measure of compulsiveness. In an angular hand it often reveals mechanical ability. Even though the handwriting might show a preponderance of weakness otherwise, if this sign appears we know the writer will eventually get what he goes after.

16. The *g* that looks like the figure *9* and the *y* that looks like a 7 give us a clue to mathematical ability; it's seen in the *z*, too. Appears in the hand of a person who can deal with facts and figures, but essentially it shows good judgment.

17. Initial strokes omitted on upper loops, so first stroke is a single line, are the work of mentally developed individuals. Called a mental formation, it shows rapidity of thought, and in many instances facile literary expression, especially when accompanied by the Greek *d* and *e*.

18. Wide upper loops show sensitivity, an emotional nature, musical responsiveness; often found in the handwriting of singers and dramatic actresses. (See chart on loops.)

19. High upper loop, where rest of the letter (as in *k*) is cramped, shows religious tendencies with superstitious overtones.

20. Rounded tops of letters show childish tendencies, lack of mental acuity, immaturity, yielding, and submissive traits in a person who is obedient and strictly follows the rules.

21. Angular tops and rounded bottoms show a keen mind and a gentle nature, with yielding emotions. This combination of mental maturity and emotional immaturity often results in inner conflict.

22. When both tops and bottoms are angular it points to an unyielding, exacting, often demanding and intolerant person; one who is set in his habits, rigid and inflexible, and usually without humor. (The typical German script tends toward this type of angularity, and though it may be indicative of Teutonic scientific efficiency, it also reveals other traits that are less laudatory.)

23. The open formation of the small *p* shows simplicity and gentleness; it is frequently found in the handwriting of old-fashioned older people.

24. Long downstroke on *p* shows love of sports and outdoor activity. When loop is wide and rhythmic, as in the second letter, there is an absolute need for physical activity; it shows the ability to dance gracefully, as well as a natural responsiveness to rhythm through the senses when the writing is heavy in pen pressure.

25. *Q* made like *g*, or *g* made like *q*, shows altruistic tendencies. The instinctive desire is to give. It often shows generosity of mind and nature combined, an empathy that exceeds mere sympathy. But it has other connotations, such as a clue to a messianic or martyr complex, depending upon other signs in the writing. It's usually found in handwriting of enlightened people, but it is more instinctive than developed. Also found in the handwriting of those who have something to contribute toward enriching the world, though they may not use it to that purpose. The *g* or *y* that comes down in a single line and then goes back to cross that line tells us that the impulse is to give, but that caution overtakes the writer and he closes the giving channel.

26. The broad *r* in handwriting always points to the person's strong visual sense, and consequently he is interested in what he sees. He is therefore concerned with appearances—whether of objects, people, or surroundings. In a constructive hand it may show the person's ability to create those objects that relate to appearances, as with a dress designer. The painter comes within this category, since painting is largely the ability to put on canvas what the artist sees and how he sees it. The graphologist, too—always looking, observing, visually exploring—comes under this heading. Where there are two or three kinds of *r*'s in one handwriting, we have versatility.

27. The quick *r* in writing, the one made by most people, is often seen where there are other signs of rapid writing, though it may also appear in a slowly written hand. When it appears in the same hand that shows the broad *r*, our conclusion is still that the person is visual to some extent; the versatility is often corroborated by other letters made in different ways.

28. The closed small *s*, often found with the closed *a* and *o*, augments the caution in the nature. When open at the bottom it has the same significance as the small open-lipped *b* and reveals gullibility.

29. Printed small letters, whether *s*, *r*, or *a*, show constructive ability and when accompanied by signs of imagination tell us the writer can formulate ideas independently. It is the sign of talent, although it may not always be put to use; waste of talent is noticed when there is a lack of consistent drive in the writing, shown in forms of weakness or laziness.

30. The inverted *b* often appears in the same handwriting as the inverted *d*, and shows some inversion in the nature, often found in the writing of homosexuals and in handwriting that shows a variety of neurotic symptoms.

31. Greek formations of *d* and *e* and the *g* made like a figure *8* all appearing in the one specimen, along with mental formations of *b*, *l*, and *k*, belong primarily to the person of cultured background and good education. The *g* made like an *8* has a significance of its own: When found in any hand, cultured or otherwise, it shows an ability to adapt oneself to various and varied circumstances. People making this kind of *g* usually manage, no matter what they encounter, to see the way clear ahead. It indicates rapidity of thought, literary tastes, and often dormant talent along literary lines. There is an intellectual flexibility in those who make such a *g*; they can make themselves at home in a tent or in a palace, besides making the best of any difficulty that arises and gaining something from the experience. They sometimes learn more from experience than from books, although books are of great importance to them.

Small letters, or even the center part of letters that are looped (as *l*'s and *y*'s), relate to the middle zone in handwriting; it is in this zone that we find clues to how practical and how much of a realist the person is, and how his approach affects his everyday life. Each of us writes in three zones—upper, middle, and lower —and they must be taken into consideration when preparing an analysis.

Capital Letters

1. The old-fashioned, protective *A* is usually found in a handwriting that also has the old-fashioned capitals *M* and *N*. When rounded (often ornamented) it shows a maternal (or paternal) instinct that is often prevalent over reason. In an angular hand it is frequently streamlined; it shows the same instinct but is often sublimated into accomplishments of one kind or another. Found in welfare workers, philanthropists, veterinarians, farmers; when simplified or printed, it is found in artists and writers, many of whom love animals.
2. This large capital *B*, with the lower bulb larger than the upper one, shows generosity, a measure of expansiveness (usually corroborated by other signs); it is often found with the gullible small *b* and rounded formations.
3. In this formation the upper bulb is larger than the lower one, which closes cautiously, showing just that—caution and skepticism; it is often found in combination with the closed *b*, *a* and *o*.
4. Capitals that start with an initial stroke show concern with outer trappings and appearances, often impatience with trifles about which the writer may be fussy even though larger problems do not bother him so much.
5. Simple, constructed, printed capitals show mental independence, a capacity for formulating ideas that can be put to practical use, manual constructiveness. Severe *E* and *I* show severity and lack of frills and furbelows in the choice of dress. The capital *I* that starts from the left and goes around to the right—just the oppo-

1.

A A A A   *M N M N*

2.

B B

3.

B B

4.

B R E

5.

T L N K J

6.

I I E

7.

D N

8.

D A

9.

D D

10.

11.

12.

H H

13.

CHART D

CHART D (CONT.)

site of what we're taught in school—indicates the complete rebel, and there will be other signs in the handwriting to reinforce this conclusion.

6. The capital *I* that is a single stroke shows clarity of thought, real sophistication (not pseudo), and mental clarity; there is no overestimation of the ego. The person usually realizes his capabilities as well as his limitations. It's found usually in handwriting showing signs of culture and is a clue to a strong aesthetic sense. Some simple *I*'s are made with a serif above and below and reveal constructive thinking.

7. The capital *D* open at the top shows frankness, openheartedness, and orality; the writer finds it hard to keep confidences. Often small *a*'s and *o*'s will be open, too, though there may be closed cautious ones in the same handwriting.

8. The capital *D* closed at the top, often with a loop, shows caution, a measure of reserve, the ability to keep one's own counsel as well as confidences. Shows secretiveness when the next letter is enclosed within the capital letter; usually more definite when the closed formation appears in a vertical or backhand.

9. If the *D* is closed with a flying loop that reaches above the letter, we have a sign of coquettishness, somewhat muted by reserve. (Found in men's handwriting as well as in women's and it has the connotation of flirtatiousness.)

10. Ornamented, vulgar-looking capitals, often found in a semiliterate hand, show vulgar tastes, unnecessary ornamentation in both appearance and surroundings; the speech may be vulgar, too. This kind of unaesthetic capital is more often found in a heavy, muddy, or "pasty" handwriting than in a light, sensitive one.

11. Capital *G* made like the figure *8*, usually accompanied by the small *g* made the same way, augments the traits of adaptability, desire for culture, and rapidity of thought, and it shows a measure of self-reliance and independence.

12. Involved formation of capital *H* shows the writer's tendency for getting into involved, tight situations. Often appears in handwriting of strategists; most noticeable in the two *H*'s of Harry Houdini's signature. Houdini was the magician who got himself into impossible situations and by clever manipulation always managed to extricate himself.

13. Inflated lower portions of capitals *L* and *I* show vanity, often in regard to personal appearance. (Usually found as a compensation for an inferiority complex.) In an untutored hand, it shows conceit, with an overestimation by the writer of his importance.

14. Exaggerated wide upper portion of capital *L* shows sensitivity, expansiveness, and generosity. (Make the gesture with your hand and see what an expansive one it is.)

15. Angular tops of capitals and rounded bottoms have the same

connotation as in small letters; they show keenness of mind, gentleness of nature, and moral resistance to obstacles.

16. Where the first mound is higher than the others in capital M and N, starting with an incurve, we have evidence of family pride, sensitivity, and dignity. (The incurve in any formation is a sign of a conscious desire to protect oneself and in some instances the family name.)

17. Where the final (third mound in M, second in N) becomes higher than the others, if rounded (as in a rounded hand), there is a desire for self-assertion and a position of authority, although the approach is gentle because the person is. But where the last mound is sharp and pointed, it is quite a different story. The person can be self-assertive when least expected; will prefer to show his authority, in fact will act like an authority in situations where he may have only superficial knowledge; is capable of treachery, is querulous, and becomes disagreeable. It is, essentially, a neurotic sign and is found in the handwriting of neurotics of every degree. It also reveals an element of self-righteousness.

18. Printed capitals, unusual in formation like these, show artistic potentiality; in heavy-pressure writing, manual dexterity.

19. Such modern simplified formations of M and N point to a strong aesthetic sense that often conditions the person's choices in clothes, food, surroundings. Shows good taste, appreciation of art, structure, line, and form. The writer usually dislikes clutter of any kind.

20. The wide-looped S open as the bottom shows expansiveness, one portion of the formation augmenting the other. The rhythmic S, which in some instances looks like a musical clef, is often found in the handwriting of musicians and those with musical appreciation.

21. This kind of S without an upper loop, often found in handwriting where other formations are slurred, the rhythm lagging, and t bars weak, shows mental laziness.

22. Of special significance is the capital I formed in the opposite direction of the way it was taught; it starts at the left and goes

to the right, often ending in a blunt stroke (the major clue to how it was made). It will appear in handwriting that has other signs of rebelliousness and is, in fact, the sign of the complete rebel. You can see this being done if you watch the writer, otherwise you may not recognize it. But as this kind of capital *I* belongs in the neurotic category, the beginner will have to conclude rebelliousness from the obvious downstroke of the *t* bar in the handwriting specimen.

Loops

A LOOP is an avenue of emotion, so if loops are wide the person is emotional and sensitive and permits himself emotional expression. Where the loops are compressed, repression is indicated; this is often accompanied by signs of caution, fearfulness, and emotional tension, so that the pen pressure is also intensified and likely to be heavy. (Pen pressure may vary, however, depending upon moods, the stability of the writer, and other factors.)

In the height of the upper loops is seen the extent of the writer's idealism, dreams, fantasies. This relates to the upper zone in handwriting; here we can see what the person's reach is and whether he has set up realizable goals or if his reach exceeds his grasp. If the upper loops are higher than any other letters and immediately noticeable, we have the sign of visionary idealism, which sometimes gives rise to distortion of the imagination. Such exaggerations are usually clues to a neurosis, yet from them some unique ideas have had their inception.

Speaking symbolically, upper loops may represent hands reaching up, or in the case of lower loops, reaching down, since handwriting is an instinctive gesture. Loops consistently high show an imaginative, idealistic nature. When the lower loops are equal in size (and they belong in the lower zone), the writer is not content to merely

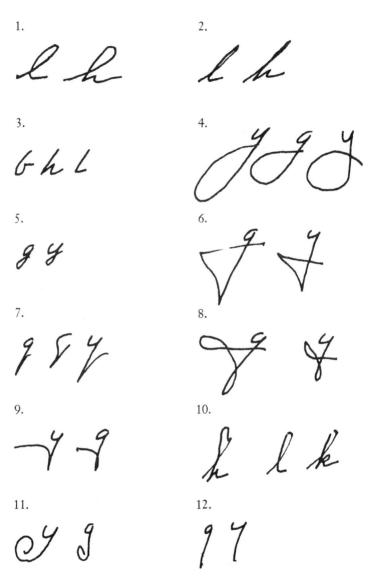

CHART E

dream, but seeks concrete realization of his dreams in some form.
High upper loops show high standards (which the person has set up

or which have been set up for him during his youth). How he attempts to realize them will be revealed in the extent of his will power (shown in *t* bars), and whether he is a well-organized, adjusted individual will show in the spacing, margins, small letter forms—in fact, in the *gestalt*, or over-all specimen.

Long lower loops accompanied by heavy pen pressure show essentially the materialistic side of the person's nature. But they also reveal physical attributes, including a love of physical activity and the sex impulse. When the writing reveals signs of mathematical ability, the exaggerated loops in the lower zone often point to mechanical ability. The musician who plays an instrument with technical virtuosity has such mechanical ability, which shows in such loops.

The long swinging loops almost always are found in the handwriting of people with strong primitive impulses who respond to jazz, rhythm, and so on. The generous impulse that impels the hand to make a large lower loop is a sign of generosity in the writer's nature.

Short upper loops denote practicality and are often accompanied by other signs that corroborate this trait and have a relation to the realism expressed in the middle zone.

Extremely short loops when found in a light handwriting point to a lack of physical vitality or robustness; if found in a heavy-pressure hand they show physical inertia. (Sometimes a former athlete takes on fat where he once had muscle, and as he grows in girth his handwriting changes, especially in lower loop formations.)

1. This is the wide upper loop and shows an emotional, sensitive person—expansive and expressive—who loves to sing.
2. This loop is compressed and indicates emotional repression, the result of inhibitions and fears (some of them nameless).
3. These are mental formations. The initial stroke on the loop is eliminated.
4. This is the materialistic (earthy) lower loop. In heavy pressure it shows strong sex impulses, animal spirits, with corresponding physical appetites. In a light or medium-heavy pressure hand it indicates sensuousness to music, color, rhythm; often found in graceful dancers. Also indicates tendency to make generous gestures.

5. This short ineffectual lower loop made jerkily, indicating lack of muscular coordination, is often found in the handwriting of sick, devitalized people. The rest of the writing will show signs of tremulousness and weakness. (A good example is shown in the heart patient.)

6. The angular lower loop here shows aggressiveness and obstinacy and may be accompanied by other angular formations. When appearing in an otherwise rounded hand, it shows an unexpected aggressiveness—and takes the person out of the yielding category. When extremely long and out of harmony with the rest of the writing (whether angular or rounded) it shows pretentiousness and an exaggerated importance of material things, of position and prestige. When it runs into the line below it shows confusion, self-centeredness, a sense of the dramatic, and showmanship, and the writer is attracted to the novel and unusual.

7. Here again is the rightward turn on the downstroke of the *g* and *y*, showing generosity, sympathy, an interest in people, and a desire to contribute in some way to bring the greatest good to the greatest number. (This formation has a number of meanings, depending on what kind of handwriting it appears in.)

8. Such double loops in the lower part of the looped formations (a loop within a loop, so to speak) are indications of a peculiarity that stems from physical factors, but they are also indicative of compulsiveness. The person can be described as being compulsively persistent. (It is frequently a neurotic sign.)

9. The return stroke to the left on the lower part of the downstroke shows clannishness; also an exacting quality in the writer and a tendency to be ceremonious about petty details. (In a vertical hand it shows snobbishness.)

10. Broken upper loops show heart ailment. Where there is a consistent break in the lower loops, we may find that the writer limps, or has something wrong with one of his legs.

11. This kind of incurve on the stem of the *y* or *g* shows sensitivity, points to some peculiarity or eccentricity.

12. No lower loop (straight line) shows good judgment.

Zones

WE ALL REACH OUT for something in life, whether it be love, understanding, physical comforts, or even the basic necessities. Each person has his own goals for which he strives, and whether they are realizable or not will show up in handwriting in signs of strength and weakness, as well as whether there is a genuine desire to reach the goal or whether it is just wishful thinking. We may discover we have long wished for something beyond our reach, and when we change our direction and shift our values, we can have success—the success that has previously eluded us because we lived too much in fantasy.

In the upper zone of handwriting, where the upper loops appear, we see the extent of the writer's dreams, fantasies, and ideals. Other high strokes (reaching up) corroborate our findings. The middle zone, where most of the small letters appear, gives us clues as to how he copes with the reality of everyday life and to what extent he adjusts to it. We can also recognize if he is using his fantasies to guide (or misguide) himself, and how well he functions in relation to the outside world. His work may be a practical solution to his problems yet not fulfill him emotionally, but having made the compromise, he may accept it philosophically and find expression for his repressed needs in hobbies. Or he may regress into childhood and become dependent on others without realizing his potential for enjoying independence. If his physical demands are stronger than he can cope with, he may be in conflict; this will become evident in the lower loops, which appear in the lower zone.

Many of us become aware of the dissonances between our ideals and their realization; when this happens either we can set up other ideals that are more nearly attainable, or we can live lives of quiet desperation. The fact remains that we have a choice. And upon our choice rests success or failure, depending on what these words means to each of us.

Since we are dynamic entities and not machines, few of us function in a balanced way. Thus, there are few handwritings that do not show some measure of inconsistency, whether it be because our dreams are beyond our reach, or because our primitive urges remain unsatisfied.

The lower zone gives us some major clues as to how an individual copes with his sexual drives and what effect his efforts have on both his fantasy world and the real world as he sees it. Where there are extreme manifestations in any of the zones—if the middle zone is outstanding because of an absence of upper and lower loops; or if the upper zone has unusually high or very inflated loops; or if the lower zone is filled with loops that run into the line below—we can be sure the writer has some abnormality. It is, therefore, important to look for other signs to substantiate a suspicion that we might be dealing with a disturbed individual.

The following three specimens illustrate the three zones and how three individuals function within them:

UPPER

MIDDLE

LOWER

SPECIMEN 162

We see good evidence of the high upper loops here, showing the kind of unrealistic drive that is definitely abnormal in its exaggeration. What saves this writer from living in a world of confusion to complicate her fantasies is that she manages to clear her lines, being careful not to let the lower loops run into the line below. Keeping order in her realistic world becomes something of an obsession.

ER
)LE
ER

I have been fairly cheerful, as, if cloudy thoughts occur, as they do with all of us imaginative people, I usually bounce up again pretty quickly.

SPECIMEN 163

Here the letters almost hug the middle zone, and upper and lower loops are inconsequential. Thus, the person can cope with reality on a common-sense basis. Fantasies do not push him to strive for goals beyond his reach. He has felt secure and loved from childhood and does not need to retreat into fantasy for love and security.

ER
)LE
ER

ended Fordham University e leaving New York Bre + other locations while r Westinghouse. My ost enjoyable ... Cité and Sales promotion ic and Industrial

SPECIMEN 164

In this specimen, fantasies spill over into the person's world of reality, as seen in the long, wide, swinging loops that run way past the line below. However, the pen pressure is fairly light, and this puts a different connotation on the direction his fantasies take, for his values have something spiritual about them. He wants to be rich materially and to have some power, but he takes other people into consideration and would bestow lavish gifts on those he feels are deserving. He has a gentle, gracious demeanor (roundness, coupled with even pen pressure, and an easy, graceful rhythm in the writing; also, many terminals rise). Although somewhat self-centered, he wants to better himself so as to perform efficiently in his work and fulfill his responsibilities toward others. He is trying to compensate (exaggerated loops) for something he wanted, dreamed of, and missed in his childhood, and he has the drive to achieve a modicum of it.

When such long lower loops in the same context appear in a heavy-pressure handwriting the picture is changed, as are the values of the individual. The heavy pressure tells us that there is a striving for lavish, expensive material possessions—which he may or may not be able to afford, for he must have the illusion of being rich and powerful. (The power drive is intensified when the pen pressure is heavy, especially where *t* bars are strong.) Such people get a terrific sense of power when driving a high-powered car (which is their choice). The individual dramatizes himself in a heroic role very often. (I knew a man who wrote in this manner who pictured himself a Robin Hood and thoroughly enjoyed the role.) Often we find such lavish spenders save on pennies while they squander dollars.

The kind of exaggerated lower loop that does not clear the line below has other meanings, which are: a subjective way of reasoning, which we have come to believe is a feminine way of reasoning; extroversion, a measure of showmanship, and a dislike for the commonplace and ordinary. Where there are signs of weak will power, the person often spends more than he earns, is usually in debt, and is greatly preoccupied with money.

Basic Line

Optimism, Buoyancy, Hopefulness, Rising Spirits

SUCH POSITIVE EMOTION as produces optimism and buoyancy, making one feel as if he were walking on air, affects the hand when it is writing, and the result is lines that soar on the paper. Even temporary moods of depression do not change the upward swing of the basic line in the handwriting of those described as incurable optimists, though occasional words may droop now and then. Fold the paper in the center, and if the writing runs uphill it will show immediately.

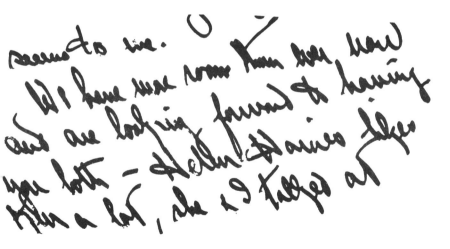

SPECIMEN 165

Such soaring lines are often found in the handwriting of ambitious people with drive and energy; this will show in the quick rhythm, accompanied by strong, often long *t* bars with a hook on the end. Temporary discouragement, the loss of a loved one, financial reverses, may all cause words to droop in an optimistic hand. It is only when discouragement has been prolonged and has a chance to wear a groove in the inner consciousness that it shows in drooping basic lines.

In most writing showing optimism and buoyant spirits, the writer is engaged in activity he enjoys. His energy is put to use, and the person is cheerful in the pursuit of his goals.

It is usually the indecisive, weak-willed, or neurotic person whose motivations are not well defined who lacks ambition and whose writing may droop. People who have long periods of inactivity, even though restlessness overtakes them and causes them to work spasmodically, show signs of boredom, despondency, and inertia in their handwriting. When the energies are tied up by a neurosis, we see signs of weak and strong *t* bars, and where the weak ones are preponderant and the basic lines droop we see the warning signal. The writer may be heading for a breakdown, may be seeking an escape from reality in drugs, alcohol, or even crime.

Some people, unsuccessful because of a lack of ambition, may be pessimistic and refuse to see the cheerful side of a situation. Their so-called failure may be the result of an unconscious will to fail, and they are achieving negative (or secondary) benefits. Their reasoning goes something like this: "Why should I make an effort? I'll only fail if I do." The optimist, on the other hand, tells himself if he makes the effort there is bound to be success at the other end. "If I look hard enough for the pot of gold at the end of the rainbow, I'll find it." His optimism is more often than not predicated upon a deep, underlying faith that everything works together for good.

Not all cynics are failures, although many failures are cynics, embittered by disappointment. The emotional person whose emotionalism outweighs his thinking is more likely to become the embittered pessimist, and his writing will consistently swing downward.

Where misfortune has affected the attitude and viewpoint of an individual and caused continual unhappiness, though he may delude himself into thinking he is happy and contented, he will be betrayed by his handwriting, which tells the real story. For handwriting never lies, even though the individual may, unwittingly, lie to himself.

Specimen 166 is an example of such a person. She came to see me the day this specimen was written; told me she had finally divorced her husband, who (she said) had sapped her energy for ten years, and she was happy to be free of him. The writing betrayed her real feelings. She was still suffering from the impact of her enervating experiences, was really lonely and unhappy and still in love with the man she had divorced.

> ...... , the weathe
> as heavenly (around 77°) the
> ime . I made $200 at the 3
> racing (including santa ana
> the little King took quite
> to the Judson school at Phoeni
> will probably go next fall.
> Well dearest Emil ...

SPECIMEN 166

A sudden drooping of words—or some of them hanging over at the end of a line—may give us a major clue to suicidal tendencies. We must look for other signs of morbidity in "pasty" or varying pen pressure and in weak *t* bars. (See specimen of suicide in Chapter XI, "The Maladjusted.")

As in the specimen of the drug addict's writing, these are the signs of hopelessness and futility. Paradoxically we frequently see signs of melancholia and suicidal tendencies in the writing of optimists. Pessimists seldom commit suicide; optimists who realize their hopes are futile are more likely to take their own lives.

Moodiness—when a person is happy one moment and gloomy the next—will show in varying angles and pen pressure, and the tendency of the basic line to waver. Often he becomes depressed for no reason he can fathom. In the case of the manic-depressive we may have many lines that, at the beginning of a specimen, will virtually soar on the paper, disclosing his euphoria; yet before he has finished writing (it is a good idea to have him write at least a page if not more) we see that the lines have begun to droop, and by the time he signs his name, it is written as if under a weeping willow.

What if people ask: "How can you analyze someone's handwriting if she writes so many ways?" The answer is: She is probably a person of moods, perhaps great versatility, and all specimens written by one person would disclose fundamental traits, attributes, and talents.

By the same token, a person cannot disguise his handwriting for any length of time without giving himself away. There are signs, strokes, and especially the rhythm of an individual's handwriting that will show in both his natural and his disguised handwriting. If you write a rightward-flowing hand and try to disguise it by writing a backhand, your words will hike up, which will be a major clue to the disguise.

Connecting Strokes (Logic and Intuition)

Logical thinking, which is orderly and consecutive and deals with facts and figures, reveals itself in connecting letters without breaks, and sometimes in connected words, where the ideas, like the thoughts, hang together. Logic is concerned mostly with evaluating evidence and drawing proper conclusions from it. A logical person seeks such proof as can be clearly demonstrated to him. At times he may be so logical, so concerned with following the letter, that he may miss the underlying spirit that created the issue in the first place. His mind may form a pedantic pattern that renders him unable to see the forest because of the trees. Literal-minded people who demand concrete proof for everything tend to be limited in their horizons. They learn by rote more than by observation or personal experience.

I have already discussed the difference between the logical and the intuitive approach. However, I will repeat that even the most logical-thinking man may get flashes of intuition (though he may not trust them); similarly, the most intuitive woman can be capable of clear and incisive logical reasoning. Intuition enlivens the activity of the mind; it shows in breaks between letters in words. The writer's hand lifts unconsciously from the paper to permit a flash of intuition to enter. There may be a combination of logic and intuition in the same specimen of writing, and this tells us the writer is capable of both inductive and deductive reasoning. The more intuition a person has, the more likely he is to jump to conclusions, to take a short cut to a conclusion or destination, and to form quick impressions based on personal feelings more than on conventional criteria.

Where intuition is evident in writing without signs of good judgment, we have a person who forms impressions from feelings and the senses, often from some subconscious memory association, or from externals. When the mind skims the surface of a situation and forms a conclusion, if judgment is not present it may be wrong. Or it may take a negative turn and become suspicion, as shown in the handwriting of a person with paranoid trends. Where a conclusion is reached intuitively from superficialities, breaks between letters will be accompanied by long, swinging lower loops, sometimes greatly exaggerated, as in Specimen 164 in the section on *Zones*. Such people do not think things out clearly, are apt to say things like: "I don't know why, but there's something about the way she wears her hair that I don't like." The exaggerated lower loop is often an indication of prejudice against some external (or material) manifestation; the breaks show the instantaneous reaction, and when the pen pressure is heavy, showing emotional intensity, this combination (breaks, long loops, heavy pressure) reveals a person who forms strong likes and dislikes from appearances. The senses, in such instances, may be offended, which brings to mind Emerson's remark: "At short distances the senses are despotic." The emotions of intuitive people are often intensified through the senses.

Terminals

When the terminals of words rise it is a sign of aspiration, of even disposition, and of pleasantry. When found in a rounded handwriting, it indicates definite social trends. These people must have other people around to be happy, and they tend to act in such a way that others are attracted to them. A good example appears in Specimen 59.

When the final stroke on a word is flung downward, sometimes ending in a thick, black blob, we have indications of obstinacy, aggressiveness, and bad temper. The downward trend points to the negative direction the disposition takes, tells us there is sadism in the individual. There will usually be other signs of temper in the same specimen. A good example is Specimen 62. (Wait till you see the final stroke on the signature of Machiavelli, which appears further on! It speaks volumes.)

A long horizontal terminal indicates generosity (it's a generous, outgoing stroke) and curiosity, and if it's hooked, as often happens, it shows tenacity of purpose. In a heavy-pressure hand it reveals possessiveness and is frequently accompanied by signs of suspicion. See a good example of this in Specimen 65.

Short, blunt terminals show abruptness and bluntness. In a vertical hand this may mean curtness—sometimes to the point of rudeness—repressed sadism (and sometimes not so repressed). The person is usually opinionated and not easily swerved from his convictions. See Specimen 73.

Other terminals are usually a variation of these, and if you imitate them with a gesture of your hand, you will get some idea of what they mean. Make a graceful gesture with your hand (with or without a pen) and you feel a certain rhythm, almost as though you were keeping time to music. People who make graceful terminals are usually very fond of music, harmony, beauty in nature, and are themselves in harmony with it.

Roundness and Angularity

W<small>E HAVE SEEN</small> many examples of roundness as it is revealed in the handwriting of children, as well as of adults who are still children in many respects. So we know that maturity or immaturity, strength of character or lack of it, is revealed by angularity or roundness or a combination of both.

SPECIMEN 167

Mention has been made of the German script, which is characterized by angularity. Above is an example of a typical writing of this kind, and in it we see the unyielding, rigid, exacting, and efficient person who has been cast into a sharp mold. It is an extreme example, to be sure, and we know that any extreme is bound to have neurotic overtones. We see this here. There is a slight hint of roundness in the upper parts of letters (as in the *m*), which saves her from being an automaton. The writing looks like a design in its consistency, and the writer is skillful at handwork. In the home she has a place for everything and everything in its place.

Most handwriting influenced by Teutonic education or language has a strong element of angularity, but the Scandinavian, Swiss, and Austrian hands have more elements of roundness, so we regard them as being more flexible than the German.

Uniformity of Letter Formations

Impetuosity

A SPECIMEN OF HANDWRITING in which all the letters are the same size gives evidence that the writer has a balanced evaluation of the things that interest him. Where letters are completely clear and legible, we have a person who hides nothing, one whose subconscious is in harmony with his conscious mind, one who can communicate clearly.

SPECIMEN 168

Where the letters become larger toward the end of a word, we see a tendency to blurt things out, impetuosity and impulsiveness overcoming caution. This will most often appear in a rightward-flowing hand, corroborating the impulsiveness and spontaneity of the writer. (See Specimen 168). We think of this as a childlike trait, arising from the tendencies of the emotions to override cool reasoning. It is a sign of naïve honesty, like that of the child who says, "My mother says to tell you she isn't home."

Discretion

Discretion, tact, diplomacy, and finesse are all shown in the tendency of the letters to taper toward the end of words. The writer has the inclination to close in, tone down, become cautious—at which point the mind steps in to take charge of the emotions. The smaller the letters become toward the end of a word, the more the evidence of diplomacy, but there is a difference in the tact of the diplomat and the tact of the ordinary person. The diplomat's handwriting will show keenness of intellect (or should), awareness through intuition, and an ability to communicate with other people, though the route may be a subterranean one. It often turns out to be a match of wits. Thus, in the handwriting of diplomats, statesmen, and strategists of any kind, we look for and usually find similar combinations of signs. Napoleon's handwriting is a good example (shown in an earlier chapter). Disraeli's is an excellent one (he was an amateur graphologist in his day). In Chapter III, the handwriting of a diplomat appears with all its ramifications.

Tactfulness

Tactfulness is more evident in handwriting that discloses consideration and kindness in rounded formations. It differs from diplomacy in being inspired by feelings of sympathy—often empathy—for people, where diplomacy concerns itself with issues. The following example shows tact.

SPECIMEN 169

Diplomacy

In writing that shows mental formations, often in a vertical hand, diplomacy will be evident. (Disraeli's was forward leaning, and from his biography we know he was something of a sentimentalist.) The ends of words will sometimes taper to mere strokes, which is the sign of evasiveness, sometimes dissimulation. Diplomacy implies courtesy, but it will be of a disinterested sort; and signs of intuition, when present, tell us the diplomat in question often sees through the person he is dealing with and gauges his conclusions accordingly.

Secretiveness

This will show in tapering formations when the writing flows to the right and is accompanied by tightly closed small *a*'s and *o*'s representing caution. Capitals *D* and *O* will be tightly closed, often with a loop. Frequently the signature will show the first capital somewhat involved, or the second letter tied in with the capital. The person "covers up his tracks," as it were, hides something, as in the following specimen, where he hides the small *r* within the capital *D*.

SPECIMEN 170

Shrewdness

When letter forms dwindle and become mere strokes rather than clear-looking letters, we have evidence of shrewdness, or what we have heard described as smoothness. In a semiliterate hand, this would be tantamount to dishonesty. (Here extreme care must be taken not to confuse the nervous hand with the shrewd one, though some shrewd people are nervous about being found out.) Specimen 171 is an example of the smooth article against whom we must protect ourselves, as he would not be averse to robbing orphans and widows. You're not likely to know what he's thinking, for he may give lip service to an idealistic purpose but act in an underground way. This specimen was written by a person who is no mental slouch, as can be seen in mental formations, intuition, signs of good judgment, and mathematical ability. Because of his superior intellect, he is that much more dangerous.

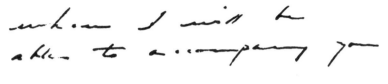

SPECIMEN 171

Legibility and Illegibility

LEGIBLE OR ILLEGIBLE WRITING in itself tells us little or nothing about the mentality of the writer. A great many professional men and women, top executives, statesmen, authors, musicians, certainly doctors (as their prescriptions often show) write illegibly.

Young children attempt to write legibly because their attention is concentrated on forming letters. The desire of the detail worker is also to write clearly, for he feels that to slur letters or to be sloppy with details is to turn out a slipshod piece of work. These people have patience, and they are found in the ranks of clerical workers, bookkeepers, often kindergarten teachers. It is not usually in the nature of detail workers to write an individualized script different from what they were taught. The mechanical accuracy seen in the handwriting of such people shows an ability to follow a prescribed pattern of thought and action, as well as an effort to perfect themselves in following the copybook script. These people are rarely leaders; their very desire to follow a pattern of writing laid down by someone else is the same desire that makes them followers.

But legible writing doesn't belong only to detail workers. Other people may be capable of doing detail work of a different sort. The clear-thinking scientist, with a direct approach to his research, often has simple tastes and may write a legible hand. Professor Einstein comes under this heading, and his handwriting analysis (in an earlier chapter) reveals the simplicity of his nature. Handwriting is, after all, a means of communicating with your fellow man, and if you want to be understood and are cooperative and want other people to understand you, you will make the effort to write in such a manner as to make it easier for them to do so. It is a clue to the illegible writer that something within him does not care whether or not he is easily understood. Writing illegibly is a way of saying: "This is the way I am; try to understand my meanings if you can; if not, too bad."

Illegible writing belongs, first of all, to the uneducated (illiterate) person. With training, the formations may become more readable, but education itself does not necessarily result in legible writing.

One might be able to express his thoughts with clarity in conversation or in literature, yet not write legibly. On the other hand, he might be awkward, even inarticulate in conversation yet his handwriting might be quite legible.

Mental confusion is indicated in handwriting that shows great disorder and is disturbing to the eye, but this type of illegibility is in a class by itself, and we may be dealing with the mental and emotional disturbances of psychoneurotics or psychotics.

Illegibility that belongs to the dishonest person is often determined by very ordinary letter formations and by awkward and ungainly capital letters, usually accompanied by signs of a weak will and signs of rebelliousness (the downstroke of the *t* bar). The variety of *t* bars in the neurotic's writing will appear in the dishonest person's hand, too, though this does not mean that neurotics are dishonest. (When they are, it is apt to be with themselves.) In the dishonest person, pen pressure tends to be muddy or pasty, showing his emotional instability. Letters will be slurred and not readily determined; there will be signs of manipulativeness in uneven letters, and many times the writ-

Horace Greeley

SPECIMEN 172

ing will be cramped and poorly spaced, showing a narrowness of vision and a person who lives in a world of private meanings. He does not communicate with the outside world and often considers other people his enemies. His dishonesty is his way of taking revenge on a world he feels rejects him. His viewpoint is obviously distorted, and the distortions are bound to show in his handwriting.

A nervous person may write illegibly because his nervousness transmits itself to his hand. His lack of control and his restlessness make it difficult for him to focus his attention on one thing for any length of time; his nerves keep him on the jump. To the practiced eye of the expert, the nervous person's handwriting will not be confused with that of the shrewd or dishonest person.

In estimating dishonesty in handwriting, other factors besides letter formations must be taken into account. Pen pressure is extremely important (which is why a ball-point pen should not be used for a specimen for analysis). Strength of will power and the pattern of the mentality are equally important in such a diagnosis.

Horace Greeley, noted for his illegible handwriting, was a keen intellect. His writing reveals mental formations, with the sign of intuition in breaks between letters, and the altruistic turn of the *y*. This was his last letter, written in bad health which included a mental breakdown. He had lost the election, his wife, and his usual enthusiasm for life itself.

Margins and Spacing

Margins have, primarily, an aesthetic significance. They are said to have originated with the monks who, when they did illuminated writing, held the thumb of the left hand along the margin to keep the parchment from sliding about.

The impulse of the economical person is to make use of all the paper's space available to him. Even when he uses hotel stationery he leaves no margin, sometimes filling the page to overflowing, even writing over the hotel imprint. Such people place comfort and practical needs ahead of good taste. An economical woman may select a sofa primarily because it is comfortable and resonably priced, with little regard for its appearance. Where there are signs of both a sense of economy and good taste, the margins may be slight, but the practicality will show up in cautious or closed letter formations. Some people write large hands (which show expansiveness, sometimes extravagance) yet leave no margin on the left; they are apt to save on little things. (Specimen 173 is an example of a narrow-minded, repressed person, tight with money, intolerant, and greatly concerned with saving—old clothes as well as money.)

SPECIMEN 173

The consistently wide margin on both sides of the paper, where the specimen of handwriting looks as if it were framed by the space around it, signifies a person of innately good taste, one whose aesthetic sense conditions everything she does. These are the people who have a setting for everything they do, a frame for every picture. They possess a sense of the fitness of things, and their good taste extends to their behavior. Such specimens will usually be consistent in the expression of good taste by the use of wide spacing between words and lines. It shows an instinctive love (even an almost neurotic need) for order, harmony, and balance in their surroundings and often in their thinking, too. It is unlikely that such an individual could approach any task without first creating order in the surroundings. She may be considered fussy by some people and neat as a pin by others. (She reminds me of the woman who sets about cleaning her house on the day her cleaning woman is due to arrive, so that the maid will not consider her disorderly.)

When margins start out narrow on the left and grow wider as the writer becomes more interested in the thoughts being expressed than in the looks of the writing, we have evidence of a person who starts out cautiously in many resolves, but whose aesthetic sense overpowers his caution. Signs of extravagance also begin to appear as the widening left margin leaves more blank paper on one side. Such people may save money for necessities yet spend it on some beautiful

1. 16. 67

Dear Friend:

Thank you for your kind
words of sympathy which always helps at a time like this.
When I have put my house in
order, I will see you.

                    Sincerely
                    Eva

SPECIMEN 174

The weather held out and we
skiing. You should have seen
mountain top. The sun was s
The colors were breath-taking.
We were hungry as bears and o
set before us, devouring every
we'd never seen food before. Th
we relaxed in front of we o
and sat around singing all t

SPECIMEN 175

object that satisfies them aesthetically. The overriding desire here is to possess something of beauty rather than something of practical value. In such people, their generosity will often overcome their desire to be sensible.

Such writers seem to spend instinctively—and this includes energy as well as money.

Where the left margin starts out wide and grows narrower toward the bottom of the page, we have evidence of the sense of economy overcoming the aestheticism in one's nature. The person may desire to surround himself with objects of beauty, but his practical side asserts itself, and though he may splurge momentarily, he begins to feel the necessity to make up for his lavishness and economizes in other things.

Often this happens with people whose experience has taught them to be thrifty, no matter how much money they have. So they compromise by splurging on some things and economizing on others. (I knew a man who would walk five blocks to save a few pennies on a pack of cigarettes, yet he entertained lavishly at home.)

SPECIMEN 176

Where the margin on the left is uneven and untidy, we will usually find that the writer is inconsistent and not always concerned with keeping order around him. There may be clutter in some places and then a compulsive neatness in others. This is often found where the rest of the writing reveals inconsistencies, capriciousness, and a measure of emotional instability. The person has no rationale about spending money or energy and is often referred to as mixed up. In Specimen 177 we have such a man, but he is not without talent, and, paradoxically enough, the type of R he makes ("sorry" and "forget") shows a kind of artistic concern with appearances.

SPECIMEN 177

There is also a psychological connotation that relates to the way a person sets his margins. A wide margin on the left may mean that the writer allows other people a wide margin for error, whereas a narrow margin or none at all may be construed as narrow-mindedness and intolerance, which are usually substantiated by other signs in the writing. However, a wide margin often means that the writer desires to keep a distance between himself and other people, whereas the writer who leaves no margin at all may allow more intimacy. Here again we must examine the rest of the writing before making a positive statement. The actor, for instance, who needs people, nevertheless keeps a distance between himself and his audience.

So much depends on other factors in the handwriting (as to how an individual relates to other people) that it is wiser to analyze the margin solely for its aesthetic significance and to judge other traits from the handwriting itself.

Signatures

YOUR SIGNATURE is your individual stamp. It reveals what you think of yourself, what you would like others to think of you, or what you think they think of you. A signature expresses the personality of the individual, showing individual marks of importance; it gives an important clue to the writer's inferiority complex, whether he is making definite efforts to compensate for it or whether he considers himself too superior to strive consciously.

When analyzing a specimen of handwriting, it is best to include the natural signature of the writer. There may be a distinct contrast between the personality and the character of the writer, who may not be at all like what he appears to be; this may show in a signature that has more force than the body of the specimen. Where the personality is modest or meek and the character is stronger than might be supposed, this will show in a modest signature even though the body of the writing will reveal signs of strength.

Where the writing flows to the right, but the signature is written at a vertical angle, we have a person whose façade is reserved and aloof, even though underneath he may be warm and responsive. Circumstances may have forced him to adopt a calm, dignified exterior.

In instances where the body of the writing is vertical and the signature spontaneously flowing to the right, we have a reserved person who gives the impression of being warm and spontaneous, but who does not warm up or easily become intimate with other people. The nature of a person's work may force him to develop an outgoing personality in order to win people over, but there will always be some barrier between him and other people. This is the introvert with an extroverted personality.

When the signature is larger than the rest of the writing, we are dealing with a person who considers himself important. He believes that what he does or says is important because he did it and said it. He is the authority, and he makes his authority felt when he exerts it over others.

We regard the personality as negative when the signature is ineffectual, perhaps smaller than the rest of the writing. Such people tend to underestimate their importance, and the body of the specimen will reveal signs of self-abnegation and masochism. There are instances where such retiring individuals have, through their work, impressed the outside world.

An illegible signature is a sign that the writer does not really want the world to know him well. He may have something to hide, or he may not really care whether others understand him or not. Where the signature is so complicated and involved that it isn't legible, we can be sure that the writer has an involved and perhaps unique personality, and we wonder what sort of person he is.

When a signature is written so that the last stroke goes backward through it, something in the individual impels him to cancel himself out. We cannot guess at what it might be; we must know something of his habits, his early history, to find the clues to this paradox.

Though it is not definitive to make an analysis from only a signature, a great deal of the character is congealed in the signature. It takes more perspicacity and a great deal of experience to draw definite conclusions from the signature alone. (I have had to do this when someone's handwriting was not available, and in many instances I have had marked success.)

Following are the signatures of many well-known people about whom we are curious, and everything possible is deduced from the way they sign their names.

The Underscore

The underscore is in itself a sign of self-assertiveness. It also tells us what type of personality we are dealing with—forceful and magnetic, unique, or unusually extroverted. It is an attention-getting device and is usually found in the handwriting of people who are in the public eye—or who wish they might be.

Roman Polanski

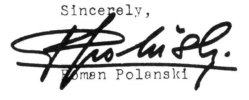

SPECIMEN 178

The forceful, positive personality is expressed in a heavy, straight line under the signature. We see this in the signature of Roman Polanski, who directed the pictures *Knife in the Water* and *Rosemary's Baby*. He is a very young man, unusually talented, forceful, intensely emotional, yet quite disciplined and controlled, whose signature shows intuition that would no doubt be seen in the body of his handwriting.

Gamal Abdel Nasser

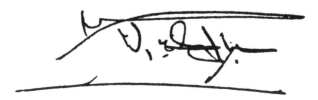

SPECIMEN 179

Another signature with this kind of underscore is that of Gamal Abdel Nasser. He encloses himself within a frame, so to speak (see the overscore) and shows persistence in doing this. His vertical angle tells us he considers himself a person apart, in a class by himself, and one whom few people can get really close to. Here is evidence of illegibility, and it is a fact that Nasser is a riddle to many people. (That is the way he wants it to be.) The power drive is shown in hooks on the end of long strokes, yet implicit within this force is his weakness, which is fear of failure. (That the writing was done from right to left in no way changes our conclusions.) It is primarily the underscore that gives the important clue to his deep-seated inferiority complex, for which he overcompensates through his political power.

Ravi Shankar

SPECIMEN 180

Some signatures are so flamboyant they need no underscore to show that the writer is an exhibitionist. And an excellent example of this is Ravi Shankar, the East Indian who plays the sitar. His signature is involved and pervaded with rhythm; it reveals the man's showmanship, his concern with appearances, in the broad and unusual *r* at the end of his name. His uniqueness in the circle dot over the *i* simply intensifies our impression. The capital *R*, larger than any other letter in the signature, is a definite indication of his inflated opinion of himself—an overcompensation for a deep-seated inferiority complex.

We see in the vertical, heavy-pressure handwriting of Lyndon B. Johnson an emotionally intense man who does not usually act im-

Lyndon B. Johnson

SPECIMEN 181 (ENLARGED)

pulsively, who deliberates before taking action; but when he does act he goes after what he wants with persistence and determination. He is rigid and unyielding, often believes he can accomplish the impossible, finds it hard to believe he is ever wrong. He has an insatiable drive for power and is not averse to following a circuitous route to achieve it.

In this kind of hand, the obvious altruistic formations disclose a messianic faith in a self-appointed moral mission. The final stroke on his last name, in which letters are obliterated, shows his secretiveness. Anyone who makes this kind of formation, whether in the body of a handwriting specimen or in the signature, has no intention of communicating his thoughts to anybody.

The squared-off upper loop in the capital *J* shows extreme tenacity in holding to a point of view. Once he has formed an opinion he is apt to consider the matter settled, and it is difficult for him to go over the same ground twice. He plays his cards close to the chest, but this may occur because of his own uncertainty about his plans. The vertical writing combined with the forcefulness (especially in the downstrokes) bespeak a person who can switch from being a misunderstood saint into being an avenging angel.

In the signature of Nelson Rockefeller we see flair and energy— and tenacity of purpose in the long hook on the capital *R*. The rhythm is quick and the pen pressure is medium heavy to heavy, revealing both sensuousness and spontaneous reactions; and there are signs of intuition and sound practical judgment. Letters taper in his first name, start to taper in his last name, and then broaden in the

Nelson A. Rockefeller

SPECIMEN 182

small *r*. So we have here a man who can be diplomatic but who will do or say some things for the sake of appearance. He is essentially outgoing, and although he has a drive for power, he is really concerned with how his actions affect others. He will, therefore, cut the cloth to fit the garment, economizing where he thinks necessary and finding valid reasons for spending.

A man of perspicacity, foresight, and planning, plus a good sense of timing, in positions of high responsibility he might even distinguish himself. He can be noncommittal up to a point, but in the end he shows his hand and does so fearlessly, with courage and a sense of rightness in his own decisions. And he has a sense of humor, which he can share with others.

Hubert H. Humphrey

SPECIMEN 183

We see in the signature of Hubert Humphrey a compulsive, somewhat unreasonable obstinacy in the final letter of his name, and the hook on the end of the *y* augments this conclusion. The entire signature is written with a continuous stroke, without his hand lifting from the paper, and this shows his persistence, as well as logical approach. (If he has intuition, it does not show here.) He backs up his conclusions with his own form of logic, as if to say, "That's my story and I'm stuck with it." Formations are mostly angular, with only a hint of roundness, and this tells us he can be inflexible except where sentiment enters. Caution is indicated in the small *b*, and the vertical angle suggests that despite his outward friendliness there are not many people who can get really close to him.

He appears to be a simple man, but there are unconscious strivings of which he is not fully aware, and we therefore conclude that he has some unresolved problems on the emotional level.

John F. Kennedy

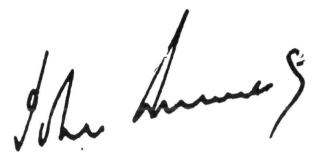

SPECIMEN 184

Autographing a photograph for the inaugural ceremonies, the late John F. Kennedy wrote his name informally, leaving out his middle initial. The rhythm here is quick, showing the speed with which his keen, razor-sharp mind worked. The high capitals reveal a combination of idealism and a strong, unwavering ego. In the single downstroke of the *y* we observe sound practical judgment, and the open *o* shows he was generous and articulate.

But there is a contradiction in his last name, illegible as it is, reminding us of the handwriting of many outstanding statesmen whose small letters are mere strokes. The break before the *y* indicates intuition, and it is reasonable to believe that his handwriting would reveal many such breaks because of his rapid perception and insight.

The capital letters show originality, noticeable in the small twist in the center of the capital *J* and the sharp, tentlike angle of the *K*. Certainly there was more to the late President than met the eye.

The formations in Senator Morse's signature are rounded and

Wayne Morse

SPECIMEN 185

could be described as gentle. The signature shows the simplicity, un-wavering honesty, and unpretentiousness that characterize him. Every letter is clear; the *o* is open, showing generosity; the *e*'s on both first and last names are slightly larger than the other letters, a sign that he can be direct and outspoken. The connected letters show logical reasoning. Here is a man who says what he thinks, who puts his cards on the table—somewhat unusual for a politician. His interest in people is expressed in a deep concern for their welfare—and not because of any advantage to himself, for his lower loop is normal.

Martin Luther King, Jr.

SPECIMEN 186

The signature of the Reverend Martin Luther King shows unique-ness in the *g*'s ending stroke; it also reveals a compulsive persistence, substantiated by the long *t* bar that starts with a hook. The high upper loops and capitals are signs of his idealism. That his final letters taper a bit is a sign of his tact and consideration, and the *i* dot to the right of the *i* reveals enthusiasm. The rightward angle tells of an outgoing man, interested in people and concerned with their welfare. The connected letters show logical thinking, and great pride and self-assurance are seen in the combination of high capitals and strong *t* bars. There is no doubting the integrity and sincerity of the late

Dr. King. And the way the last name is circled by the *g* stroke reveals many things, among them a flair for the dramatic, as well as a clue to the uniqueness of the man.

Jeannette Rankin

With highest hopes,

JEANNETTE RANKIN

SPECIMEN 187

The even pen pressure, on the heavy side, is our major clue to Jeannette Rankin's consistency. She was an exponent of peace in the First World War and still holds the same view today. The angle of her writing shows her concern for people. She is dependable, direct, and courageous, and fights for what she believes is right. Emotional though she is, she has a capacity for clear reasoning and possesses a sense of justice, as her angular formations show. Despite her directness, she is secretive about very personal matters, as shown in the way the capital *J* and the *ea* run together. Here is a woman with a mind of her own—the first woman to sit in Congress.

Nikita Khrushchev

SPECIMEN 188

For an apparently robust person, Khrushchev's handwriting is oddly light in pen pressure, though it varies from light to medium heavy. There is a slight wavering in the lines, which tells us he was not in the pink of condition when he wrote this. Nevertheless, it shows unusual sensitivity, high hopes, and optimism in the way the signature rises, and the sign of altruism is very apparent. Here we see his concern with the welfare of his people, an innate generosity with an element of masochism (sometimes giving until it hurts), and a uniqueness that sent this man of peasant temperament to a position of great power. There is pride shown in his capital *N* (in Russian it is an *H*), and there is some illegibility, which tells us he did not always show his hand.

Barry Goldwater

SPECIMEN 189

The large capitals in Barry Goldwater's signature are the sign of his strong ego, pride, and independence, and the angular formations in the other letters tell us he can be rigid and unyielding once he's convinced he's right. Some open formations, even in this seemingly tight hand, indicate generosity; it is based on judgment, and he gives when he deems it wise to do so. The literary capital *g* discloses cultural leanings and shows he can adapt himself within the framework of his beliefs. He has flashes of intuition, as shown in the break after the letter *w*, but does not trust them, preferring to back them up with logic. The blunt stroke of the *y* shows he can be blunt at times, and combined with an element of humor, it tells of his talent for practical joking. The curve at the top of the capital *G* looks like a hook and suggests persistence, but it has another connotation, relating to family pride and a protective instinct for those close to him. The compressed loop in his last name shows some repression, substantiated by the closeness of letters; but there is strength in his *t* bar, and this means he has a will of his own and can persevere in the face of difficulty.

The rightward-leaning, heavy-pressure writing of Dr. Benjamin Spock tells us immediately that he is an intensely emotional person,

Dr. Benjamin Spock

SPECIMEN 190

utterly sincere and wholehearted, with a strong sense of justice. The altruistic formation of the *j* points to his concern for the welfare of other people; he is capable of making sacrifices for a cause in which he believes, and he is selfless. The critical *i* dot indicates sharp vision in one who is as critical of himself as he is of others. Yet the letters taper in both names, and we see in such formations a tactful, considerate human being who will, however, express himself with firmness when his sense of justice is outraged. We wonder about the ragged upper loop in the *k*, and hope it is just a temporary condition, the result perhaps of his latest brush with the law!

Adolf Hitler

SPECIMEN 191

This signature's veering downward tells of Hitler's morbid, depressed states, and the carefully dotted *i* is a sign of his exactness with detail. The involved capital *H* indicates the strategist—the person who gets himself into tight situations from which he usually manages to emerge, no matter what the cost. It is a tight, somewhat restrained writing, for he was less a man of action than a planner who got others to do his bidding. Small, almost imperceptible upper loops reveal that he dreamed of earthly conquests; the one high loop in his last name, along with a bowed *t* bar, tells us of his God-like self-image. The droop of his signature is a clue to his suicidal tendencies; he killed himself when he realized he had failed, for here was a man who could not accept failure. (Notice the ego emphasis in the aggressive period after his name.)

Joe McCarthy

SPECIMEN 192

The signature of the late Joe McCarthy reveals secretiveness. Notice how some of the letters are enclosed in his final stroke and that this same stroke ends in a flair: It is tantamount to an underscore. The way part of the stroke goes over the stem of the letter *t* gives us a clue to his rich fantasy world, and we must conclude that many of his fantasies dominated his thinking.

The blunt way his *e* ends (in "Joe") shows his capacity for blunt outspokenness, especially as this letter is larger than the one before it. He was contradictory, however, considering his caution in the closed *o* and *a*, combined with the secretiveness mentioned. Our conclusion must therefore be that here was a man who was cautious and secretive, yet who wanted to give the impression that he was fearlessly outspoken. So we describe him as inconsistent. His capital *J* is a sign of personal vanity, and the small *r* in his last name tells us that he was not always aboveboard in his communication with others. In clinical terms, we would call him a psychopathic personality.

Fidel Castro

SPECIMEN 193

A person of tremendous energy, drive, and persistence, Fidel Castro has visionary ideals, as revealed in his very high upper loops, and intuition (shown in the break between the *i* and *d*). His unique self-image is evident in the way he makes his capital *F*, with its complicated cap and tenacious middle bar. But notice a substantiation of this in the way he connects his *l* to his capital *C*, making the *l* part of the *C!* Furthermore, the persistence with which he continues after the *o*, where he crosses over to cross his *t*, then continues to the right with a loop, a downstroke, a star-shaped formation, and the tail for an underscore tells us he does not give up, no matter what the obstacles.

Here is certainly the classic strategist: a man who can get himself into tight situations from which he finally emerges victorious and with flair. However, we have another meaning in the final strokes on his signature: It is that of a man who lives in a world of his own making in which he is the ruler. It is a fantasy-laden world that, through concerted effort, he means to bring to fruition. He does not give up without a struggle, yet he manages to maintain a measure of dignity, as the *d* in his first name shows. He is strong, purposeful, and resolute—but also outgoing, for his writing leans to the right. And this tells us he is concerned with other people and not afraid to take some of them into his confidence. In other words, he is not afraid. And what a sense of humor—he can laugh at himself.

John Gielgud

SPECIMEN 194

The handwriting of John Gielgud as revealed in his signature is that of the instinctive poet, what with the consistent breaks seen between letters. The Greek *d* is the sign of a cultured man, and the simple large capitals tell us he is distinguished in his profession— which brings him into the public eye, as revealed in the underscore. A simple line underscores his name, and the *i* dot, which is a tentlike formation, indicates a keen critical faculty. He is critical of his own performance, for being a perfectionist (as the very high stroke on the capital *J* shows), he is not satisfied with just good enough. That the writing slants upward tells us of his optimism, vision, spirituality; all in all we have an actor who is in a class by himself and who works best when inspired from his inner depths. (The colon after his name is a form of ego emphasis, as if he had more to say but chose to withhold it.)

Noel Coward

SPECIMEN 195

Distinguished by originality and versatility, Noel Coward's signature looks like a design. In the underscore, which is a continuation of the final stroke on his name, we see his persistence, coupled with his strong dramatic instinct. The elongated downstroke on the *l* in his first name tells us he can be willful and determined to do things in his own way, and the hook on the end of this stroke reveals his tenacity. His capital *N*, certainly original, also shows his awareness of his importance in the theater; but he has earned his accolades with his original songs, his acting and his plays. Intuition, which plays a part in his compositions, is evident in the handwriting of all great artists.

Despite her friendliness, there is a measure of reserve in Beatrice Lillie that prevents too much intimacy on the part of others, although she gives the impression of being warm, spontaneous, and responsive.

Beatrice Lillie

SPECIMEN 196

And she is all of these, but she is infinitely more sensitive than most people realize, as shown in the way she forms her *t*.

High *i* dots show her vivid imagination, and one of them is so plainly tent-shaped, indicating a keen critical faculty, that we only have to recall her type of humor to recognize the barbs that are often implicit in it. Nevertheless, there is a gentleness shown in the roundedness. Keenness shows in the *e*, which looks like an *i*, in both her names. She has intuition, shown in the breaks in her first name; generosity in the open *a;* high ideals (seen in the high strokes, as in the capital *L* and smaller ones); but because of the vertical angle she can also be realistic. The underscore is a simple line and is an assertion of a personality that is not easily forgotten.

Cornelia Otis Skinner

SPECIMEN 197

Vertical in angle and written with a heavy pressure, the signature of Cornelia Otis Skinner reveals positive force, coupled with a sensuousness to forms, colors, music. She is controlled, as revealed by a strong *t* bar, which also shows determination and a capacity for hard work. There is obvious talent in the constructed capital *S*, intuition in breaks between letters, and a retentive memory in careful *i* dots.

She appears friendly, but she is also discriminating, selective, and self-sufficient—a woman who would not go out of her way to make new acquaintances, but who would always be gracious, well-mannered, and in good taste at all times. Despite the angle of reserve, the underscore reveals her dramatic instinct and is a sign of exhibitionism, which in Miss Skinner's case is greatly toned down.

Olivia de Havilland

SPECIMEN 198

Even though the handwriting specimen of Olivia de Havilland is greatly reduced, it reveals a person of great sensitivity, in the fairly light pen pressure; vivid imagination amounting to a spirit of adventure and a rich world of fantasy in the *t* crossing above the stem of the letter; signs of culture in the Greek *d*, coupled with mental formations, and some originality in her capital letters.

The underscore is made with a persistent stroke and shows a dramatic instinct, along with a capacity for hard work. The *i* dots are either extremely high or close to the letter, which shows her retentive memory. There still remains something of the little girl in Miss de Havilland, seen in the many rounded strokes. She is a very gentle person, above average in intelligence, with a sense of humor that shows in the curving of the capital *O*, which also reveals her love of music in its unusual rhythm. In practical matters her judgment is often sound, but her fantasies can lead her far afield and give rise to ultimate disillusionment. She is, however, quite optimistic, vital, and interested in many subjects, including the occult.

The signature of magician and former radio personality Randi is distinguished by its ultra-exaggerated capital *R*, a major clue to his

Randi

SPECIMEN 199

inflated opinion of himself. Coupled with the wide, swinging lower loop of the *y*, it means he is notional, possesses showmanship, and is attracted to anything novel or unusual. His desire is to be involved in something outstanding where he might be the center of attraction.

He makes lavish gastures, but in reality is somewhat cautious; yet many of his actions appear consistent, as shown in small letter forms which are roughly the same size. Optimism and ambition are revealed in the tendency of the writing to veer upward. The broad *r* in "sincerely," coupled with his unmistakable exhibitionism, tells us that appearances count for a great deal with him. He is visual and goes in for photography of an unusual sort.

Randi is an admirer of the outstanding magician Harry Houdini, whose signature is shown on page 342.

The first things we notice in Harry Houdini's signature are the involved capital *H*'s, which give us the major clue to the master of escape technique. It is the sign of the strategist, and it took unusual strategy for Houdini to get out of the seemingly inextricable situations he got himself into. His flagrant underscore tells us of his showmanship, magnetic personality, and persistence, and his broad *r*'s indicate his strong visual sense; with his retentive memory, Houdini seldom forgot anything he saw that impressed him. The heavy pressure indicates his sensuous reaction to forms, colors, and music;

Harry Houdini

SPECIMEN 200

it is also a sign that he was a person of strong physical attributes without which he could not have performed as he did.

Tallulah Bankhead

SPECIMEN 201

Though she signs only her first name, she knows this will identify her, for there is only one Tallulah—Bankhead, that is. Most noticeable is her large capital *T* with a hook at the end of the bar showing tenacity; the rare breaks between letters indicate intuition. We see here a talented person with a quick mind and a rich world of fantasy. Upper loops are high and fairly wide, indicating idealism and sensitivity; the final stroke on the *h* shows curiosity. The writing swings upward, then seems to go down toward the end, telling us that she has moods of elation and depression. She may act cheerful even when a depressive mood threatens to overtake her, but this is because she is an excellent actress. There is force and frankness even in this brief specimen of her handwriting, for the *h* at the end is large, and from the clarity of all the letters we have a person who makes no attempt to hide anything.

The small writing of Alan Burke, the TV personality, tells us he has good reasoning powers as well as concentration. His curiosity

Alan Burke

SPECIMEN 202

is evident in the elongated final at the end of his last name and shows a desire to make investigations, not being satisfied with hearsay. The terminal on his first name darkens and shows an occasional flare-up of temper when he gives emphasis to what he says. He is quite intuitive and is quick to distinguish a phony from the genuine article.

His intuition gives him a rather keen insight into his interviewees. That he can be abrupt at times is shown by the small *l* in his first name not coming down to the basic line. Nevertheless, the capital *A* in his first name, a version of the protective formation, tells us he is, in some respects, old-fashioned, and also indicates that if you appeal to his paternalism you are sure to arouse his sympathy. However, many of his letter forms are not well defined, as in his last name and the dwindling *n* in his first, and this is a clue to his evasiveness and to his wish not to reveal intimate elements about his personal life. The vertical angle indicates his reserve and detachment.

Alexander Schneider

SPECIMEN 203

The quick, harmonious rhythm of Alexander Schneider's signature tells us he is a natural musician of unusual talent, a man whose background is one of culture, as seen in the Greek *d*. He thinks quickly and logically, but his emotions predominate, even though his reason can be appealed to. As a conductor, he shows great promise because of his sincerity and consistency, the latter shown in firm and even pen pressure. Its heaviness gives a clue to his sensuousness, not only to music but to form, color, structure. The ending stroke resembles the hand waving the baton, a gesture he makes while conducting, which is transferred to his expressive handwriting. The *i* dot resembles part of a circle and shows his sense of humor, but the angularity of the writing tells us that, were the specimen longer, we would see many *i* dots that are tentlike and indicate his critical faculty. Intensely emotional, he is given to varying moods, which is shown in the fact that the angles vary slightly; but there is nevertheless good coordination in the writing, and this tells us that he has self-discipline.

James Baldwin

SPECIMEN 204

The vertical angle, coupled with both light and medium-heavy pen pressure, in the handwriting of James Baldwin tells us of a reserve that covers up turbulent emotions. He is intensely sensitive, perceptive, intuitive; his tapering letters in the first name show his ability to be tactful—but in this cultured hand it is better described as subtlety. Take into consideration the dwindling of the last stroke and you see a person who does not tell all about himself, who learned from childhood to be manipulative, and who uses this acquired trait in his literary output. We see the Greek *d*, which rises upward, signaling inspiration, along with the capital *J*—a simple slightly curved line. This is the signature of an intellectual who can deal with reality, in which there is a hint of the gentle cynic in the closing down of the lower mound of the capital *B*.

Writers of fiction, romance, sentiment, usually write with a rightward slant; the realist usually writes at a vertical angle.

The handwriting of P. G. Wodehouse is rounded, belonging to a gentle, kind person, and his humor shows in the dots after his initials. That peculiar little sideward tent under the last letter is his own private insignia, giving individuality to his choices and personal

P. G. Wodehouse

SPECIMEN 205

habits. He is a bachelor and has a few of the peculiarities that people living alone can develop. (He does have a dog, however.) Notice how the letters in his name taper toward the end, and in this rounded, pleasant-looking hand, it means consideration and the ability to be discreet. The G is a curtailed formation of the literary *g*, which also shows Mr. Wodehouse's ability to adapt himself to changing environs; his handwriting shows him to be extremely flexible.

Paddy Chayevsky

SPECIMEN 206

Try to imitate the handwriting of playwright Paddy Chayevsky and you will realize how rapidly it is done. This shows what energy he has, along with a keen, quick, incisive mind, accelerated by intuition that gives him insight into more than the obvious. He has very high ideals, as seen in the high upper loop; originality is revealed in unusual letter forms; caution in that closed-up *a* in his second name. And yet he can be generous—usually when his emotions are aroused. The writing veers upward, indicating his optimism, animated spirits, uplift, and yet he has good practical judgment, which prevents him from living entirely in a dream world. His plays are unusual; the analytical approach he takes shows a more than superficial interest in what makes people tick. He has humor, can be gentle and flexible in some instances, but is essentially an independent thinker whose thoughts have vibrance, just as many of his characters do.

Ernest Hemingway

SPECIMEN 207

At one time a man of great control and tenacious drive, Ernest Hemingway was not in the best of health when this was written. There is a going-over of strokes in the final letter, and if you examine the specimen under a magnifying glass you will see some tremulousness. The vertical angle of reserve tells us he could cover up his deeper feelings, and the same angle gives us the clue to his realistic approach to life and people. Perhaps life became too harsh and uncompromising for so sensitive a man, and he could not face his waning energies. The brief underscore, made from habit, is a sign of self-assurance. He had to keep reassuring himself because of his uncertainty, and having achieved his goals a long time before, there seemed nothing left but to make a dramatic exit.

Frank Lloyd Wright

SPECIMEN 208

A man of some eccentricity and originality, Frank Lloyd Wright has a handwriting that reveals his energetic, tenacious drive; his versatility is seen in angles that vary slightly, though for the most part he wrote a vertical hand. His preoccupation with line, form, and structure are all here in his signature. And we see a man of cultured tastes and literary ability in the Greek *d* and literary *g*.

He was not a man many people could get close to, and his goal of architect substantiated this. The *i* dot resembles a circle and expresses his feeling for design, along with a dislike for the mundane and commonplace. The writing is spread out, which tells us that he needed a large stage on which to perform. He was frank, direct, and outspoken, also uncompromising, and the buildings he designed will stand for a long time as monuments to an outstanding architect.

Emile Zola

SPECIMEN 209

We remember the well-known French writer Emile Zola as much for his role in the Dreyfus case as for his literary achievements. And in his angular handwriting we see a measure of rigidity—a man who stood fast once he took a position; a man in whom a sense of justice prevailed over other traits. The down-flung final shows obstinacy, as well as defensiveness, and tells us he could be argumentative. The mind is keen and intuition evident, and a retentive memory shows

Anatole France

SPECIMEN 210

in the exact dotting of his *i*. Very much the realist, he did not rest until he felt sure that Captain Dreyfus would receive justice.

We really see evidence of a unique personality in the under-score (more of a tail) of Anatole France, the French writer. The whimsical curve on his capital *F* tells of his humor, while the protective *A* (a classic example of it) shows his paternal instinct. He usually held a brief for the underdog, the downtrodden, and the underprivileged, and his writings reveal this. His keen mentality is indicated in small, concentrated formations, and the broad formation of the small *r* shows his concern about appearances. You may be sure he wore something unusual to call attention to himself besides his beard!

Salvador Dali

SPECIMEN 211

Dali signed with a brush—as many artists do—disclosing in his high upper loop his vivid imagination, further seen in the *i* dot, which is something of a laughing mouth and shows his sense of humor. He is an excellent draftsman, exacting and particular, as shown in that angular stroke between the *a* and *l*—it looks as if a letter *v* were inserted. Certainly we see originality here, but we wonder if in his paintings he is laughing at us or just amusing himself.

Even the brushstrokes in Henri Matisse's signature could be framed for their beauty! See the many breaks between letters, indicating his intuition—without which he would be less of an artist. The *i* dots are exactly over the letter, showing attention to detail and excellent memory. Originality marks the entire display, and we have only

Henri Matisse

Henri-Matisse

SPECIMEN 212

to look at his paintings to understand why this master writes as he does. It really needs no analysis, for it speaks for itself.

Picasso signs with an underscore, and his capital *P* shows original-ity; there are signs of intuition in the breaks in his name. The down-stroke in the center of his name tells us he can be willful, at times demanding, yet there is evidence of some roundness tempering his demands and suggesting he is gentle and responsive. This example does not show his dynamic force, but it does reveal that he does

Pablo Picasso

SPECIMEN 213

things quickly, giving meaning with a few strokes to what a lesser artist might labor over. He is versatile, optimistic, and still energetic, with a sense of humor as well as a practical side, which enables him to deal with reality in everyday life.

Nahum Tschacbasov

SPECIMEN 214

As with many artists who feel more at home with a brush than a pen, Tschacbasov signed in a rightward-flowing hand, showing his leaning toward people, many of whom have been subjects of his paintings. The consistent breaks between letters indicate intuition, which is also the source of his inspiration. His feeling for strong colors shows in the extremely heavy pressure (though his handwriting which I have examined is fairly light and tells us of his acute sensitivity). He is both sensitive and sensuous, possesses originality, desires to spread out over a large unconfined space, and has an expansiveness that includes an innate generosity. He is also versatile and inventive.

Cartoonist Vip, the originator of "Big George" and Princess, the

Virgil Partch

Very sincerely,

Virgil Partch

SPECIMEN 215

amusing Siamese cat, signs his name with the same broad-nib pen that he uses to draw his cartoons. The humor that permeates his comic strips shows in the way he dots his *i*—more of a circle than a dot. There is a quick rhythm, even in these three letters, showing his energy and feeling for harmony, line, and structure. Although a deeply emotional person, he has an element of reserve, seen in the vertical angle leaning just a bit to the right. There is roundness, which expresses his gentleness, and an exactness in detail, as shown in the dot placed right above the *i*. Virgil Partch has originality and is one of the top cartoonists in the country.

William Shakespeare

𝓌ᵐ ℂ𝒽𝒶𝓀ſ𝓅𝑒𝒶𝓇𝑒

SPECIMEN 216

This signature of Shakespeare, written in a slow rhythm, would indicate a slowing down of his energy; we see raggedness and breaks in the upper loops. We have no record of his illness, but it seems possible he may have had a heart condition. The evidence is here, but specimens of this genius' handwriting are rare, so we don't know. The consistent breaks, which we've seen before in the handwriting of the poet and musician, are here, and we see originality in his capital letters and in the small *h*, which curves under the letter and acknowledges his introversion. (Did you ever see a capital *S* made like this? He was indeed in a class by himself, unless we could compare him to Dostoevski.)

Niccolo Machiavelli

SPECIMEN 217

The noted Italian author and statesman Niccolo Machiavelli wrote with the same original flair that distinguished him as a writer and diplomat. He had a remarkable talent for viewing military problems in connection with politics; this shows in his ending stroke, almost as though he were fencing—for he was very adept at matching wits. He wrote, besides many books and treatises on politics, several poems and plays; the last were mostly ribald comedies. His intuition shows in the breaks between letters, and his streamlined though still old-fashioned capital *M* tells us that his Renaissance ideas could be and have been used in more modern times. (Mussolini and Hitler were said to have been influenced by his writings.) He could be sober and concise in expressing himself, but his reputation suffered because of his contact with one of the Borgias. He is the original exponent of power politics.

Nicolaus Copernicus

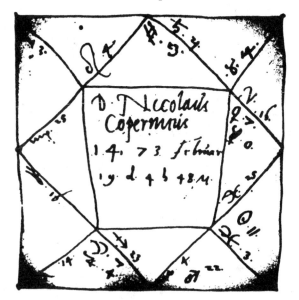

SPECIMEN 218

Polish astronomer, doctor of medicine, and student of canon law, Nicolaus Copernicus was a mathematical genius whose signature shows his intuition and exactness in the angularity of his letter forms. They are simple, legible, and without ornamentation, although his capital *N* has a hook on one of the strokes, which means he had tenacity. Modern astronomy was built upon the foundation of the Copernican system. This versatile man also practiced medicine in his scientific approach, and even held forth as a canon in a cathedral in East Prussia. He had definite ideas about anything he undertook, as happens with a genius whose usefulness persists long after he is gone.

Count Gilles de Rais (Retz) de Laval ("Bluebeard")

SPECIMEN 219

A noted soldier who was at Orleans with Joan of Arc, Count Gilles de Rais signed his name in a confusing mass of curves and strokes, rendering it unintelligible in its symbolic structure. He was a patron of the arts, a onetime marshal of France. After his retirement to his castle, he practiced satanic and vicious deeds on over one hundred boys whom he kidnapped, then murdered after maltreating them. He was called Bluebeard, although there has been no reference to wives in his biography.

You can make of this unique signature anything you wish, even to seeing in it Freudian symbols. It is included here because of its total originality, even though the heavy black strokes suggest he may have dipped his pen in the blood of his victims. To say he was emotionally unstable would be both an understatement and a euphemism. It may have been his unconscious lust for blood that originally led him into the French army.

Obviously under great tension, General Grant shows in his angular writing how unswerving he could be in his duty. But it took its toll. Here we see a nervous tremulousness, though there are also signs of a rigid self-discipline. Lines are well spaced on the page; we see the left margin that grows wider, showing his tendency toward extravagance. The last stroke, flung down from the *t* in his

Ulysses S. Grant

GRANT'S "UNCONDITIONAL SURRENDER" LETTER.

By permission of General James Grant Wilson.

SPECIMEN 220

signature, tells us he had a need to make the final gesture in order
to feel victorious.

The History of Graphology

SOME OUTSTANDING PERSONAGES OF ANTIQUITY WHO advocated the study of handwriting in order to understand other individuals include Aesop, Aristotle, Julius Caesar, and Cicero. More recent exponents were Sir Walter Scott and Disraeli, George Sand, Dostoevski, and Robert Browning, among others.

Three thousand years ago Nero said he did not trust a man in his court because "his handwriting shows him treacherous." About A.D. 120 Suetonius Tranquillus, in a book on the Caesars, described a peculiarity in the handwriting of Octavius Augustus: "He does not hyphen his words."

There are references to handwriting and character in the writings of the East. The ancient Chinese had insight into the psychology of handwriting. King Jo-Hau, a philosopher and painter of the Sung Period who lived between 1060 and 1110, declared that "handwriting infallibly shows us whether it comes from a vulgar or a noble-minded person."

The oldest book on the subject of graphology was written in Capri in 1622 by a famous scholar of his day, Camillo Baldi, who was doctor and professor at the University of Bologna. It was named: *Tratto come da una lettera missiva si cognoscano la natura e qualita de scittore.* (*How to Judge the Nature and the Character of a Person from His Letter.*) In this work the author declared it was obvious that all persons wrote in their own peculiar way, and that in private letters everyone used characteristic forms that could not accurately be imitated by anyone else.

In 1792 a professor of theology and philosophy, J. Charles Grohman, wrote in a treatise: "It is just as difficult to disguise one's handwriting as one's physiognomy."

Then, in 1871, Abbé Jean Hippolyte Michon coined the word

355

"graphology" from the Greek "graph," which means writing, and the suffix "ology," which is applied to the names of scientific studies. So little was known about graphology in intellectual circles of that day that until 1872 the knowledge was mainly speculative and controversial. But in that same year, the Abbé Flaudria wrote a systemized textbook in which he considered carefully all that had been done since the time of Baldi, clarified seemingly contradictory findings, and amplified what had been elementary. In the following year his friend and colleague the Abbé Michon wrote the first popular book on graphology; it had a tremendous sale.

The study of graphology was continued by these two Abbés, and it was about that time that the Abbé Michon joined forces with another graphologist, M. Crepieux-Jamin, to bring out a new and revised edition of Michon's earlier work, and this has remained a standard ever since.

From 1872 to 1885 the Germans were busily engrossed in the science of graphology, correlating their findings and establishing most of the empirical rules that graphologists follow today. Adolf Henze, Hans Basse, and L. Meyer are names that will always be associated with the development of graphology in Germany. These men concluded that graphological findings could be of invaluable assistance in vocational guidance. They established a technique that is still used in their country; at the head of every personnel department in every large company, a graphologist's findings determine the final selection of an employee.

England began to show an interest in graphology, too. It has been reported that Elizabeth Barrett Browning and Lord Beaconsfield included graphology as a subject for polite discussion. And it was in that period that Rose Baughan, a well-known writer and society luminary, wrote the first book on graphology in English.

Around 1860 a group of scientists throughout the world began to show a heightened interest in criminology, which had received scant attention up to that time. Up until then criminals had been identified as madmen and treated as such. Lombroso in Italy, Krafft-Ebing in Germany, and Havelock Ellis in England were the outstanding scientists. These men began their scientific study of the criminal, and this led them to consider graphology as a means of classifying different types of criminals. Lombroso and Krafft-Ebing used graphology as a positive guide in their researches. Then along came Alphonse Bertillon, who was in the process of perfecting the system of identification through fingerprints. Sir William Herschel, the father of the fingerprint system of personal identification, gave graphology his close attention, considering it as important to character deduction as fingerprints were to personal identification.

Sir William Wilks and Doctor Henry Maudsley then became interested in graphology as a means of discovering whether a person's handwriting showed signs of disease. Their researches were continued by Doctor William Hammond, whose specialty was nervous diseases; he gave many illustrations of the deterioration that set in after a neurotic condition had made inroads into the patient's psyche and how it was revealed in handwriting. Dr. Hammond stressed that in instances of diseases of the brain or spinal cord, the change of the writing from its usual formations is the first sign of physical deterioration, and that such changes are often found in the handwriting of a person who seems in perfect health but who later shows definite signs of such disease.

Physicians in this country have been much slower than those in Europe to appreciate the value of graphology to their profession, in both physical and pathological diagnoses. But with the influx of so many refugees from Hitler's Germany, a number of whom had practiced graphology in their native land, the picture changed. A larger number of psychiatrists and clinical psychologists use graphology in connection with other projective tests (Rorschach, T.A.T., Stanford-Binet, etc.) to gain further insight into their patients' behavior. And many graphology books have been written in English.

A course in graphology is being given [1968] by Daniel S. Anthony at the New School in New York City. And graphology is being used extensively by many large business firms and banks throughout the country in the selection of their personnel.

Sigmund George Warburg, a member of the old and powerful banking family now living in England, has endowed The European Foundation of Graphological Science and Application in the University of Zurich. It is hoped that some of American universities may, in the not too distant future, add the study of graphology to their curricula.

Among knowledgeable people in the arts and sciences are many amateur graphologists who derive much pleasure and information from their graphological findings. One is General James M. Gavin, whose handwriting is discussed in this book.

The painter Gainsborough while he was working on a portrait kept before him the handwriting of his subject when the latter was not actually posing.

The Difference Between a Handwriting Expert and a Graphologist

GRAPHOLOGY, AS IT STANDS TODAY, IS BASED ON A SET of empirical rules, the result of definite data amassed over the years, from which deductions are made. These are the result of all the time from Nero to Baldi, when people merely speculated and hazarded guesses about the relation of handwriting to character. In the time from Baldi to the present, a large number of books on the subject have been written in many languages and many articles have been published.

But much confusion seems to have arisen as to the similarity or difference between the handwriting expert and the graphologist.

The handwriting expert deals primarily with the physical structure of handwriting, examining it almost as an intern might a cadaver, with no thought that this might once have been a human being. The graphologist is concerned with the human equation, which includes the feelings, hopes, goals, and talents of the individual, the sum of his character. Often he has to read between the lines to arrive at a conclusion, whereas the handwriting expert is concerned only with the lines. However, the expert graphologist also examines the lines and structure of a handwriting to reach his conclusion, and he can therefore do everything the handwriting expert can do, whereas the latter cannot do everything the graphologist can do.

The graphologist has in his extended knowledge an added advantage, for he can evaluate the writer's character and conclude whether he might have performed a dishonest act or whether it was not in his character to do so. This can be of great assistance in tracking down a culprit or in proving someone's innocence. Many an innocent person has been convicted on circumstantial evidence. Some of this might have been avoided if a graphologist had been called in to study the essential character of the suspected person. Some people are constitutionally incapable of committing certain crimes, and their handwriting will reveal this.

The forger (those whose handwritings I have examined) is in a class by himself. Some forgers show little or no character structure in their handwriting. I remember one who wrote an exact copybook hand of the Palmer method. He took on the character of the person whose signature he was forging, much as an actor takes on the character of a role he is playing.

Often the forger is a frustrated artist, for he can copy a handwriting as some artists copy masterpieces and pass them off as originals.

Forgers who use a tracing of a signature will be detected when a number of the signatures of one person are examined. For no one writes his signature exactly the same way twice. There is always some slight variation. So if all versions of a signature are identical, they are tracings. The strongly visual person, with genuine talent, who does freehand forgery is more difficult to detect. He might give himself away by an unconscious minor stroke or by a punctuation mark or *i* dot which the real owner of the signature did not make.

Anonymous or poison-pen letters are easy for the graphologist to detect when specimens of the suspect's handwriting are available to be compared with the questioned documents. More than anything else, the rhythm of the writing may turn out to be the most valid clue. A person might be able to disguise the angle of the writing and the letter forms, and may even resort to printing, but even in printing the astute eye of the expert graphologist can discern the rhythm

—whether slow, quick, disturbed, or whatever—and make the deduction.

In written confessions made by a suspect under duress, the graphologist can discern whether the text was dictated, or was done spontaneously or under threat, for the handwriting of the confessor will show the extent of the tension he was under. The idea of making such confessions invalid is a good one, as it might eliminate mistakes and prevent an innocent man from convicting himself.

BIBLIOGRAPHY

Allport, Gordon Willard, and Vernon, Philip E. *Studies in Expressive Movements*. New York: The Macmillan Co., 1933

de Sainte Colombe, Paul, *Grapho-Therapeutics*. Hollywood, California: Laurida Books Pub. Co., 1966

Jacoby, Hans J. *Analysis of Handwriting*. London: Allen & Unwin, Ltd., 1939

————. *Self-Knowledge Through Handwriting*. London: J. M. Dent & Sons, Ltd., 1941

Kanfer, Alfred. *A Guide to Handwriting Analysis*. New York: Dell, 1962

Lewinson, Thea Stein, and Zubin, Joseph. *Handwriting Analysis*. New York: King's Crown Press, 1942

Mendel, Alfred O. *Personality in Handwriting*. New York: Stephen Daye, 1947

Myer, Oscar N. *The Language of Handwriting*. New York: Stephen Daye, 1951

Marcuse, Irene. *Guide to Personality Through Your Handwriting*. New York: Arc Books, Inc., 1965

Olyanova, Nadya. *The Psychology of Handwriting*. New York: Sterling Pub. Co., Inc., 1960. London: Mayflower

Rice, Louise. *Character Reading from Handwriting*. New York: Frederick A. Stokes Co., 1927

Roback, A. A. *Writing Slips and Personality*. Zurich: 1932

Roman, Klara G. *Handwriting—A Key to Personality*. New York: Pantheon Books, Inc., 1952

Sara, Dorothy. *Handwriting Analysis for the Millions*. New York: Bell Pub. Co., 1967

Saudek, Robert. *Experiments with Handwriting*. New York: William Morrow & Co., 1928

Schermann, Rafael. *Secrets of Handwriting*. Translated by Prince Sebastian Lubomirski. London: Rider & Co., 1937

SINGER, ERIC. *Personality in Handwriting*. Westport, Connecticut: Associated Booksellers, 1954

SONNEMANN, ULRICH. *Handwriting Analysis*. London: Allen & Unwin, Ltd., 1950

TELTSCHER, HERRY O. *Handwriting—A Key to Personality*. New York: G. P. Putnam & Sons, 1942

WOLFF, WERNER. *Diagrams of the Unconscious*. New York: Grune & Stratton, 1948

INDEX

A PERSONAL WORD FROM MELVIN POWERS
PUBLISHER, WILSHIRE BOOK COMPANY

Dear Friend:

My goal is to publish interesting, informative, and inspirational books. You can help me accomplish this by answering the following questions, either by phone or by mail. Or, if convenient for you, I would welcome the opportunity to visit with you in my office and hear your comments in person.

Did you enjoy reading this book? Why?

Would you enjoy reading another similar book?

What idea in the book impressed you the most?

If applicable to your situation, have you incorporated this idea in your daily life?

Is there a chapter that could serve as a theme for an entire book? Please explain.

If you have an idea for a book, I would welcome discussing it with you. If you already have one in progress, write or call me concerning possible publication. I can be reached at **(818) 765-8579.**

Sincerely yours,

MELVIN POWERS

12015 Sherman Road
North Hollywood, California 91605

MELVIN POWERS SELF-IMPROVEMENT LIBRARY

ASTROLOGY

____ ASTROLOGY: HOW TO CHART YOUR HOROSCOPE *Max Heindel*	5.00
____ ASTROLOGY AND SEXUAL ANALYSIS *Morris C. Goodman*	5.00
____ ASTROLOGY AND YOU *Carroll Righter*	5.00
____ ASTROLOGY MADE EASY *Astarte*	5.00
____ ASTROLOGY, ROMANCE, YOU AND THE STARS *Anthony Norvell*	5.00
____ MY WORLD OF ASTROLOGY *Sydney Omarr*	7.00
____ THOUGHT DIAL *Sydney Omarr*	7.00
____ WHAT THE STARS REVEAL ABOUT THE MEN IN YOUR LIFE *Thelma White*	3.00

BRIDGE

____ BRIDGE BIDDING MADE EASY *Edwin B. Kantar*	10.00
____ BRIDGE CONVENTIONS *Edwin B. Kantar*	7.00
____ COMPETITIVE BIDDING IN MODERN BRIDGE *Edgar Kaplan*	7.00
____ DEFENSIVE BRIDGE PLAY COMPLETE *Edwin B. Kantar*	15.00
____ GAMESMAN BRIDGE—PLAY BETTER WITH KANTAR *Edwin B. Kantar*	5.00
____ HOW TO IMPROVE YOUR BRIDGE *Alfred Sheinwold*	7.00
____ IMPROVING YOUR BIDDING SKILLS *Edwin B. Kantar*	7.00
____ INTRODUCTION TO DECLARER'S PLAY *Edwin B. Kantar*	7.00
____ INTRODUCTION TO DEFENDER'S PLAY *Edwin B. Kantar*	7.00
____ KANTAR FOR THE DEFENSE *Edwin B. Kantar*	7.00
____ KANTAR FOR THE DEFENSE VOLUME 2 *Edwin B. Kantar*	7.00
____ TEST YOUR BRIDGE PLAY *Edwin B. Kantar*	7.00
____ VOLUME 2—TEST YOUR BRIDGE PLAY *Edwin B. Kantar*	7.00
____ WINNING DECLARER PLAY *Dorothy Hayden Truscott*	7.00

BUSINESS, STUDY & REFERENCE

____ BRAINSTORMING *Charles Clark*	7.00
____ CONVERSATION MADE EASY *Elliot Russell*	5.00
____ EXAM SECRET *Dennis B. Jackson*	5.00
____ FIX-IT BOOK *Arthur Symons*	2.00
____ HOW TO DEVELOP A BETTER SPEAKING VOICE *M. Hellier*	4.00
____ HOW TO SAVE 50% ON GAS & CAR EXPENSES *Ken Stansbie*	5.00
____ HOW TO SELF-PUBLISH YOUR BOOK & MAKE IT A BEST SELLER *Melvin Powers*	10.00
____ INCREASE YOUR LEARNING POWER *Geoffrey A. Dudley*	3.00
____ PRACTICAL GUIDE TO BETTER CONCENTRATION *Melvin Powers*	5.00
____ PRACTICAL GUIDE TO PUBLIC SPEAKING *Maurice Forley*	5.00
____ 7 DAYS TO FASTER READING *William S. Schaill*	5.00
____ SONGWRITERS' RHYMING DICTIONARY *Jane Shaw Whitfield*	7.00
____ SPELLING MADE EASY *Lester D. Basch & Dr. Milton Finkelstein*	3.00
____ STUDENT'S GUIDE TO BETTER GRADES *J. A. Rickard*	3.00
____ TEST YOURSELF—FIND YOUR HIDDEN TALENT *Jack Shafer*	3.00
____ YOUR WILL & WHAT TO DO ABOUT IT *Attorney Samuel G. Kling*	5.00

CALLIGRAPHY

____ ADVANCED CALLIGRAPHY *Katherine Jeffares*	7.00
____ CALLIGRAPHER'S REFERENCE BOOK *Anne Leptich & Jacque Evans*	7.00
____ CALLIGRAPHY—THE ART OF BEAUTIFUL WRITING *Katherine Jeffares*	7.00
____ CALLIGRAPHY FOR FUN & PROFIT *Anne Leptich & Jacque Evans*	7.00
____ CALLIGRAPHY MADE EASY *Tina Serafini*	7.00

CHESS & CHECKERS

____ BEGINNER'S GUIDE TO WINNING CHESS *Fred Reinfeld*	5.00
____ CHESS IN TEN EASY LESSONS *Larry Evans*	5.00
____ CHESS MADE EASY *Milton L. Hanauer*	5.00
____ CHESS PROBLEMS FOR BEGINNERS *Edited by Fred Reinfeld*	5.00
____ CHESS TACTICS FOR BEGINNERS *Edited by Fred Reinfeld*	5.00
____ CHESS THEORY & PRACTICE *Morry & Mitchell*	2.00

____	HOW TO WIN AT CHECKERS *Fred Reinfeld*	5.00
____	1001 BRILLIANT WAYS TO CHECKMATE *Fred Reinfeld*	7.00
____	1001 WINNING CHESS SACRIFICES & COMBINATIONS *Fred Reinfeld*	7.00

COOKERY & HERBS

____	CULPEPER'S HERBAL REMEDIES *Dr. Nicholas Culpeper*	5.00
____	FAST GOURMET COOKBOOK *Poppy Cannon*	2.50
____	HEALING POWER OF HERBS *May Bethel*	5.00
____	HEALING POWER OF NATURAL FOODS *May Bethel*	5.00
____	HERBS FOR HEALTH—HOW TO GROW & USE THEM *Louise Evans Doole*	5.00
____	HOME GARDEN COOKBOOK—DELICIOUS NATURAL FOOD RECIPES *Ken Kraft*	3.00
____	MEATLESS MEAL GUIDE *Tomi Ryan & James H. Ryan, M.D.*	4.00
____	VEGETABLE GARDENING FOR BEGINNERS *Hugh Wiberg*	2.00
____	VEGETABLES FOR TODAY'S GARDENS *R. Milton Carleton*	2.00
____	VEGETARIAN COOKERY *Janet Walker*	7.00
____	VEGETARIAN COOKING MADE EASY & DELECTABLE *Veronica Vezza*	3.00
____	VEGETARIAN DELIGHTS—A HAPPY COOKBOOK FOR HEALTH *K. R. Mehta*	2.00
____	VEGETARIAN GOURMET COOKBOOK *Joyce McKinnel*	3.00

GAMBLING & POKER

____	HOW TO WIN AT DICE GAMES *Skip Frey*	3.00
____	HOW TO WIN AT POKER *Terence Reese & Anthony T. Watkins*	7.00
____	WINNING AT CRAPS *Dr. Lloyd T. Commins*	5.00
____	WINNING AT GIN *Chester Wander & Cy Rice*	3.00
____	WINNING AT POKER—AN EXPERT'S GUIDE *John Archer*	5.00
____	WINNING AT 21—AN EXPERT'S GUIDE *John Archer*	5.00
____	WINNING POKER SYSTEMS *Norman Zadeh*	3.00

HEALTH

____	BEE POLLEN *Lynda Lyngheim & Jack Scagnetti*	3.00
____	COPING WITH ALZHEIMER'S *Rose Oliver, Ph.D. & Francis Bock, Ph.D.*	7.00
____	DR. LINDNER'S POINT SYSTEM FOOD PROGRAM *Peter G. Lindner, M.D.*	2.00
____	HELP YOURSELF TO BETTER SIGHT *Margaret Darst Corbett*	7.00
____	HOW YOU CAN STOP SMOKING PERMANENTLY *Ernest Caldwell*	5.00
____	MIND OVER PLATTER *Peter G. Lindner, M.D.*	5.00
____	NATURE'S WAY TO NUTRITION & VIBRANT HEALTH *Robert J. Scrutton*	3.00
____	NEW CARBOHYDRATE DIET COUNTER *Patti Lopez-Pereira*	2.00
____	REFLEXOLOGY *Dr. Maybelle Segal*	5.00
____	REFLEXOLOGY FOR GOOD HEALTH *Anna Kaye & Don C. Matchan*	5.00
____	30 DAYS TO BEAUTIFUL LEGS *Dr. Marc Selner*	3.00
____	YOU CAN LEARN TO RELAX *Dr. Samuel Gutwirth*	3.00

HOBBIES

____	BEACHCOMBING FOR BEGINNERS *Norman Hickin*	2.00
____	BLACKSTONE'S MODERN CARD TRICKS *Harry Blackstone*	5.00
____	BLACKSTONE'S SECRETS OF MAGIC *Harry Blackstone*	5.00
____	COIN COLLECTING FOR BEGINNERS *Burton Hobson & Fred Reinfeld*	5.00
____	ENTERTAINING WITH ESP *Tony 'Doc' Shiels*	2.00
____	400 FASCINATING MAGIC TRICKS YOU CAN DO *Howard Thurston*	5.00
____	HOW I TURN JUNK INTO FUN AND PROFIT *Sari*	3.00
____	HOW TO WRITE A HIT SONG & SELL IT *Tommy Boyce*	7.00
____	JUGGLING MADE EASY *Rudolf Dittrich*	3.00
____	MAGIC FOR ALL AGES *Walter Gibson*	4.00
____	MAGIC MADE EASY *Byron Wels*	2.00
____	STAMP COLLECTING FOR BEGINNERS *Burton Hobson*	3.00

HORSE PLAYER'S WINNING GUIDES

____	BETTING HORSES TO WIN *Les Conklin*	7.00
____	ELIMINATE THE LOSERS *Bob McKnight*	5.00
____	HOW TO PICK WINNING HORSES *Bob McKnight*	5.00

____ HOW TO WIN AT THE RACES Sam (The Genius) Lewin	5.00
____ HOW YOU CAN BEAT THE RACES Jack Kavanaqh	5.00
____ MAKING MONEY AT THE RACES David Barr	5.00
____ PAYDAY AT THE RACES Les Conklin	5.00
____ SMART HANDICAPPING MADE EASY William Bauman	5.00
____ SUCCESS AT THE HARNESS RACES Barry Meadow	5.00
____ WINNING AT THE HARNESS RACES—AN EXPERT'S GUIDE Nick Cammarano	5.00

HUMOR

____ HOW TO FLATTEN YOUR TUSH Coach Marge Reardon	2.00
____ HOW TO MAKE LOVE TO YOURSELF Ron Stevens & Joy Grdnic	3.00
____ JOKE TELLER'S HANDBOOK Bob Orben	7.00
____ JOKES FOR ALL OCCASIONS Al Schock	5.00
____ 2,000 NEW LAUGHS FOR SPEAKERS Bob Orben	5.00
____ 2,400 JOKES TO BRIGHTEN YOUR SPEECHES Robert Orben	7.00
____ 2,500 JOKES TO START 'EM LAUGHING Bob Orben	7.00

HYPNOTISM

____ ADVANCED TECHNIQUES OF HYPNOSIS Melvin Powers	3.00
____ CHILDBIRTH WITH HYPNOSIS William S. Kroger, M.D.	5.00
____ HOW TO SOLVE YOUR SEX PROBLEMS WITH SELF-HYPNOSIS Frank S. Caprio, M.D.	5.00
____ HOW TO STOP SMOKING THRU SELF-HYPNOSIS Leslie M. LeCron	3.00
____ HOW YOU CAN BOWL BETTER USING SELF-HYPNOSIS Jack Heise	4.00
____ HOW YOU CAN PLAY BETTER GOLF USING SELF-HYPNOSIS Jack Heise	3.00
____ HYPNOSIS AND SELF-HYPNOSIS Bernard Hollander, M.D.	5.00
____ HYPNOTISM (Originally published in 1893) Carl Sextus	5.00
____ HYPNOTISM & PSYCHIC PHENOMENA Simeon Edmunds	4.00
____ HYPNOTISM MADE EASY Dr. Ralph Winn	5.00
____ HYPNOTISM MADE PRACTICAL Louis Orton	5.00
____ HYPNOTISM REVEALED Melvin Powers	3.00
____ HYPNOTISM TODAY Leslie LeCron and Jean Bordeaux, Ph.D.	5.00
____ MODERN HYPNOSIS Lesley Kuhn & Salvatore Russo, Ph.D.	5.00
____ NEW CONCEPTS OF HYPNOSIS Bernard C. Gindes, M.D.	7.00
____ NEW SELF-HYPNOSIS Paul Adams	7.00
____ POST-HYPNOTIC INSTRUCTIONS—SUGGESTIONS FOR THERAPY Arnold Furst	5.00
____ PRACTICAL GUIDE TO SELF-HYPNOSIS Melvin Powers	3.00
____ PRACTICAL HYPNOTISM Philip Magonet, M.D.	3.00
____ SECRETS OF HYPNOTISM S. J. Van Pelt, M.D.	5.00
____ SELF-HYPNOSIS—A CONDITIONED-RESPONSE TECHNIQUE Laurence Sparks	7.00
____ SELF-HYPNOSIS—ITS THEORY, TECHNIQUE & APPLICATION Melvin Powers	3.00
____ THERAPY THROUGH HYPNOSIS Edited by Raphael H. Rhodes	5.00

JUDAICA

____ SERVICE OF THE HEART Evelyn Garfiel, Ph.D.	7.00
____ STORY OF ISRAEL IN COINS Jean & Maurice Gould	2.00
____ STORY OF ISRAEL IN STAMPS Maxim & Gabriel Shamir	1.00
____ TONGUE OF THE PROPHETS Robert St. John	7.00

JUST FOR WOMEN

____ COSMOPOLITAN'S GUIDE TO MARVELOUS MEN Foreword by Helen Gurley Brown	3.00
____ COSMOPOLITAN'S HANG-UP HANDBOOK Foreword by Helen Gurley Brown	4.00
____ COSMOPOLITAN'S LOVE BOOK—A GUIDE TO ECSTASY IN BED	7.00
____ COSMOPOLITAN'S NEW ETIQUETTE GUIDE Foreword by Helen Gurley Brown	4.00
____ I AM A COMPLEAT WOMAN Doris Hagopian & Karen O'Connor Sweeney	3.00
____ JUST FOR WOMEN—A GUIDE TO THE FEMALE BODY Richard E. Sand, M.D.	5.00
____ NEW APPROACHES TO SEX IN MARRIAGE John E. Eichenlaub, M.D.	3.00
____ SEXUALLY ADEQUATE FEMALE Frank S. Caprio, M.D.	3.00
____ SEXUALLY FULFILLED WOMAN Dr. Rachel Copelan	5.00
____ YOUR FIRST YEAR OF MARRIAGE Dr. Tom McGinnis	3.00

MARRIAGE, SEX & PARENTHOOD

____ ABILITY TO LOVE Dr. Allan Fromme	7.00

____ LEFT-HANDED PEOPLE *Michael Barsley*		5.00
____ MAGIC IN YOUR MIND *U.S. Andersen*		7.00
____ MAGIC OF THINKING SUCCESS *Dr. David J. Schwartz*		7.00
____ MAGIC POWER OF YOUR MIND *Walter M. Germain*		7.00
____ MENTAL POWER THROUGH SLEEP SUGGESTION *Melvin Powers*		3.00
____ NEVER UNDERESTIMATE THE SELLING POWER OF A WOMAN *Dottie Walters*		7.00
____ NEW GUIDE TO RATIONAL LIVING *Albert Ellis, Ph.D. & R. Harper, Ph.D.*		7.00
____ PSYCHO-CYBERNETICS *Maxwell Maltz, M.D.*		7.00
____ PSYCHOLOGY OF HANDWRITING *Nadya Olyanova*		7.00
____ SALES CYBERNETICS *Brian Adams*		7.00
____ SCIENCE OF MIND IN DAILY LIVING *Dr. Donald Curtis*		7.00
____ SECRET OF SECRETS *U.S. Andersen*		7.00
____ SECRET POWER OF THE PYRAMIDS *U. S. Andersen*		7.00
____ SELF-THERAPY FOR THE STUTTERER *Malcolm Frazer*		3.00
____ SUCCESS-CYBERNETICS *U. S. Andersen*		7.00
____ 10 DAYS TO A GREAT NEW LIFE *William E. Edwards*		3.00
____ THINK AND GROW RICH *Napoleon Hill*		7.00
____ THREE MAGIC WORDS *U. S. Andersen*		7.00
____ TREASURY OF COMFORT *Edited by Rabbi Sidney Greenberg*		7.00
____ TREASURY OF THE ART OF LIVING *Sidney S. Greenberg*		7.00
____ WHAT YOUR HANDWRITING REVEALS *Albert E. Hughes*		4.00
____ YOUR SUBCONSCIOUS POWER *Charles M. Simmons*		7.00
____ YOUR THOUGHTS CAN CHANGE YOUR LIFE *Dr. Donald Curtis*		7.00

SPORTS

____ BICYCLING FOR FUN AND GOOD HEALTH *Kenneth E. Luther*		2.00
____ BILLIARDS—POCKET • CAROM • THREE CUSHION *Clive Cottingham, Jr.*		5.00
____ COMPLETE GUIDE TO FISHING *Vlad Evanoff*		2.00
____ HOW TO IMPROVE YOUR RACQUETBALL *Lubarsky, Kaufman & Scagnetti*		5.00
____ HOW TO WIN AT POCKET BILLIARDS *Edward D. Knuchell*		7.00
____ JOY OF WALKING *Jack Scagnetti*		3.00
____ LEARNING & TEACHING SOCCER SKILLS *Eric Worthington*		3.00
____ MOTORCYCLING FOR BEGINNERS *I.G. Edmonds*		3.00
____ RACQUETBALL FOR WOMEN *Toni Hudson, Jack Scagnetti & Vince Rondone*		3.00
____ RACQUETBALL MADE EASY *Steve Lubarsky, Rod Delson & Jack Scagnetti*		5.00
____ SECRET OF BOWLING STRIKES *Dawson Taylor*		5.00
____ SECRET OF PERFECT PUTTING *Horton Smith & Dawson Taylor*		5.00
____ SOCCER—THE GAME & HOW TO PLAY IT *Gary Rosenthal*		7.00
____ STARTING SOCCER *Edward F. Dolan, Jr.*		5.00

TENNIS LOVER'S LIBRARY

____ BEGINNER'S GUIDE TO WINNING TENNIS *Helen Hull Jacobs*		2.00
____ HOW TO BEAT BETTER TENNIS PLAYERS *Loring Fiske*		4.00
____ PSYCH YOURSELF TO BETTER TENNIS *Dr. Walter A. Luszki*		2.00
____ TENNIS FOR BEGINNERS *Dr. H. A. Murray*		2.00
____ TENNIS MADE EASY *Joel Brecheen*		5.00
____ WEEKEND TENNIS—HOW TO HAVE FUN & WIN AT THE SAME TIME *Bill Talbert*		3.00

WILSHIRE PET LIBRARY

____ DOG TRAINING MADE EASY & FUN *John W. Kellogg*		5.00
____ HOW TO BRING UP YOUR PET DOG *Kurt Unkelbach*		2.00
____ HOW TO RAISE & TRAIN YOUR PUPPY *Jeff Griffen*		5.00

The books listed above can be obtained from your book dealer or directly from Melvin Powers.
When ordering, please remit $1.50 postage for the first book and 50¢ for each additional book.

Melvin Powers
12015 Sherman Road, No. Hollywood, California 91605